Simpsons Comics Madness

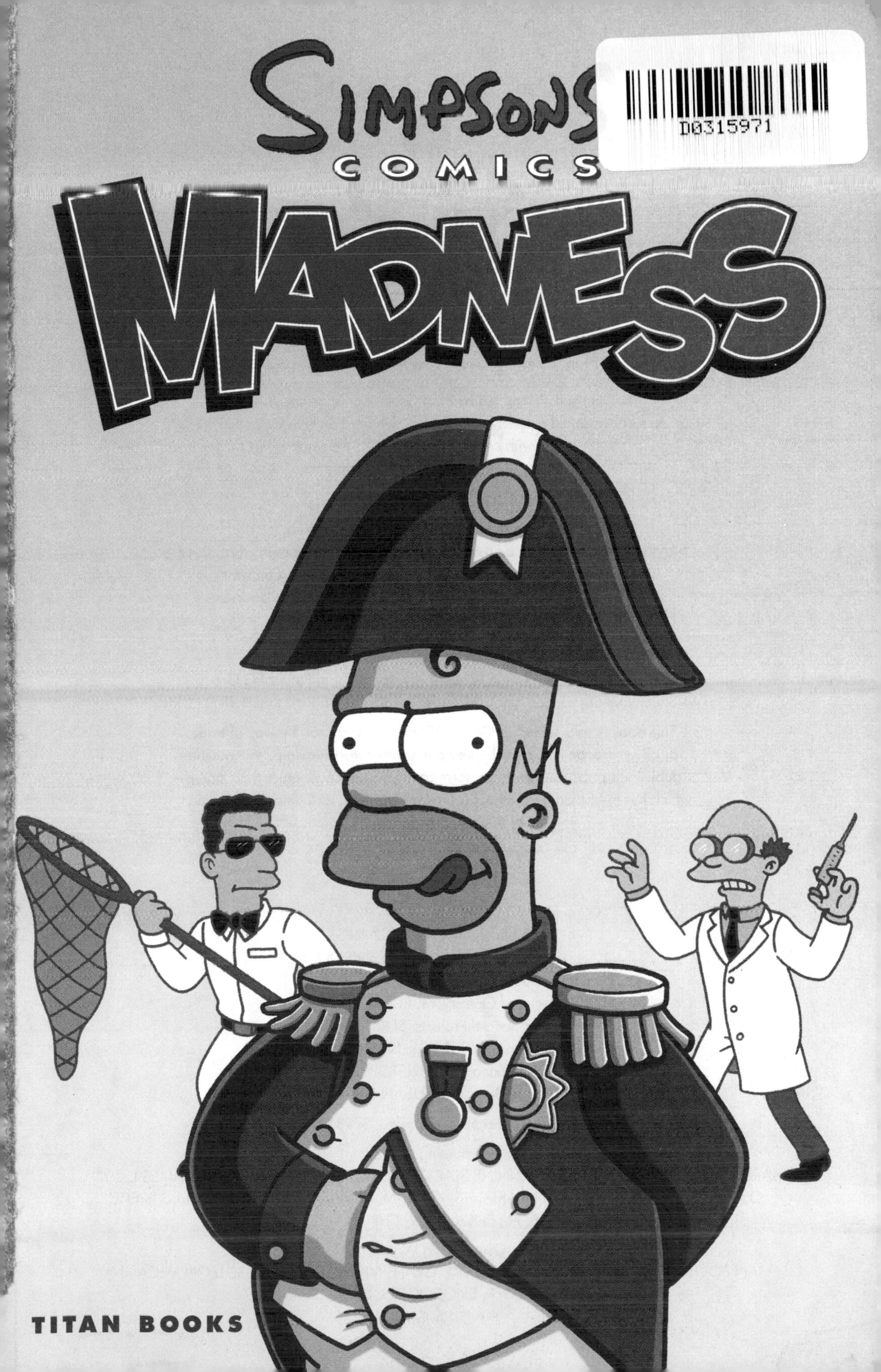

TITAN BOOKS

Dedicated to Snowball I:

You may be gone, but the extra yarn from
Mom's sewing basket never goes to waste.

The Simpsons™, created by Matt Groening, is the copyrighted
and trademarked property of Twentieth Century Fox Film Corporation.
Used with permission. All rights reserved.

SIMPSONS COMICS MADNESS

Copyright © 2000, 2001 & 2002 by
Bongo Entertainment, Inc. All rights reserved.
No part of this book may be used or reproduced in any manner whatsoever
without written permission except in the case of brief quotations
embodied in critical articles and reviews. For information address:

Bongo Comics Group c/o Titan Books
P.O. Box 1963, Santa Monica, CA 90406-1963

Published in the UK by Titan Books, a division of Titan Publishing Group,
144 Southwark St., London SE1 0UP, under licence from Bongo Entertainment, Inc.

This book is sold subject to the condition that it shall not, by way of trade
or otherwise, be lent, resold, hired out or otherwise circulated without the
publisher's prior consent in any form of binding or cover other than that in
which it is published and without a similar condition, including this condition,
being imposed upon the subsequent purchaser.

FIRST EDITION: JANUARY 2003

ISBN 1-84023-592-6
2 4 6 8 10 9 7 5 3 1

Publisher: MATT GROENING
Creative Director: BILL MORRISON
Managing Editor: TERRY DELEGEANE
Director of Operations: ROBERT ZAUGH
Art Director Special Projects: SERBAN CRISTESCU
Art Director Comic Books: NATHAN KANE
Production Manager: CHRISTOPHER UNGAR
Legal Guardian: SUSAN GRODE

Trade Paperback Concepts and Design: SERBAN CRISTESCU

Contributing Artists:
KAREN BATES, TIM BAVINGTON, JEANNINE BLACK, TIM HARKINS, NATHAN KANE, JAMES LLOYD,
OSCAR GONZÁLEZ LOYO, DAN NAKROSIS, KEVIN M. NEWMAN, PHIL ORTIZ, JULIUS PREITE,
STEVE STEERE, JR., ERICK TRAN, CHRISTOPHER UNGAR

Contributing Writers:
IAN BOOTHBY, TERRY DELEGEANE, ROBERT L. GRAFF, MICHAEL LISBE, JESSE LEON McCANN,
NATHAN REGER, ERIC ROGERS, SCOTT SHAW!

PRINTED IN CANADA

TABLE OF CONTENTS

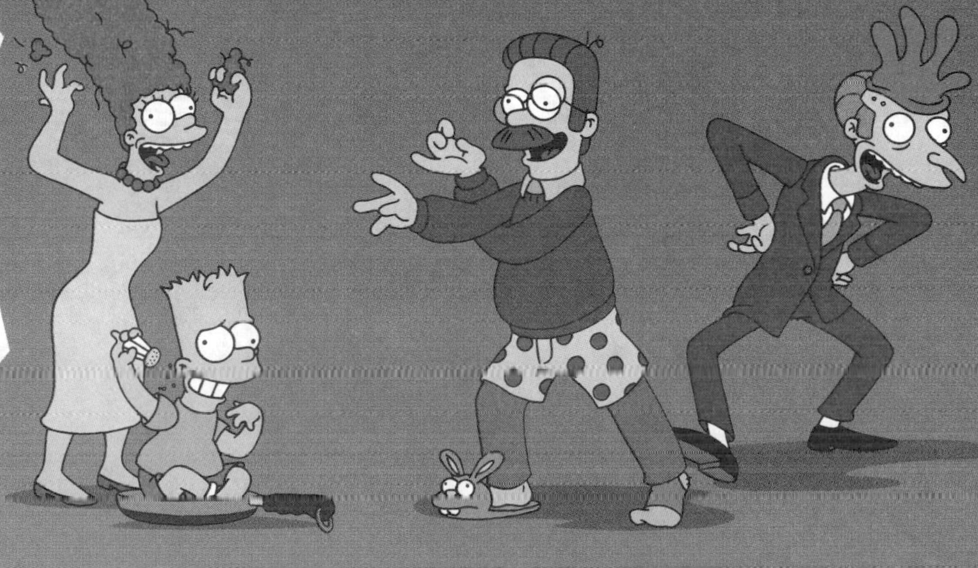

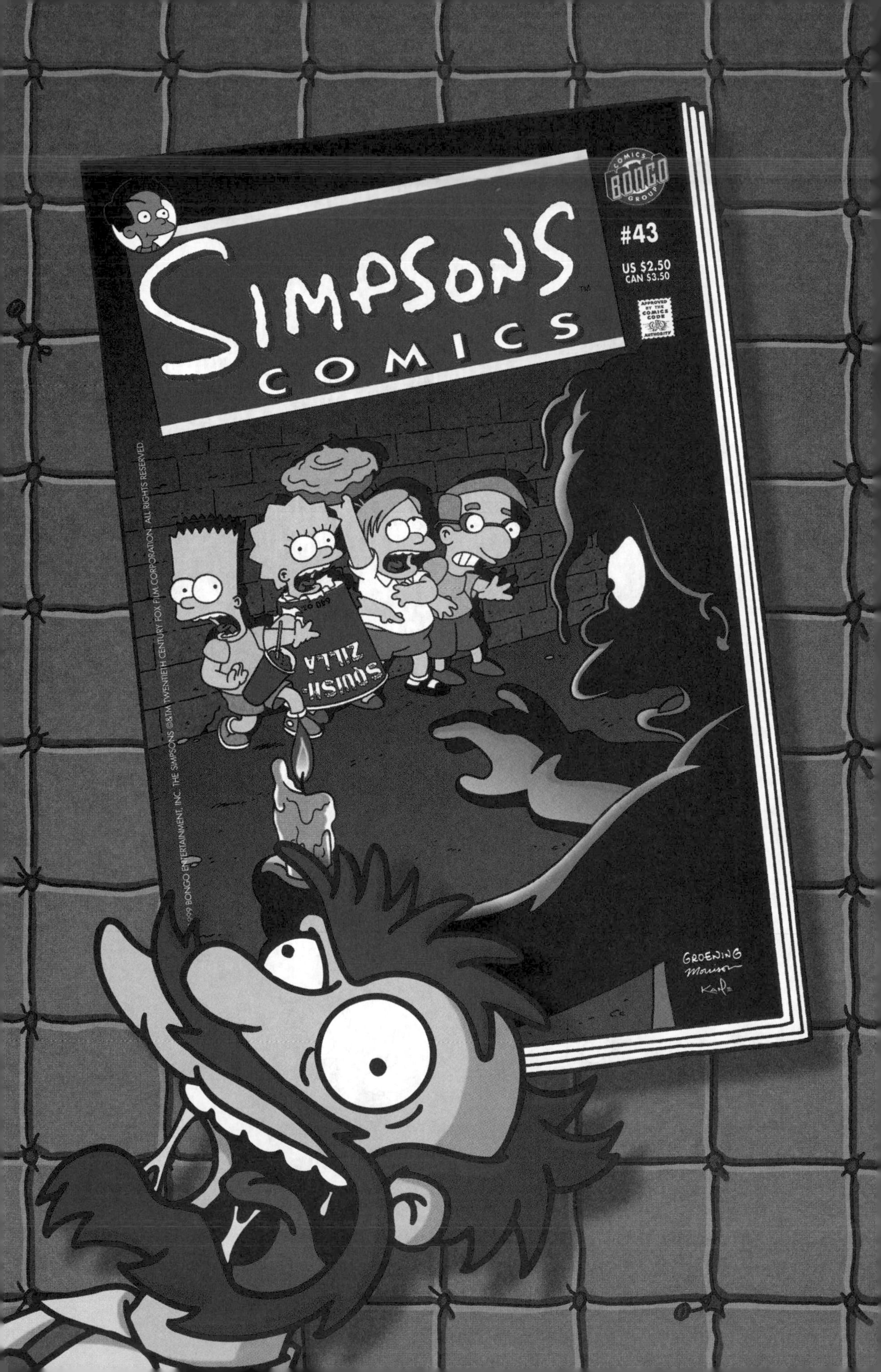
BONGO COMICS GROUP
SIMPSONS COMICS
#43
US $2.50
CAN $3.50
APPROVED BY THE COMICS CODE AUTHORITY
BONGO ENTERTAINMENT, INC. THE SIMPSONS ©&TM TWENTIETH CENTURY FOX FILM CORPORATION. ALL RIGHTS RESERVED.
GROENING

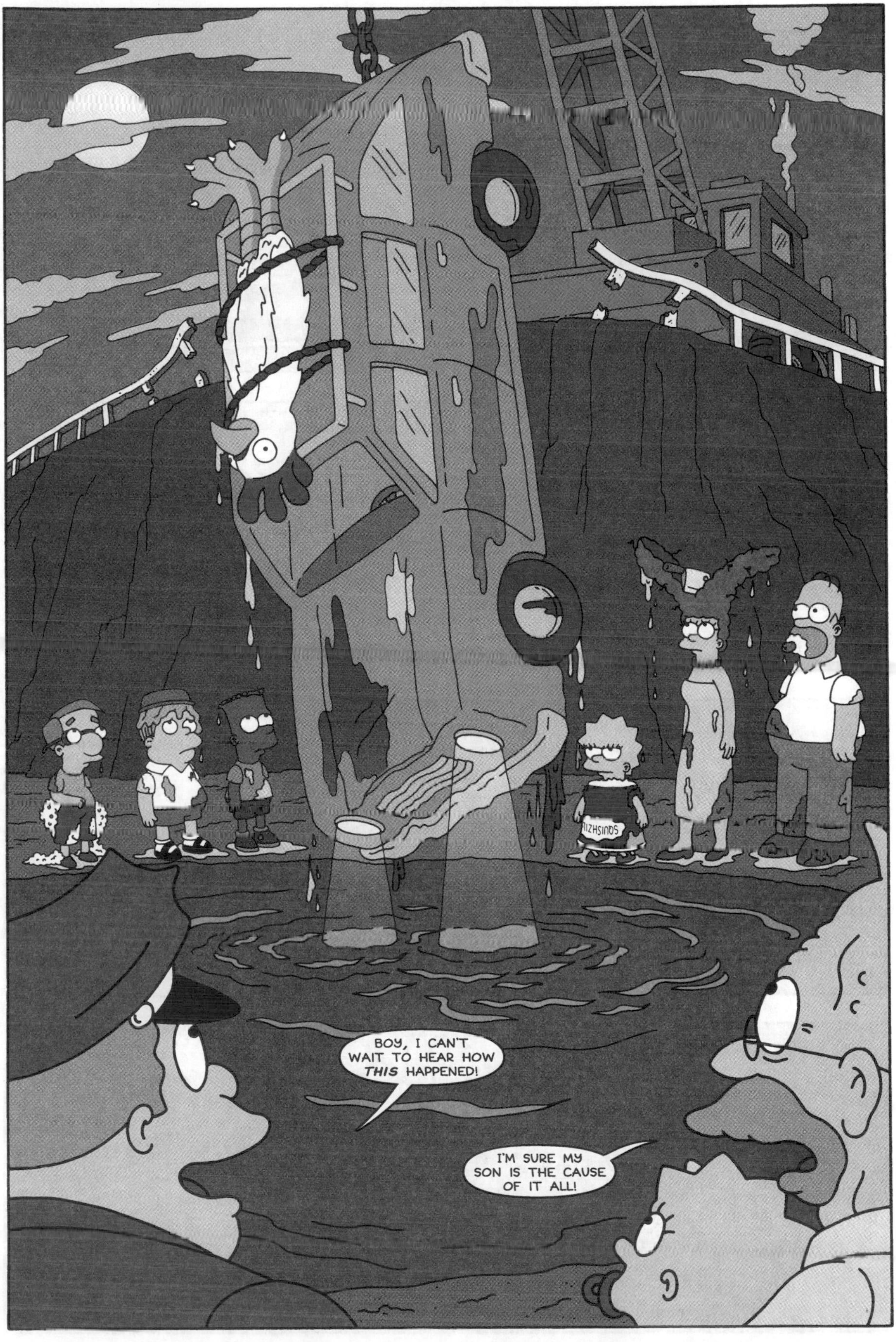
SPRINGFIELD
BOY, I CAN'T WAIT TO HEAR HOW THIS HAPPENED!
I'M SURE MY SON IS THE CAUSE OF IT ALL!

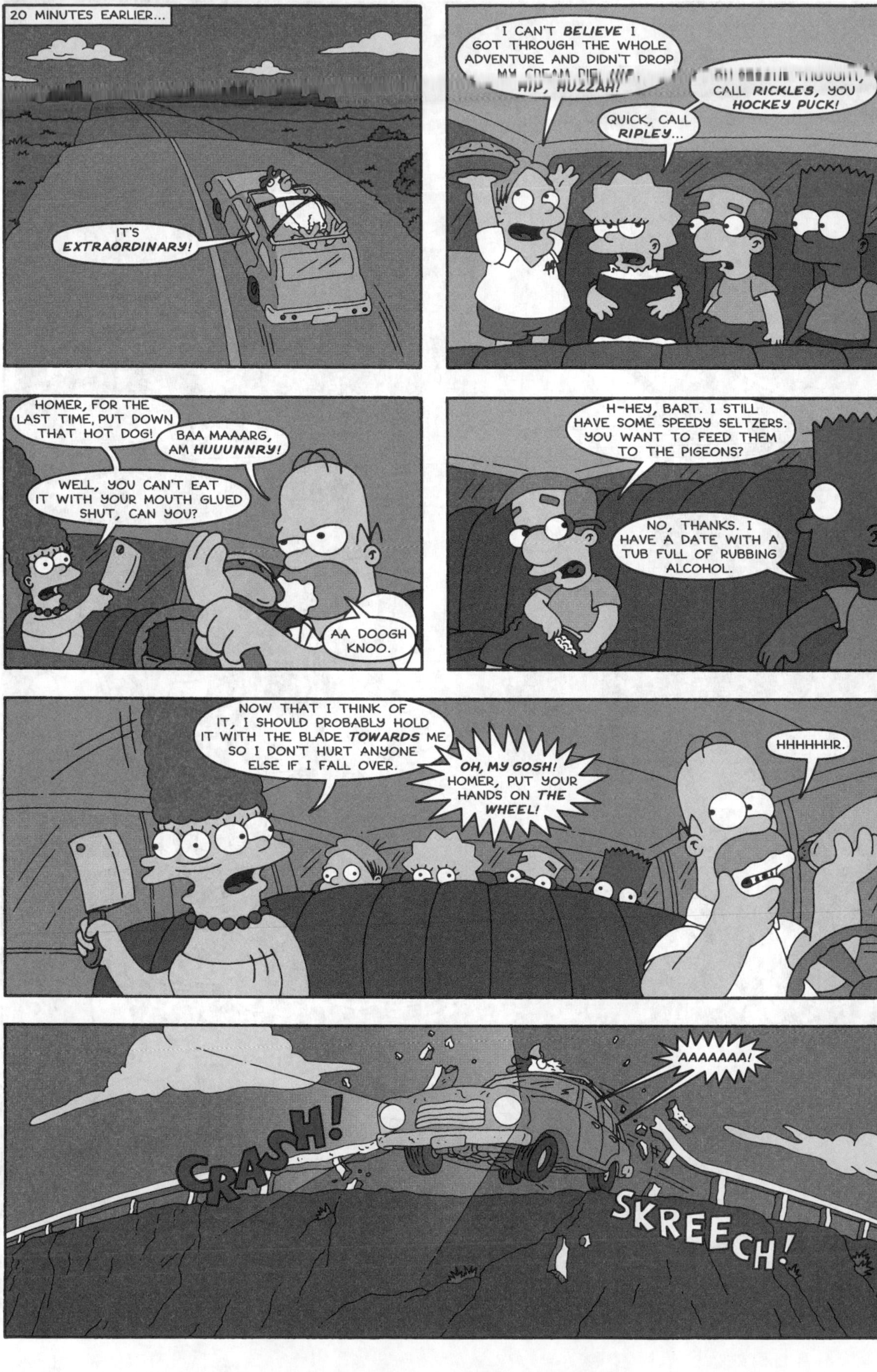
20 MINUTES EARLIER...
IT'S EXTRAORDINARY!
I CAN'T BELIEVE I GOT THROUGH THE WHOLE ADVENTURE AND DIDN'T DROP MY CREAM PIE. HIP, HIP, HUZZAH!
QUICK, CALL RIPLEY...
CALL RICKLES, YOU HOCKEY PUCK!
HOMER, FOR THE LAST TIME, PUT DOWN THAT HOT DOG!
BAA MAAARG, AM HUUUNNRY!
WELL, YOU CAN'T EAT IT WITH YOUR MOUTH GLUED SHUT, CAN YOU?
AA DOOGH KNOO.
H-HEY, BART. I STILL HAVE SOME SPEEDY SELTZERS. YOU WANT TO FEED THEM TO THE PIGEONS?
NO, THANKS. I HAVE A DATE WITH A TUB FULL OF RUBBING ALCOHOL.
NOW THAT I THINK OF IT, I SHOULD PROBABLY HOLD IT WITH THE BLADE TOWARDS ME SO I DON'T HURT ANYONE ELSE IF I FALL OVER.
OH, MY GOSH! HOMER, PUT YOUR HANDS ON THE WHEEL!
HHHHHHR.
CRASH!
AAAAAAA!
SKREECH!

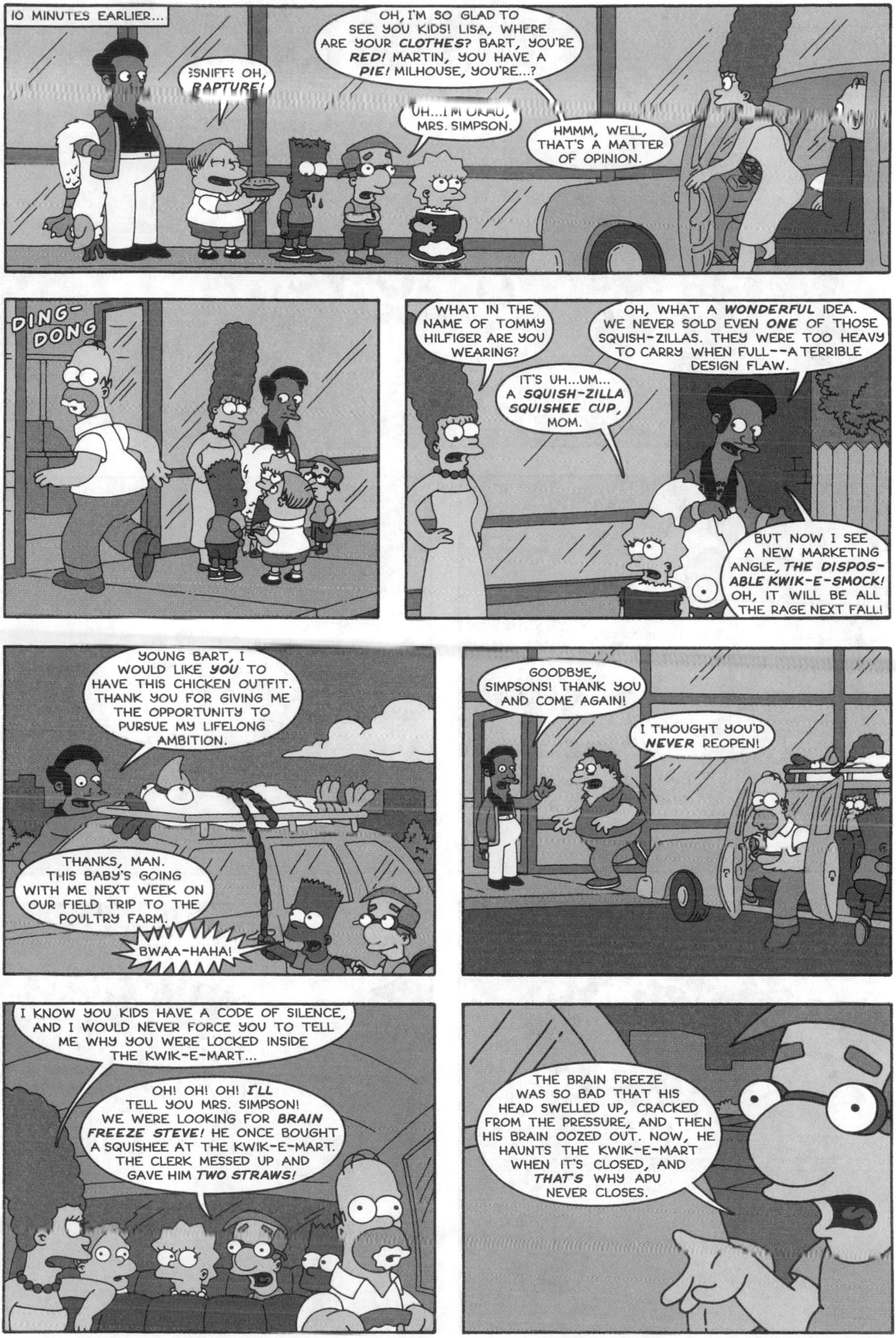
10 MINUTES EARLIER...
SNIFF! OH, RAPTURE!
OH, I'M SO GLAD TO SEE YOU KIDS! LISA, WHERE ARE YOUR CLOTHES? BART, YOU'RE RED! MARTIN, YOU HAVE A PIE! MILHOUSE, YOU'RE...?
UH...I'M OKAY, MRS. SIMPSON.
HMMM, WELL, THAT'S A MATTER OF OPINION.
DING-DONG
WHAT IN THE NAME OF TOMMY HILFIGER ARE YOU WEARING?
IT'S UH...UM... A SQUISH-ZILLA SQUISHEE CUP, MOM.
OH, WHAT A WONDERFUL IDEA. WE NEVER SOLD EVEN ONE OF THOSE SQUISH-ZILLAS. THEY WERE TOO HEAVY TO CARRY WHEN FULL--A TERRIBLE DESIGN FLAW.
BUT NOW I SEE A NEW MARKETING ANGLE, THE DISPOSABLE KWIK-E-SMOCK! OH, IT WILL BE ALL THE RAGE NEXT FALL!
YOUNG BART, I WOULD LIKE YOU TO HAVE THIS CHICKEN OUTFIT. THANK YOU FOR GIVING ME THE OPPORTUNITY TO PURSUE MY LIFELONG AMBITION.
THANKS, MAN. THIS BABY'S GOING WITH ME NEXT WEEK ON OUR FIELD TRIP TO THE POULTRY FARM.
BWAA-HAHA!
GOODBYE, SIMPSONS! THANK YOU AND COME AGAIN!
I THOUGHT YOU'D NEVER REOPEN!
I KNOW YOU KIDS HAVE A CODE OF SILENCE, AND I WOULD NEVER FORCE YOU TO TELL ME WHY YOU WERE LOCKED INSIDE THE KWIK-E-MART...
OH! OH! OH! I'LL TELL YOU MRS. SIMPSON! WE WERE LOOKING FOR BRAIN FREEZE STEVE! HE ONCE BOUGHT A SQUISHEE AT THE KWIK-E-MART. THE CLERK MESSED UP AND GAVE HIM TWO STRAWS!
THE BRAIN FREEZE WAS SO BAD THAT HIS HEAD SWELLED UP, CRACKED FROM THE PRESSURE, AND THEN HIS BRAIN OOZED OUT. NOW, HE HAUNTS THE KWIK-E-MART WHEN IT'S CLOSED, AND THAT'S WHY APU NEVER CLOSES.

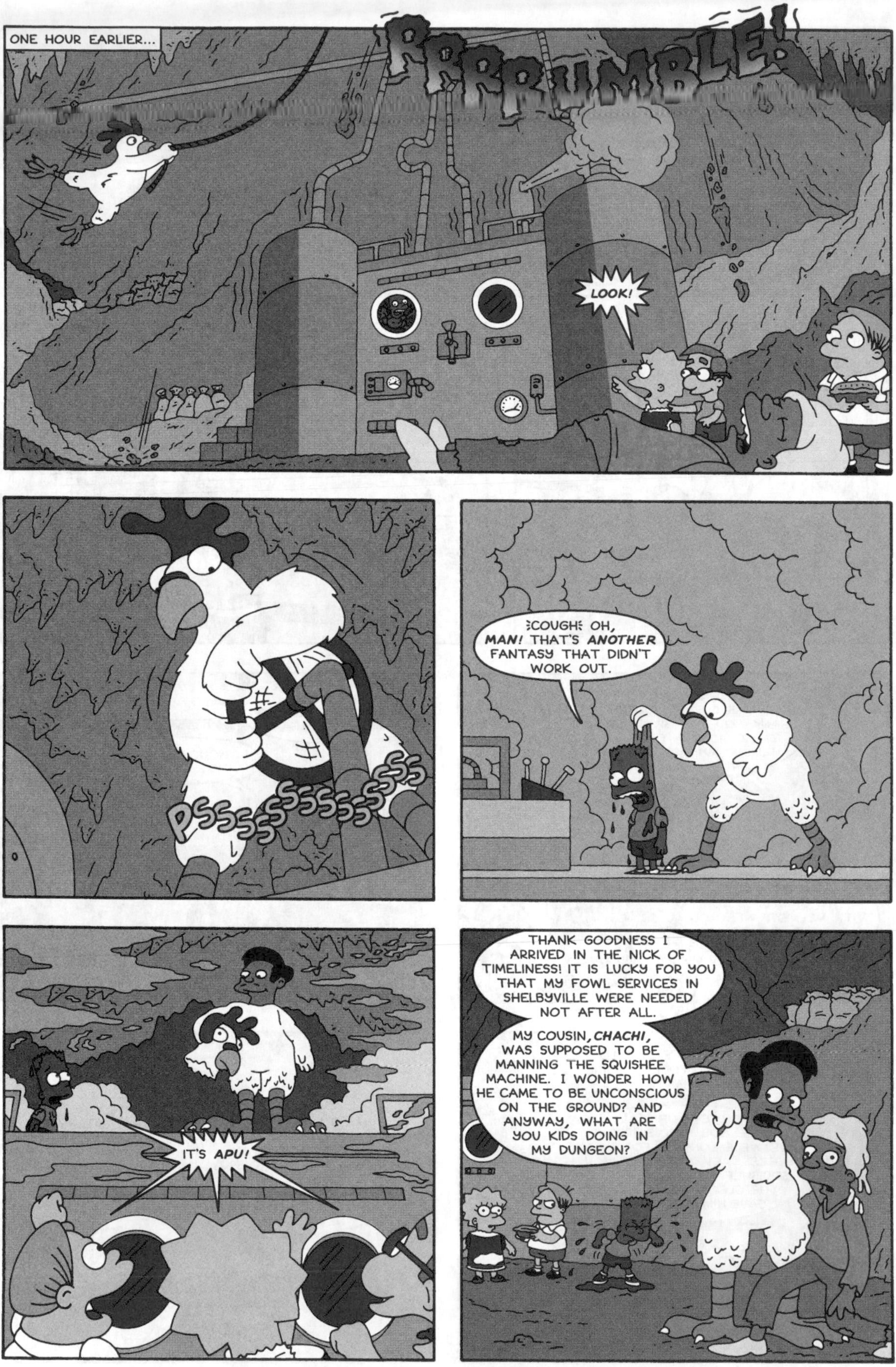
ONE HOUR EARLIER...
RRRRUMBLE!
LOOK!
PSSSSSSSSSSSSSS
:COUGH: OH, MAN! THAT'S ANOTHER FANTASY THAT DIDN'T WORK OUT.
IT'S APU!
THANK GOODNESS I ARRIVED IN THE NICK OF TIMELINESS! IT IS LUCKY FOR YOU THAT MY FOWL SERVICES IN SHELBYVILLE WERE NEEDED NOT AFTER ALL.
MY COUSIN, CHACHI, WAS SUPPOSED TO BE MANNING THE SQUISHEE MACHINE. I WONDER HOW HE CAME TO BE UNCONSCIOUS ON THE GROUND? AND ANYWAY, WHAT ARE YOU KIDS DOING IN MY DUNGEON?

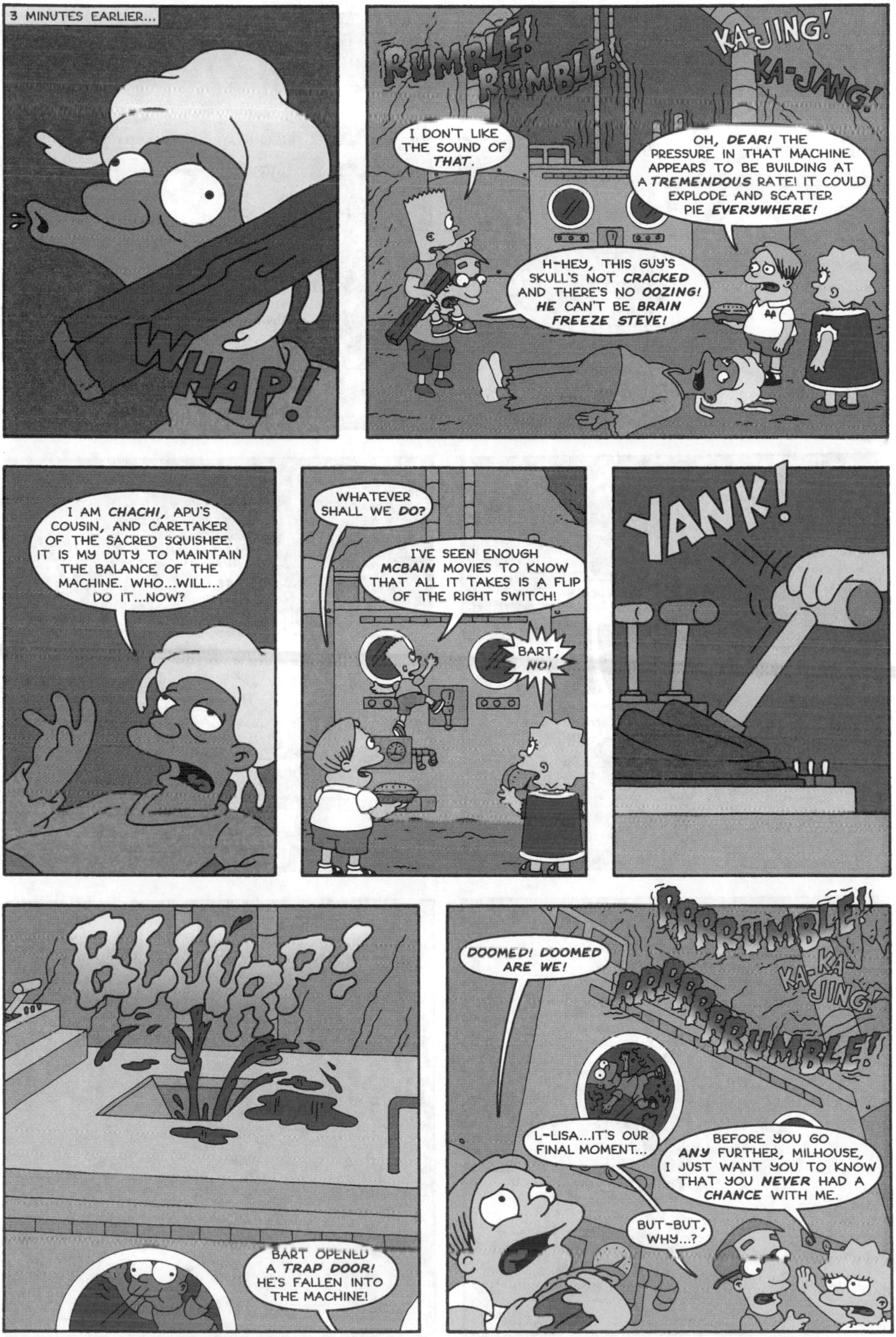

3 MINUTES EARLIER...
WHAP!
RUMBLE! RUMBLE!
KA-JING! KA-JANG!
I DON'T LIKE THE SOUND OF THAT.
OH, DEAR! THE PRESSURE IN THAT MACHINE APPEARS TO BE BUILDING AT A TREMENDOUS RATE! IT COULD EXPLODE AND SCATTER PIE EVERYWHERE!
H-HEY, THIS GUY'S SKULL'S NOT CRACKED AND THERE'S NO OOZING! HE CAN'T BE BRAIN FREEZE STEVE!
I AM CHACHI, APU'S COUSIN, AND CARETAKER OF THE SACRED SQUISHEE. IT IS MY DUTY TO MAINTAIN THE BALANCE OF THE MACHINE. WHO...WILL... DO IT...NOW?
WHATEVER SHALL WE DO?
I'VE SEEN ENOUGH MCBAIN MOVIES TO KNOW THAT ALL IT TAKES IS A FLIP OF THE RIGHT SWITCH!
BART, NO!
YANK!
BLUURP!
BART OPENED A TRAP DOOR! HE'S FALLEN INTO THE MACHINE!
RRRRUMBLE!
DOOMED! DOOMED ARE WE!
KA-KA-JING!
RRRRRRRUMBLE!
L-LISA...IT'S OUR FINAL MOMENT...
BEFORE YOU GO ANY FURTHER, MILHOUSE, I JUST WANT YOU TO KNOW THAT YOU NEVER HAD A CHANCE WITH ME.
BUT-BUT, WHY...?

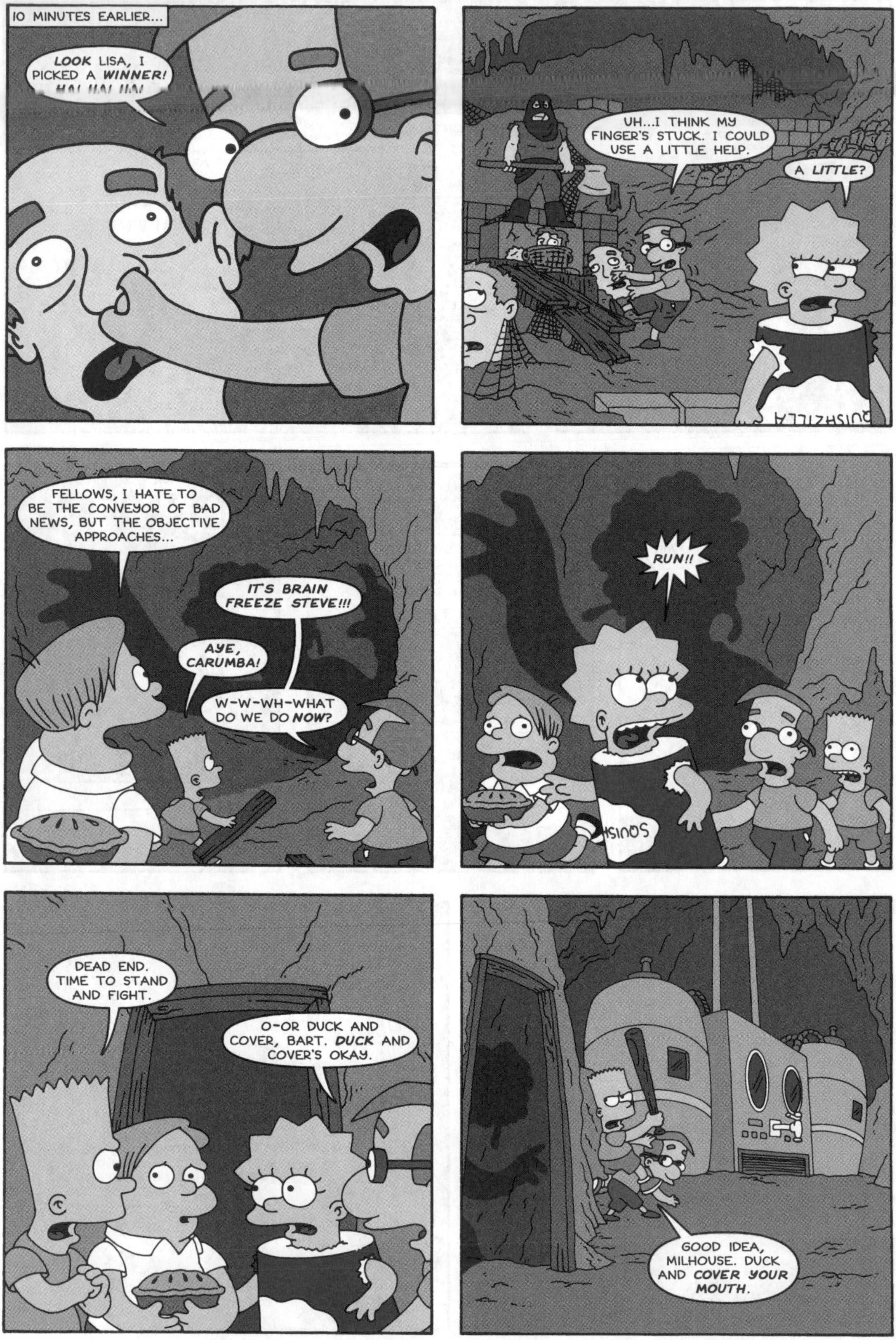

10 MINUTES EARLIER...
LOOK LISA, I PICKED A WINNER! HA! HA! HA!
UH...I THINK MY FINGER'S STUCK. I COULD USE A LITTLE HELP.
A LITTLE?
FELLOWS, I HATE TO BE THE CONVEYOR OF BAD NEWS, BUT THE OBJECTIVE APPROACHES...
IT'S BRAIN FREEZE STEVE!!!
AYE, CARUMBA!
W-W-WH-WHAT DO WE DO NOW?
RUN!!
DEAD END. TIME TO STAND AND FIGHT.
O-OR DUCK AND COVER, BART. DUCK AND COVER'S OKAY.
GOOD IDEA, MILHOUSE. DUCK AND COVER YOUR MOUTH.

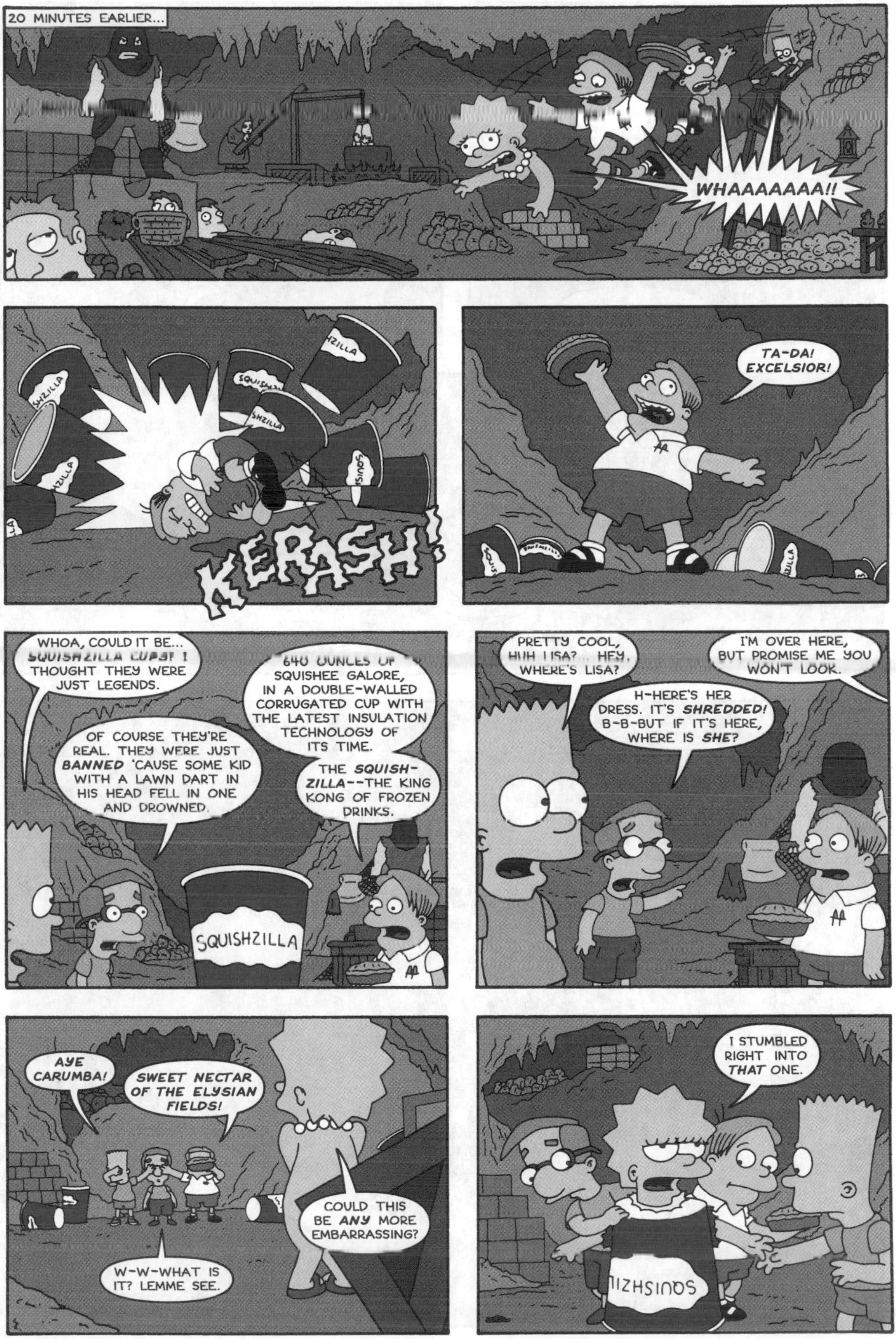
20 MINUTES EARLIER...
WHAAAAAAA!!
KERASH!
TA-DA! EXCELSIOR!
WHOA, COULD IT BE... SQUISHZILLA CUPS! I THOUGHT THEY WERE JUST LEGENDS.
OF COURSE THEY'RE REAL. THEY WERE JUST BANNED 'CAUSE SOME KID WITH A LAWN DART IN HIS HEAD FELL IN ONE AND DROWNED.
640 OUNCES OF SQUISHEE GALORE, IN A DOUBLE-WALLED CORRUGATED CUP WITH THE LATEST INSULATION TECHNOLOGY OF ITS TIME.
THE SQUISHZILLA--THE KING KONG OF FROZEN DRINKS.
SQUISHZILLA
PRETTY COOL, HUH LISA? .. HEY, WHERE'S LISA?
I'M OVER HERE, BUT PROMISE ME YOU WON'T LOOK.
H-HERE'S HER DRESS. IT'S SHREDDED! B-B-BUT IF IT'S HERE, WHERE IS SHE?
AYE CARUMBA!
SWEET NECTAR OF THE ELYSIAN FIELDS!
COULD THIS BE ANY MORE EMBARRASSING?
W-W-WHAT IS IT? LEMME SEE.
I STUMBLED RIGHT INTO THAT ONE.

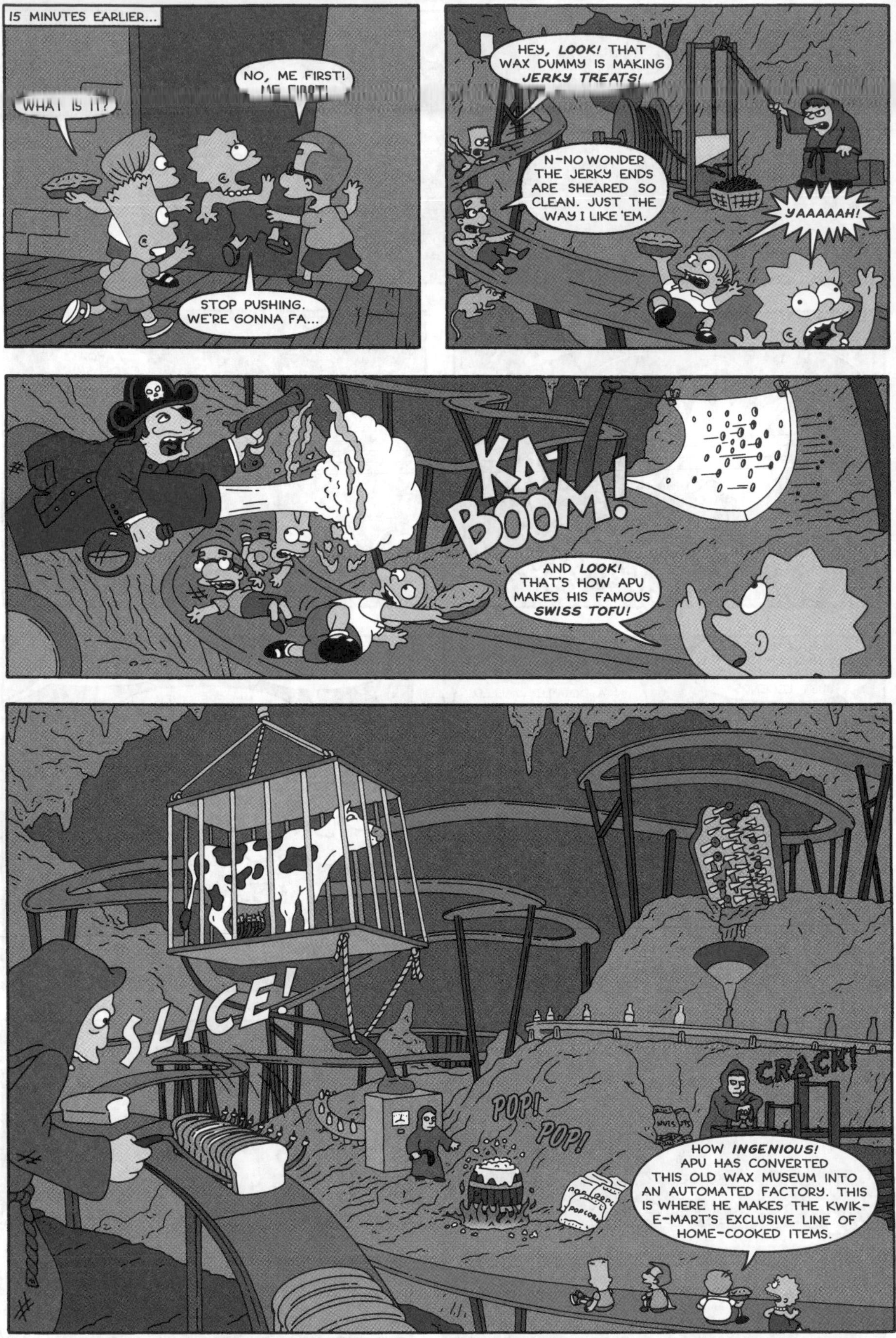
15 MINUTES EARLIER...
WHAT IS IT?
NO, ME FIRST! ME FIRST!
STOP PUSHING. WE'RE GONNA FA...
HEY, LOOK! THAT WAX DUMMY IS MAKING JERKY TREATS!
N-NO WONDER THE JERKY ENDS ARE SHEARED SO CLEAN. JUST THE WAY I LIKE 'EM.
YAAAAAH!
KA-BOOM!
AND LOOK! THAT'S HOW APU MAKES HIS FAMOUS SWISS TOFU!
SLICE!
POP!
POP!
CRACK!
HOW INGENIOUS! APU HAS CONVERTED THIS OLD WAX MUSEUM INTO AN AUTOMATED FACTORY. THIS IS WHERE HE MAKES THE KWIK-E-MART'S EXCLUSIVE LINE OF HOME-COOKED ITEMS.

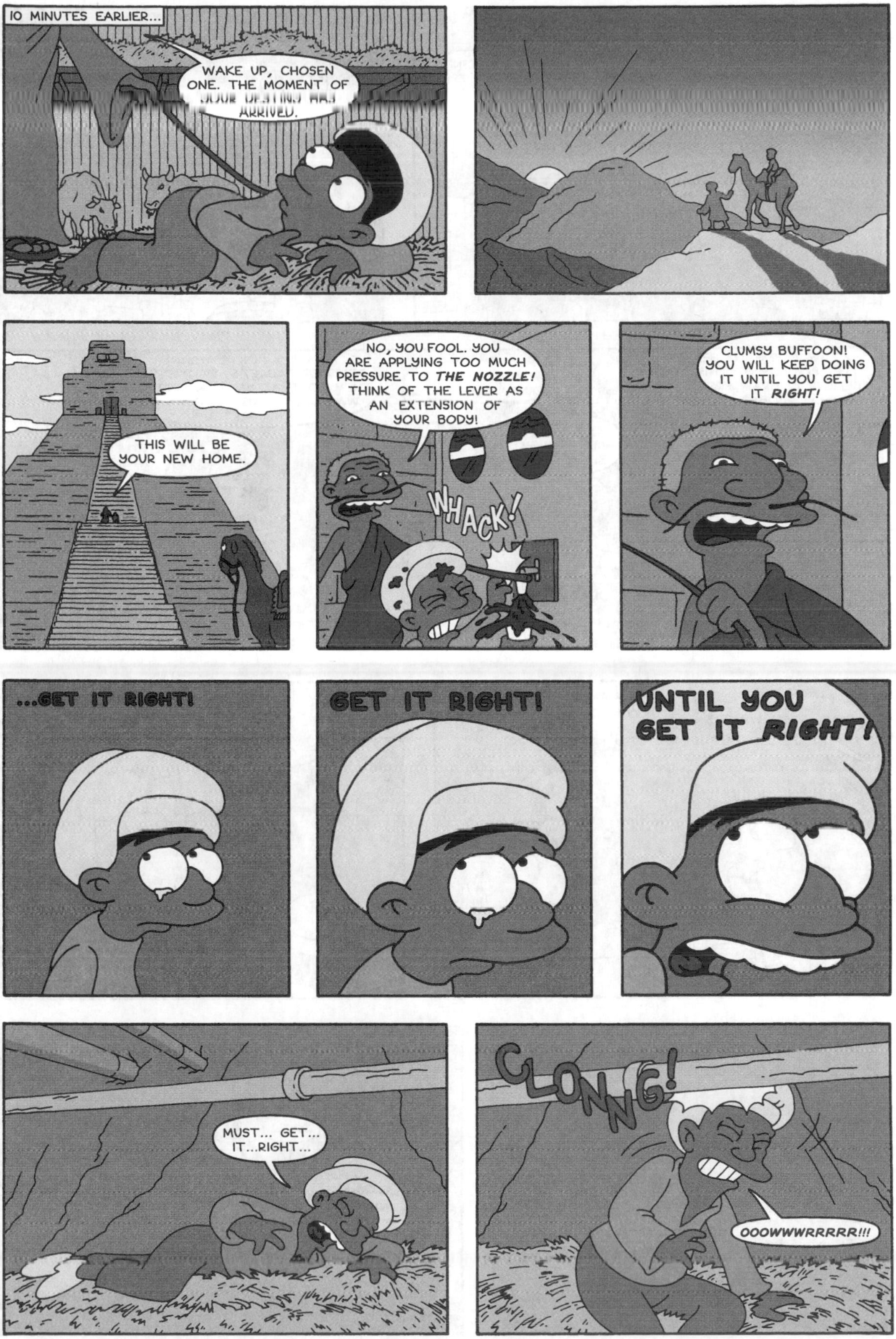
10 MINUTES EARLIER...
WAKE UP, CHOSEN ONE. THE MOMENT OF ARRIVED.
THIS WILL BE YOUR NEW HOME.
NO, YOU FOOL. YOU ARE APPLYING TOO MUCH PRESSURE TO THE NOZZLE! THINK OF THE LEVER AS AN EXTENSION OF YOUR BODY!
WHACK!
CLUMSY BUFFOON! YOU WILL KEEP DOING IT UNTIL YOU GET IT RIGHT!
...GET IT RIGHT!
GET IT RIGHT!
UNTIL YOU GET IT RIGHT!
MUST... GET... IT...RIGHT...
CLONNG!
OOOWWWRRRRR!!!

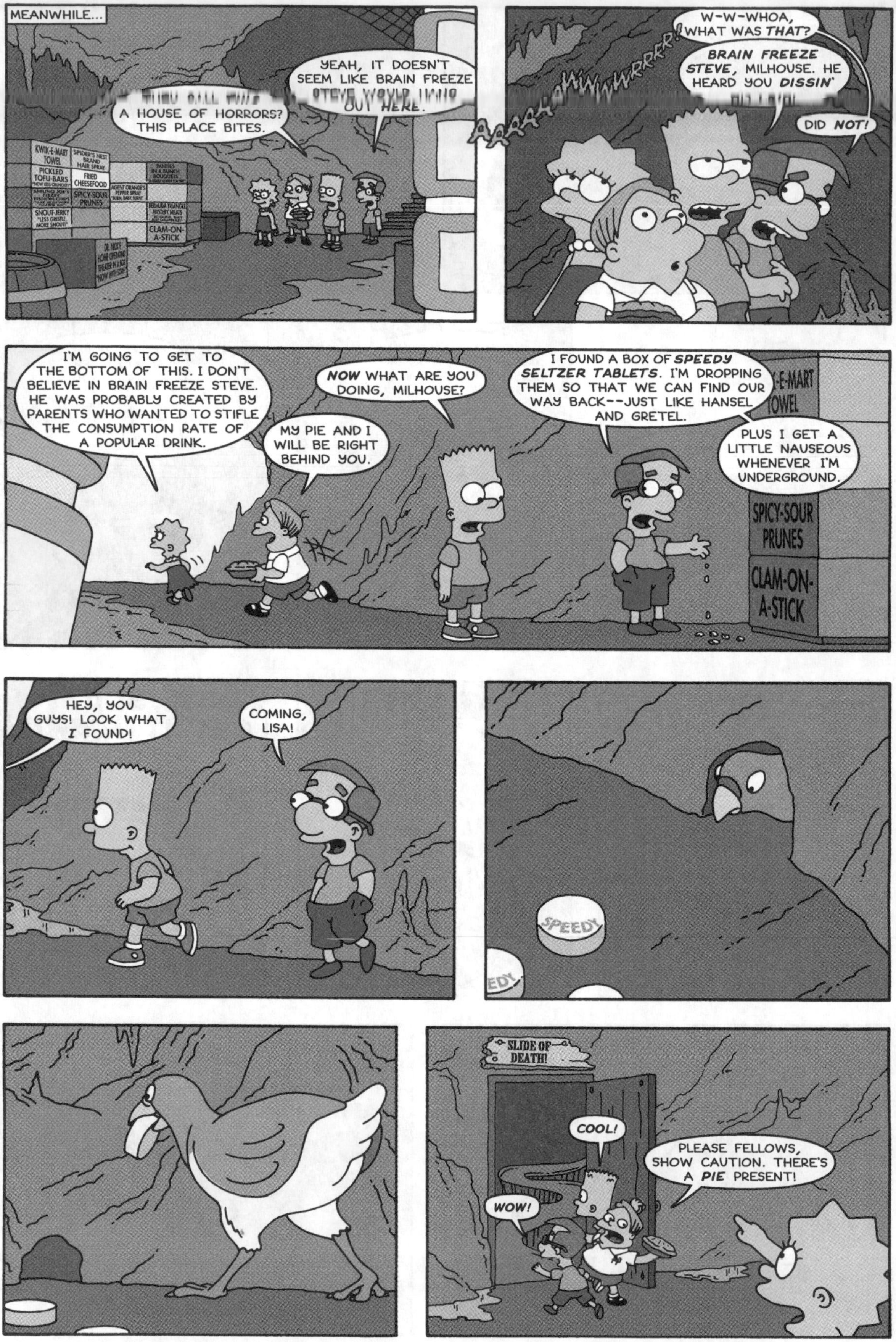

MEANWHILE...
A HOUSE OF HORRORS? THIS PLACE BITES.
YEAH, IT DOESN'T SEEM LIKE BRAIN FREEZE
OUT HERE.
KWIK-E-MART TOWEL
SPIDER'S NEST BRAND HAIR SPRAY
PICKLED TOFU-BARS
FRIED CHEESEFOOD
SPICY-SOUR PRUNES
SNOUT-JERKY "LESS GRISTLE, MORE SNOUT!"
CLAM-ON-A-STICK
AAARRAHHWWWWRRRRR!
W-W-WHOA, WHAT WAS THAT?
BRAIN FREEZE STEVE, MILHOUSE. HE HEARD YOU DISSIN'
DID NOT!
I'M GOING TO GET TO THE BOTTOM OF THIS. I DON'T BELIEVE IN BRAIN FREEZE STEVE. HE WAS PROBABLY CREATED BY PARENTS WHO WANTED TO STIFLE THE CONSUMPTION RATE OF A POPULAR DRINK.
MY PIE AND I WILL BE RIGHT BEHIND YOU.
NOW WHAT ARE YOU DOING, MILHOUSE?
I FOUND A BOX OF SPEEDY SELTZER TABLETS. I'M DROPPING THEM SO THAT WE CAN FIND OUR WAY BACK--JUST LIKE HANSEL AND GRETEL.
PLUS I GET A LITTLE NAUSEOUS WHENEVER I'M UNDERGROUND.
HEY, YOU GUYS! LOOK WHAT I FOUND!
COMING, LISA!
SPEEDY
SLIDE OF DEATH!
COOL!
PLEASE FELLOWS, SHOW CAUTION. THERE'S A PIE PRESENT!
WOW!

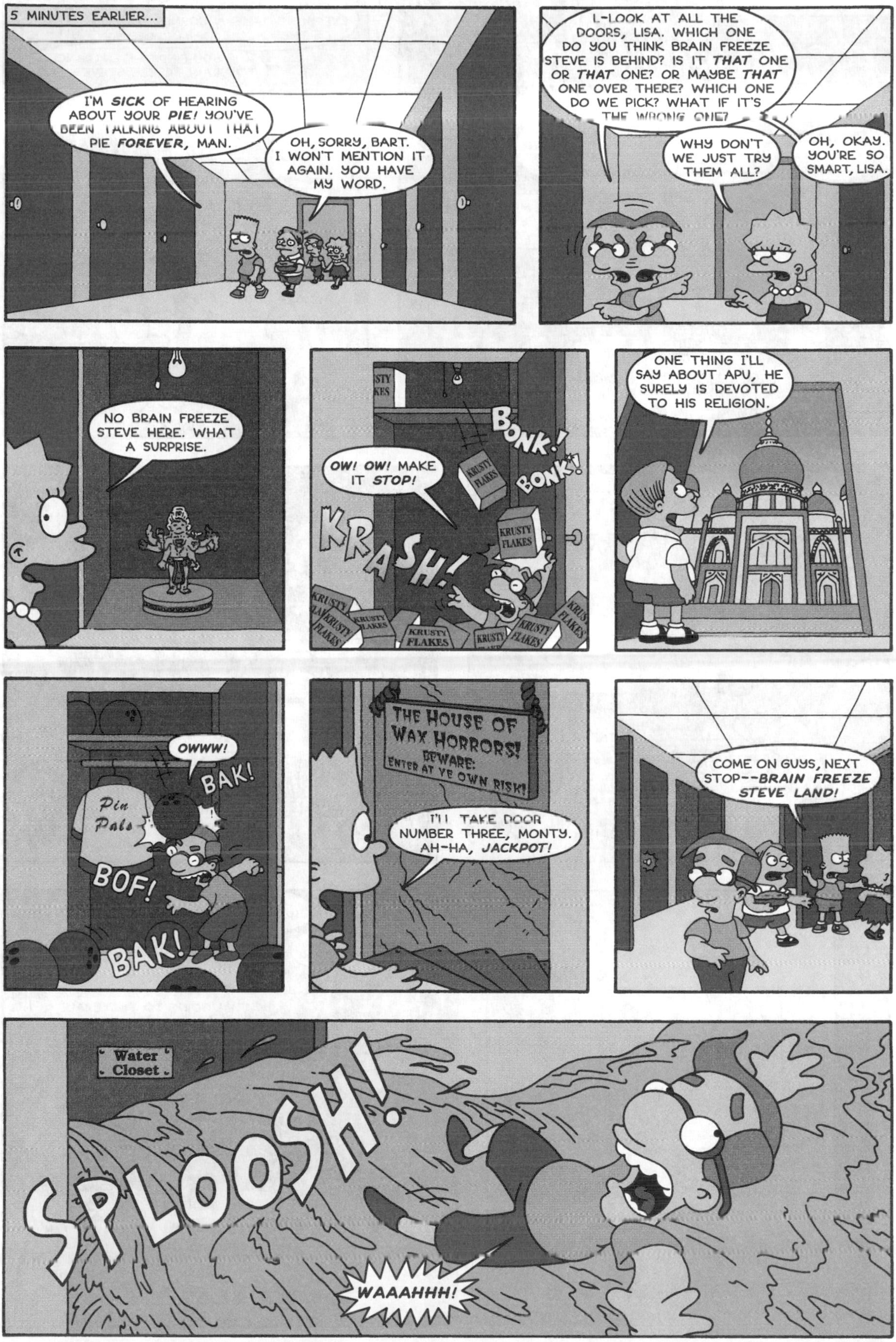
5 MINUTES EARLIER...
I'M SICK OF HEARING ABOUT YOUR PIE! YOU'VE BEEN TALKING ABOUT THAT PIE FOREVER, MAN.
OH, SORRY, BART. I WON'T MENTION IT AGAIN. YOU HAVE MY WORD.
L-LOOK AT ALL THE DOORS, LISA. WHICH ONE DO YOU THINK BRAIN FREEZE STEVE IS BEHIND? IS IT THAT ONE OR THAT ONE? OR MAYBE THAT ONE OVER THERE? WHICH ONE DO WE PICK? WHAT IF IT'S THE WRONG ONE?
WHY DON'T WE JUST TRY THEM ALL?
OH, OKAY. YOU'RE SO SMART, LISA.
NO BRAIN FREEZE STEVE HERE. WHAT A SURPRISE.
OW! OW! MAKE IT STOP!
BONK!
BONK!
KRASH!
KRUSTY FLAKES
ONE THING I'LL SAY ABOUT APU, HE SURELY IS DEVOTED TO HIS RELIGION.
OWWW!
BAK!
Pin Pals
BOF!
BAK!
THE HOUSE OF WAX HORRORS! BEWARE: ENTER AT YE OWN RISK!
I'LL TAKE DOOR NUMBER THREE, MONTY. AH-HA, JACKPOT!
COME ON GUYS, NEXT STOP--BRAIN FREEZE STEVE LAND!
Water Closet
SPLOOSH!
WAAAHHH!

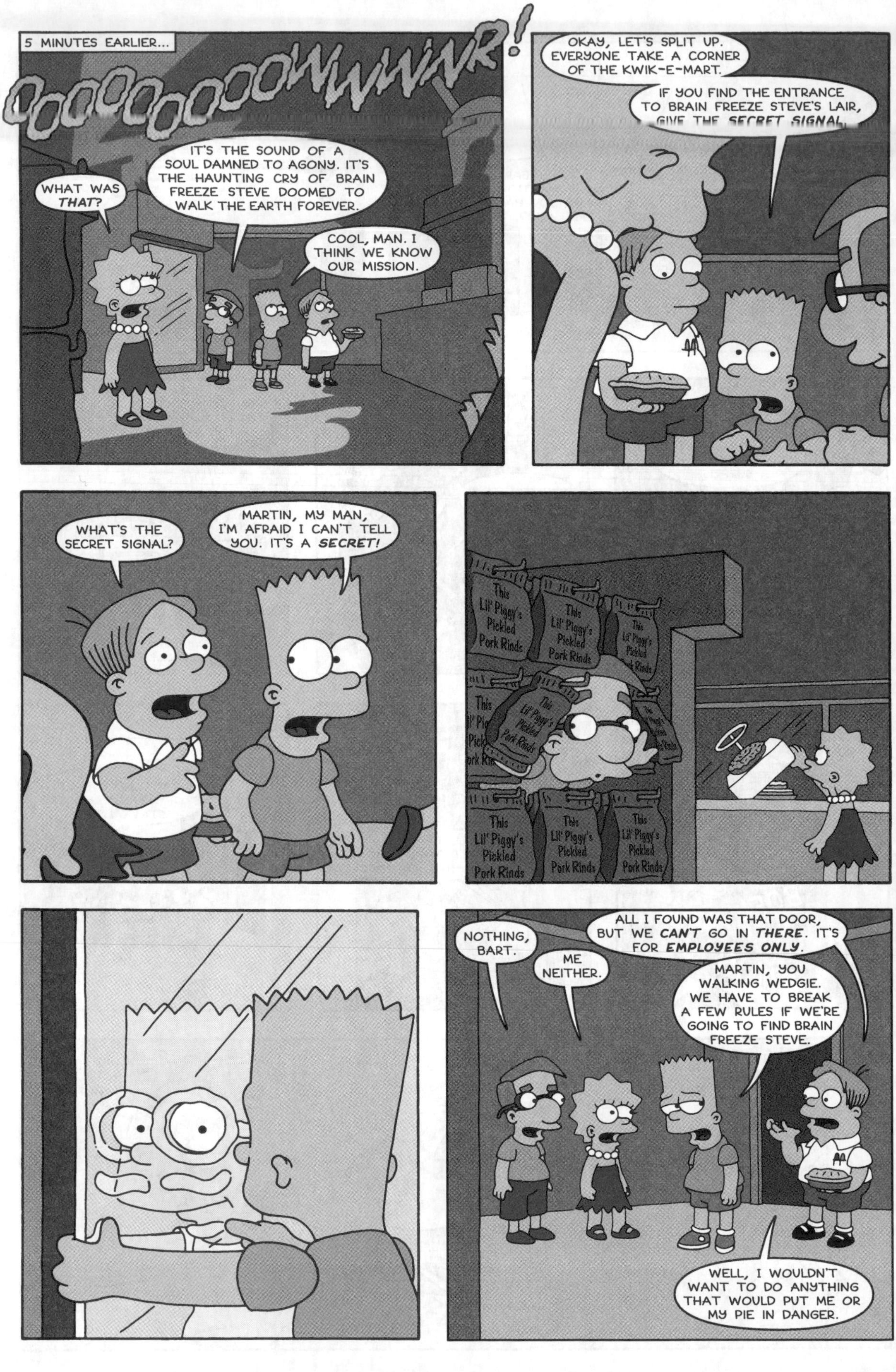
5 MINUTES EARLIER...
OOOOOOOOOOOWWWWR!
WHAT WAS THAT?
IT'S THE SOUND OF A SOUL DAMNED TO AGONY. IT'S THE HAUNTING CRY OF BRAIN FREEZE STEVE DOOMED TO WALK THE EARTH FOREVER.
COOL, MAN. I THINK WE KNOW OUR MISSION.
OKAY, LET'S SPLIT UP. EVERYONE TAKE A CORNER OF THE KWIK-E-MART.
IF YOU FIND THE ENTRANCE TO BRAIN FREEZE STEVE'S LAIR, GIVE THE SECRET SIGNAL.
WHAT'S THE SECRET SIGNAL?
MARTIN, MY MAN, I'M AFRAID I CAN'T TELL YOU. IT'S A SECRET!
This Lil' Piggy's Pickled Pork Rinds
NOTHING, BART.
ME NEITHER.
ALL I FOUND WAS THAT DOOR, BUT WE CAN'T GO IN THERE. IT'S FOR EMPLOYEES ONLY.
MARTIN, YOU WALKING WEDGIE. WE HAVE TO BREAK A FEW RULES IF WE'RE GOING TO FIND BRAIN FREEZE STEVE.
WELL, I WOULDN'T WANT TO DO ANYTHING THAT WOULD PUT ME OR MY PIE IN DANGER.

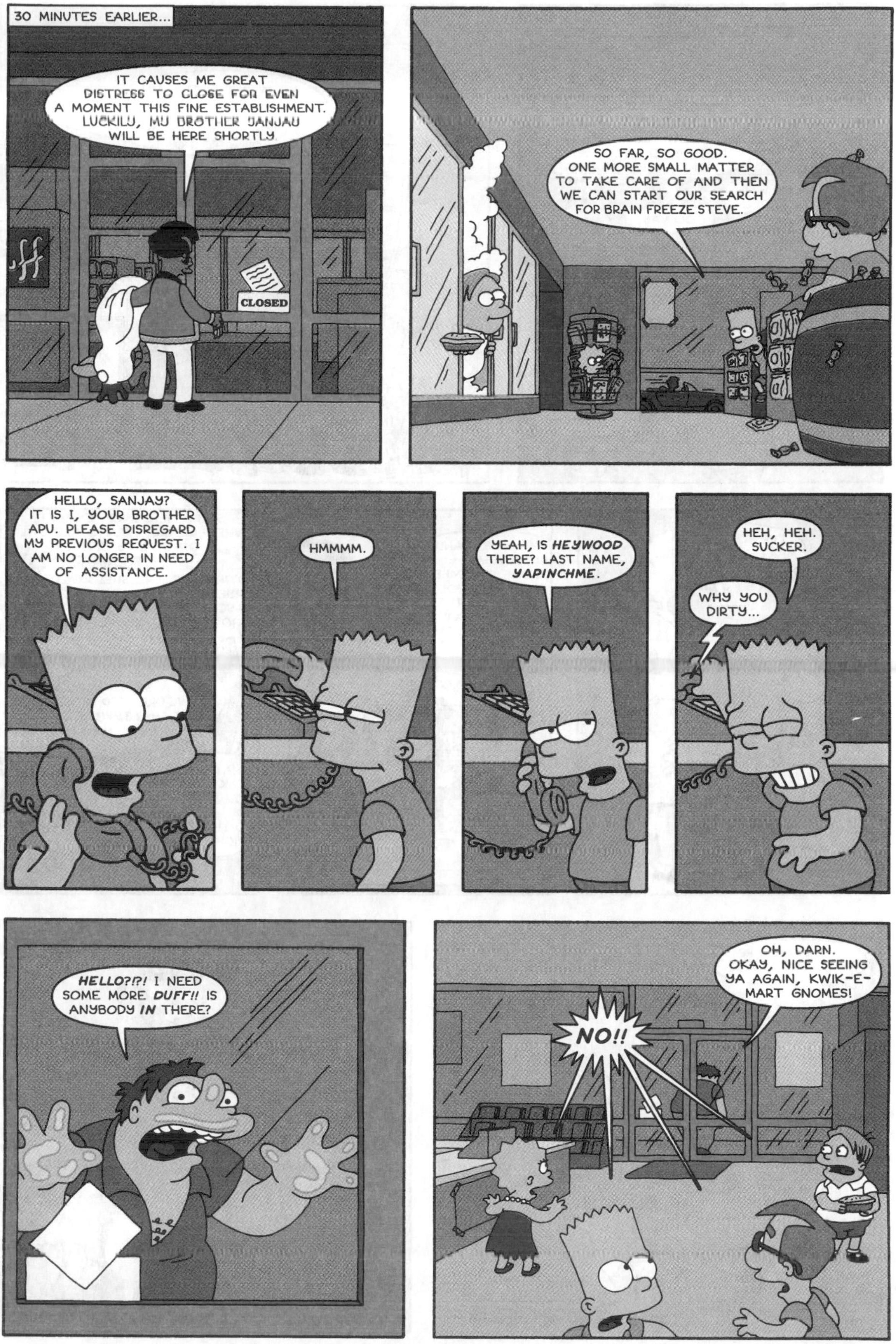
30 MINUTES EARLIER...
IT CAUSES ME GREAT DISTRESS TO CLOSE FOR EVEN A MOMENT THIS FINE ESTABLISHMENT. LUCKILY, MY BROTHER SANJAY WILL BE HERE SHORTLY.
CLOSED
SO FAR, SO GOOD. ONE MORE SMALL MATTER TO TAKE CARE OF AND THEN WE CAN START OUR SEARCH FOR BRAIN FREEZE STEVE.
HELLO, SANJAY? IT IS I, YOUR BROTHER APU. PLEASE DISREGARD MY PREVIOUS REQUEST. I AM NO LONGER IN NEED OF ASSISTANCE.
HMMMM.
YEAH, IS HEYWOOD THERE? LAST NAME, YAPINCHME.
WHY YOU DIRTY...
HEH, HEH. SUCKER.
HELLO?!?! I NEED SOME MORE DUFF!! IS ANYBODY IN THERE?
NO!!
OH, DARN. OKAY, NICE SEEING YA AGAIN, KWIK-E-MART GNOMES!

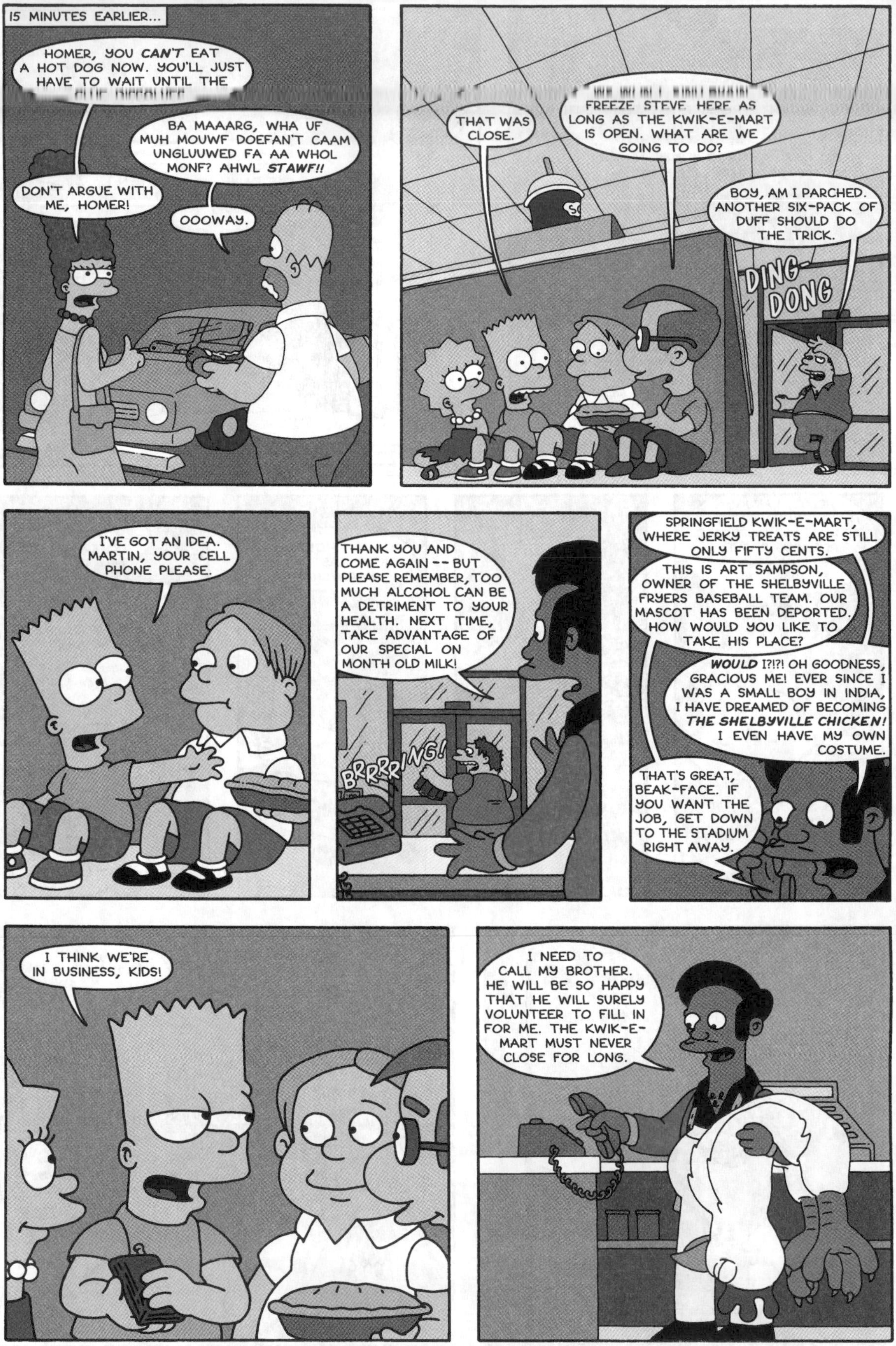

15 MINUTES EARLIER...
HOMER, YOU CAN'T EAT A HOT DOG NOW. YOU'LL JUST HAVE TO WAIT UNTIL THE
BA MAAARG, WHA UF MUH MOUWF DOEFAN'T CAAM UNGLUUWED FA AA WHOL MONF? AHWL STAWF!!
DON'T ARGUE WITH ME, HOMER!
OOOWAY.
THAT WAS CLOSE.
FREEZE STEVE HERE AS LONG AS THE KWIK-E-MART IS OPEN. WHAT ARE WE GOING TO DO?
BOY, AM I PARCHED. ANOTHER SIX-PACK OF DUFF SHOULD DO THE TRICK.
DING-DONG
I'VE GOT AN IDEA. MARTIN, YOUR CELL PHONE PLEASE.
THANK YOU AND COME AGAIN -- BUT PLEASE REMEMBER, TOO MUCH ALCOHOL CAN BE A DETRIMENT TO YOUR HEALTH. NEXT TIME, TAKE ADVANTAGE OF OUR SPECIAL ON MONTH OLD MILK!
BRRRRING!
SPRINGFIELD KWIK-E-MART, WHERE JERKY TREATS ARE STILL ONLY FIFTY CENTS.
THIS IS ART SAMPSON, OWNER OF THE SHELBYVILLE FRYERS BASEBALL TEAM. OUR MASCOT HAS BEEN DEPORTED. HOW WOULD YOU LIKE TO TAKE HIS PLACE?
WOULD I?!?! OH GOODNESS, GRACIOUS ME! EVER SINCE I WAS A SMALL BOY IN INDIA, I HAVE DREAMED OF BECOMING THE SHELBYVILLE CHICKEN! I EVEN HAVE MY OWN COSTUME.
THAT'S GREAT, BEAK-FACE. IF YOU WANT THE JOB, GET DOWN TO THE STADIUM RIGHT AWAY.
I THINK WE'RE IN BUSINESS, KIDS!
I NEED TO CALL MY BROTHER. HE WILL BE SO HAPPY THAT HE WILL SURELY VOLUNTEER TO FILL IN FOR ME. THE KWIK-E-MART MUST NEVER CLOSE FOR LONG.

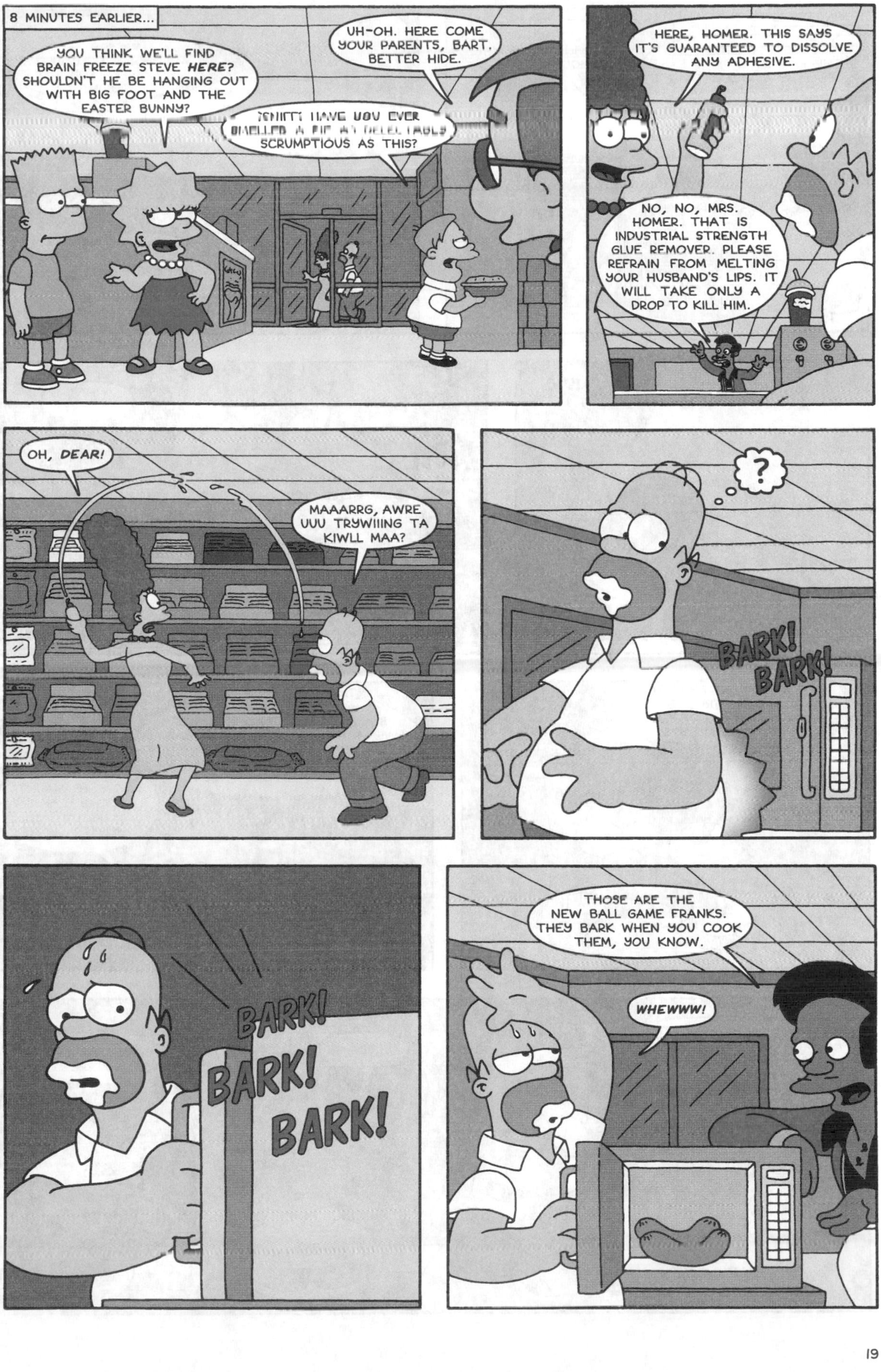

8 MINUTES EARLIER...
YOU THINK WE'LL FIND BRAIN FREEZE STEVE *HERE*? SHOULDN'T HE BE HANGING OUT WITH BIG FOOT AND THE EASTER BUNNY?
UH-OH. HERE COME YOUR PARENTS, BART. BETTER HIDE.
SCRUMPTIOUS AS THIS?
HERE, HOMER. THIS SAYS IT'S GUARANTEED TO DISSOLVE ANY ADHESIVE.
NO, NO, MRS. HOMER. THAT IS INDUSTRIAL STRENGTH GLUE REMOVER. PLEASE REFRAIN FROM MELTING YOUR HUSBAND'S LIPS. IT WILL TAKE ONLY A DROP TO KILL HIM.
OH, *DEAR!*
MAAARRG, AWRE UUU TRYWIIING TA KIWLL MAA?
?
BARK!
BARK!
BARK!
BARK!
BARK!
THOSE ARE THE NEW BALL GAME FRANKS. THEY BARK WHEN YOU COOK THEM, YOU KNOW.
WHEWWW!

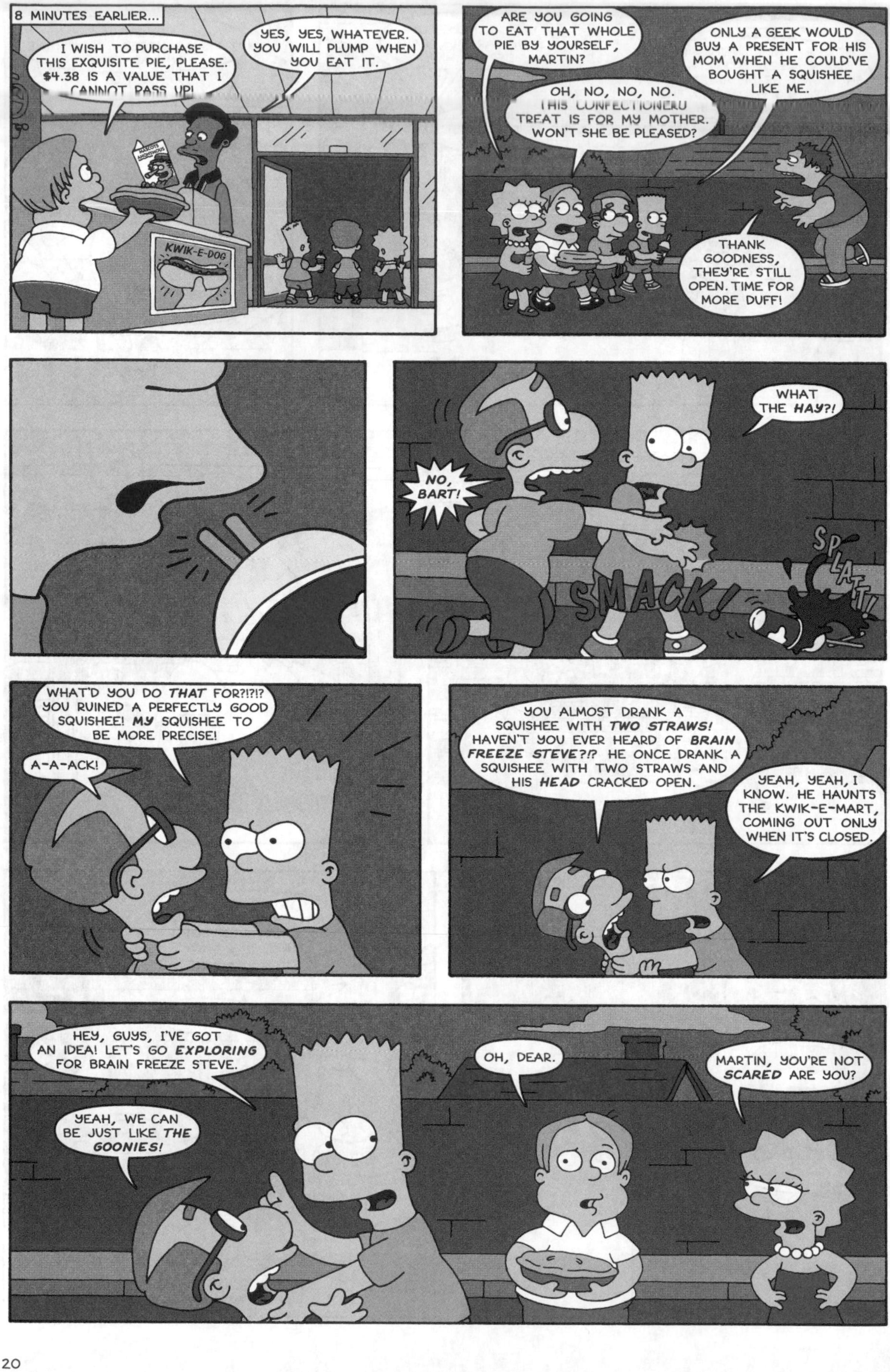

8 MINUTES EARLIER...
I WISH TO PURCHASE THIS EXQUISITE PIE, PLEASE. $4.38 IS A VALUE THAT I CANNOT PASS UP!
YES, YES, WHATEVER. YOU WILL PLUMP WHEN YOU EAT IT.
MASCOTS ANONYMOUS
KWIK-E-DOG
ARE YOU GOING TO EAT THAT WHOLE PIE BY YOURSELF, MARTIN?
OH, NO, NO, NO. THIS CONFECTIONERY TREAT IS FOR MY MOTHER. WON'T SHE BE PLEASED?
ONLY A GEEK WOULD BUY A PRESENT FOR HIS MOM WHEN HE COULD'VE BOUGHT A SQUISHEE LIKE ME.
THANK GOODNESS, THEY'RE STILL OPEN. TIME FOR MORE DUFF!
NO, BART!
WHAT THE HAY?!
SMACK!
SPLATT!!
WHAT'D YOU DO THAT FOR?!?!? YOU RUINED A PERFECTLY GOOD SQUISHEE! MY SQUISHEE TO BE MORE PRECISE!
A-A-ACK!
YOU ALMOST DRANK A SQUISHEE WITH TWO STRAWS! HAVEN'T YOU EVER HEARD OF BRAIN FREEZE STEVE?!? HE ONCE DRANK A SQUISHEE WITH TWO STRAWS AND HIS HEAD CRACKED OPEN.
YEAH, YEAH, I KNOW. HE HAUNTS THE KWIK-E-MART, COMING OUT ONLY WHEN IT'S CLOSED.
HEY, GUYS, I'VE GOT AN IDEA! LET'S GO EXPLORING FOR BRAIN FREEZE STEVE.
YEAH, WE CAN BE JUST LIKE THE GOONIES!
OH, DEAR.
MARTIN, YOU'RE NOT SCARED ARE YOU?

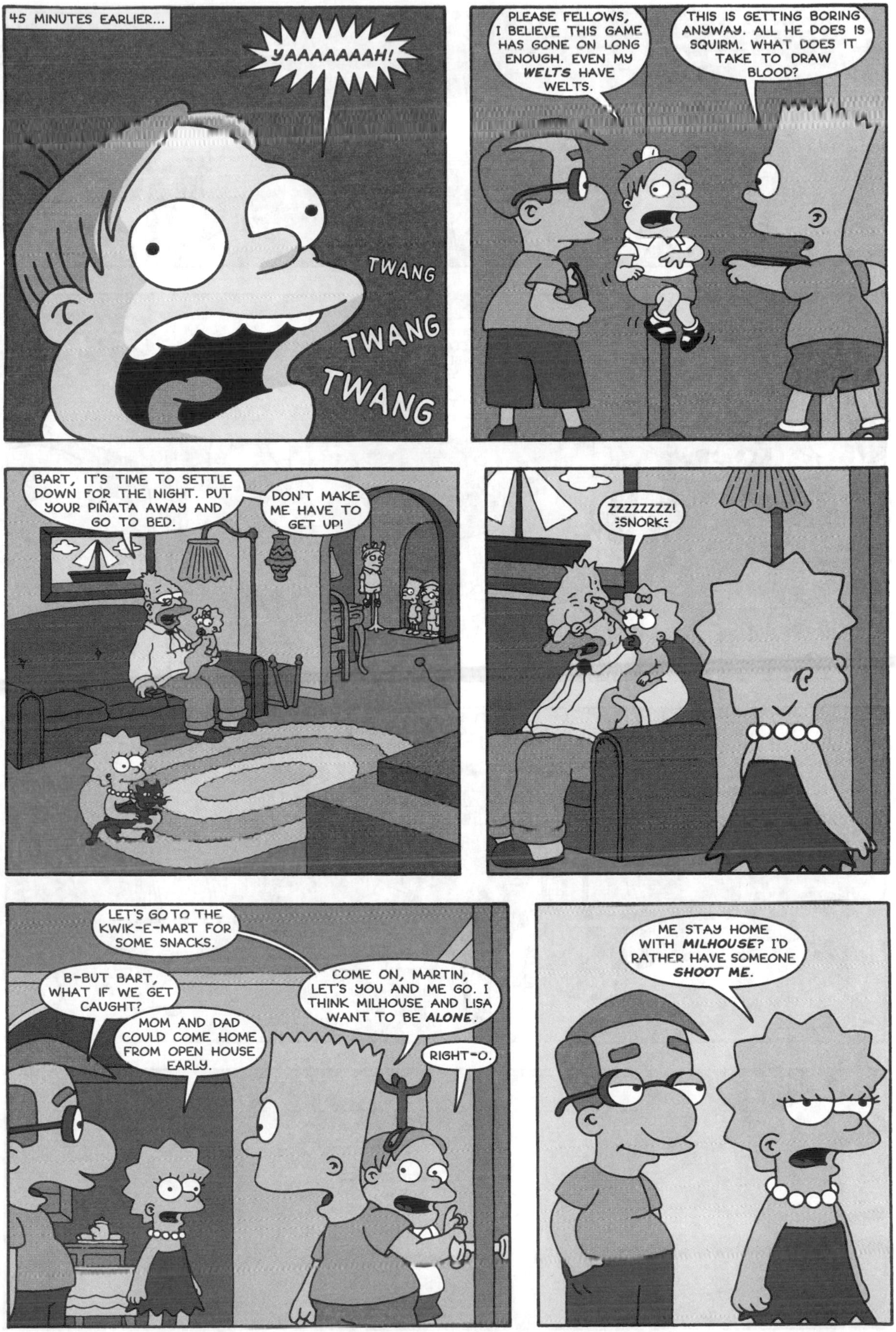
45 MINUTES EARLIER...
YAAAAAAAH!
TWANG
TWANG
TWANG
PLEASE FELLOWS, I BELIEVE THIS GAME HAS GONE ON LONG ENOUGH. EVEN MY WELTS HAVE WELTS.
THIS IS GETTING BORING ANYWAY. ALL HE DOES IS SQUIRM. WHAT DOES IT TAKE TO DRAW BLOOD?
BART, IT'S TIME TO SETTLE DOWN FOR THE NIGHT. PUT YOUR PIÑATA AWAY AND GO TO BED.
DON'T MAKE ME HAVE TO GET UP!
ZZZZZZZZ! SNORK
LET'S GO TO THE KWIK-E-MART FOR SOME SNACKS.
B-BUT BART, WHAT IF WE GET CAUGHT?
MOM AND DAD COULD COME HOME FROM OPEN HOUSE EARLY.
COME ON, MARTIN, LET'S YOU AND ME GO. I THINK MILHOUSE AND LISA WANT TO BE ALONE.
RIGHT-O.
ME STAY HOME WITH MILHOUSE? I'D RATHER HAVE SOMEONE SHOOT ME.

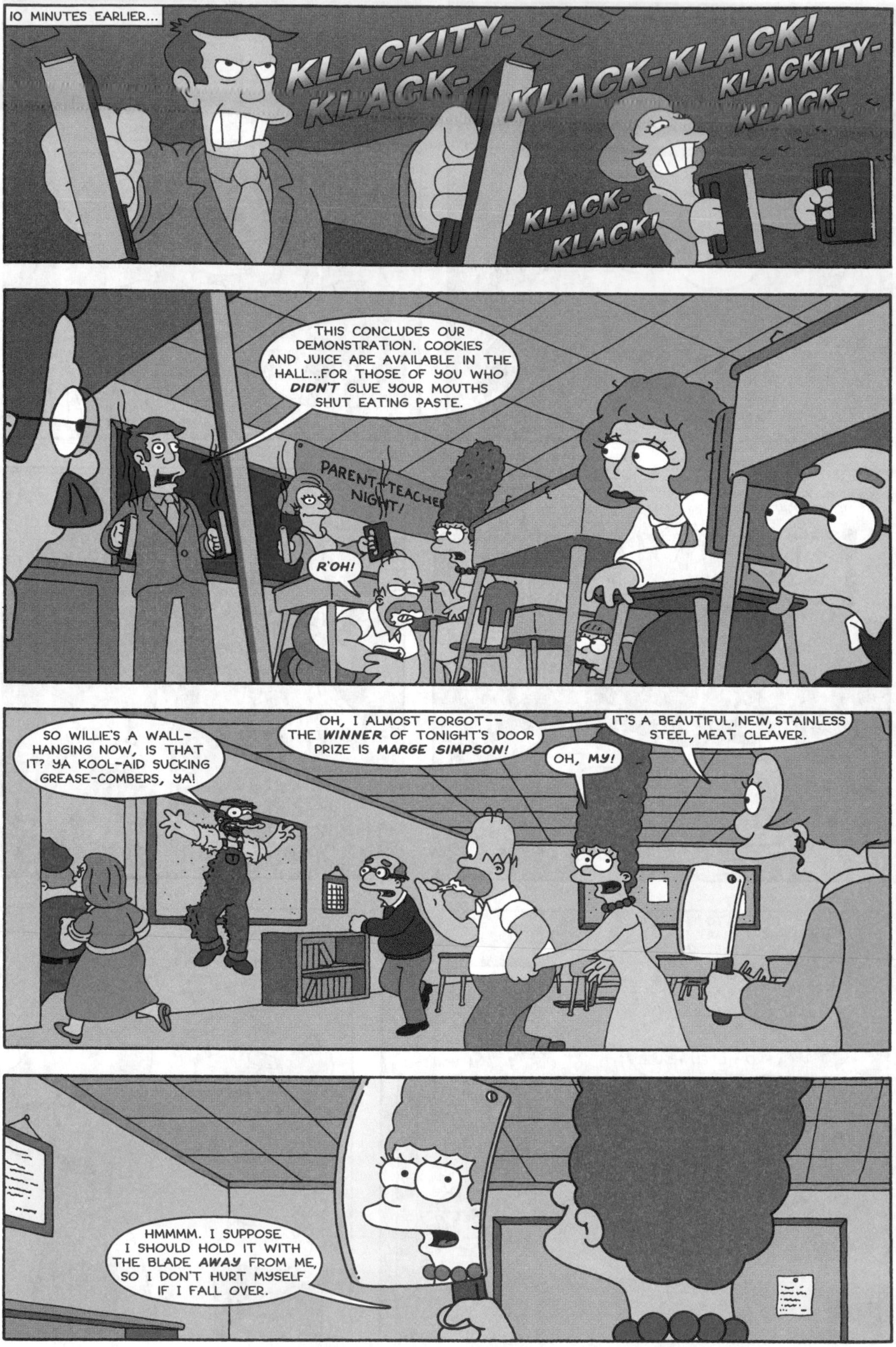
10 MINUTES EARLIER...
KLACKITY-KLACK-
KLACK-KLACK!
KLACKITY-KLACK-
KLACK-KLACK!
THIS CONCLUDES OUR DEMONSTRATION. COOKIES AND JUICE ARE AVAILABLE IN THE HALL...FOR THOSE OF YOU WHO DIDN'T GLUE YOUR MOUTHS SHUT EATING PASTE.
PARENT-TEACHER NIGHT!
R'OH!
SO WILLIE'S A WALL-HANGING NOW, IS THAT IT? YA KOOL-AID SUCKING GREASE-COMBERS, YA!
OH, I ALMOST FORGOT-- THE WINNER OF TONIGHT'S DOOR PRIZE IS MARGE SIMPSON!
OH, MY!
IT'S A BEAUTIFUL, NEW, STAINLESS STEEL, MEAT CLEAVER.
HMMMM. I SUPPOSE I SHOULD HOLD IT WITH THE BLADE AWAY FROM ME, SO I DON'T HURT MYSELF IF I FALL OVER.

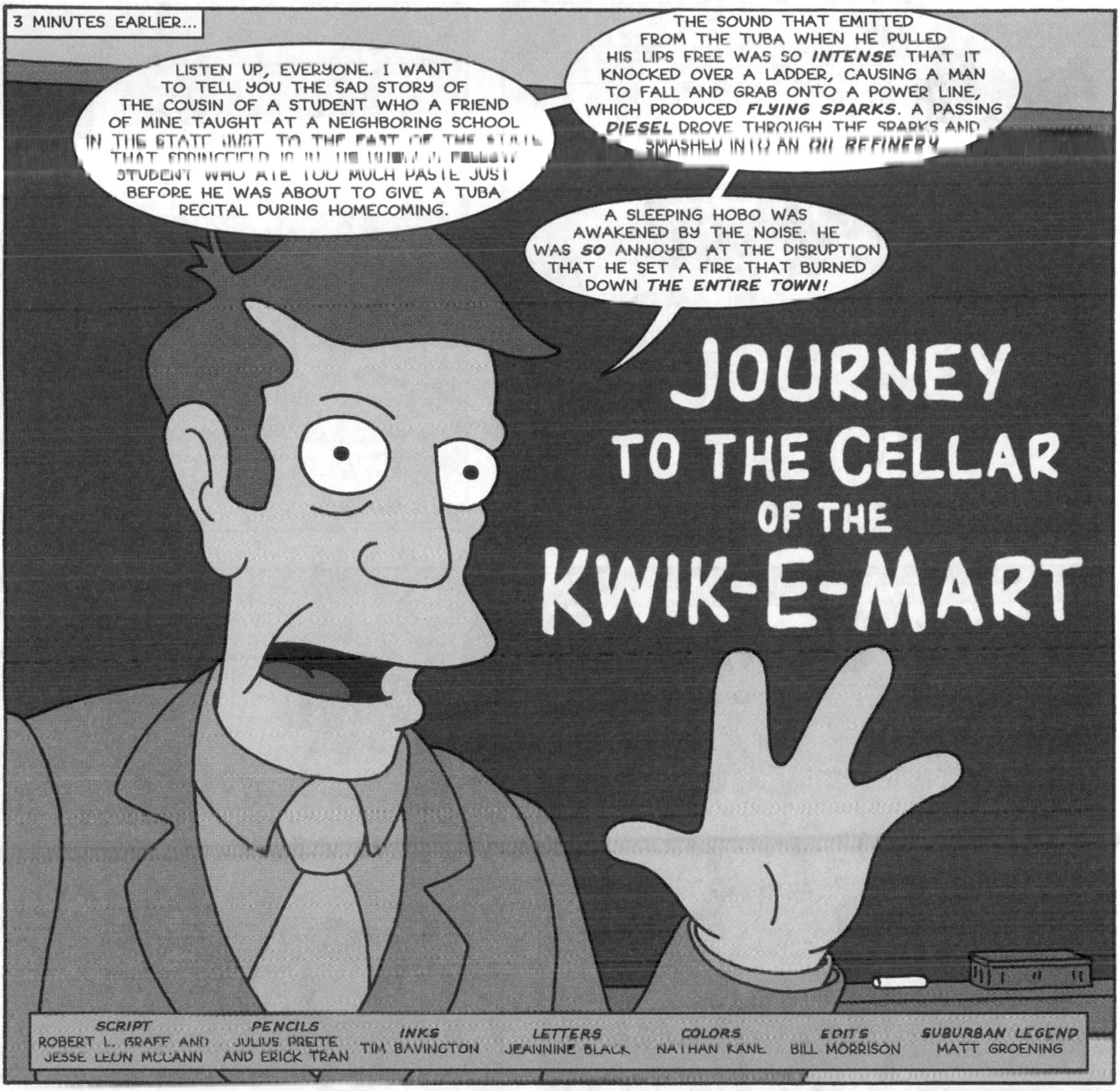
3 MINUTES EARLIER...
LISTEN UP, EVERYONE. I WANT TO TELL YOU THE SAD STORY OF THE COUSIN OF A STUDENT WHO A FRIEND OF MINE TAUGHT AT A NEIGHBORING SCHOOL IN THE STATE JUST TO THE EAST OF THE STATE THAT SPRINGFIELD IS IN. STUDENT WHO ATE TOO MUCH PASTE JUST BEFORE HE WAS ABOUT TO GIVE A TUBA RECITAL DURING HOMECOMING.
THE SOUND THAT EMITTED FROM THE TUBA WHEN HE PULLED HIS LIPS FREE WAS SO *INTENSE* THAT IT KNOCKED OVER A LADDER, CAUSING A MAN TO FALL AND GRAB ONTO A POWER LINE, WHICH PRODUCED ***FLYING SPARKS***. A PASSING ***DIESEL*** DROVE THROUGH THE SPARKS AND SMASHED INTO AN ***OIL REFINERY***
A SLEEPING HOBO WAS AWAKENED BY THE NOISE. HE WAS ***SO*** ANNOYED AT THE DISRUPTION THAT HE SET A FIRE THAT BURNED DOWN ***THE ENTIRE TOWN!***
JOURNEY TO THE CELLAR OF THE KWIK-E-MART
SCRIPT ROBERT L. GRAFF AND JESSE LEON McCANN
PENCILS JULIUS PREITE AND ERICK TRAN
INKS TIM BAVINGTON
LETTERS JEANNINE BLACK
COLORS NATHAN KANE
EDITS BILL MORRISON
SUBURBAN LEGEND MATT GROENING

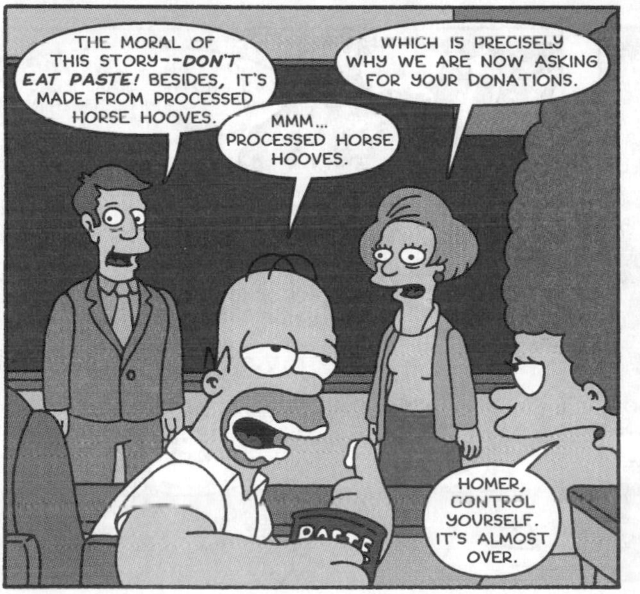
THE MORAL OF THIS STORY--***DON'T EAT PASTE!*** BESIDES, IT'S MADE FROM PROCESSED HORSE HOOVES.
MMM... PROCESSED HORSE HOOVES.
WHICH IS PRECISELY WHY WE ARE NOW ASKING FOR YOUR DONATIONS.
HOMER, CONTROL YOURSELF. IT'S ALMOST OVER.

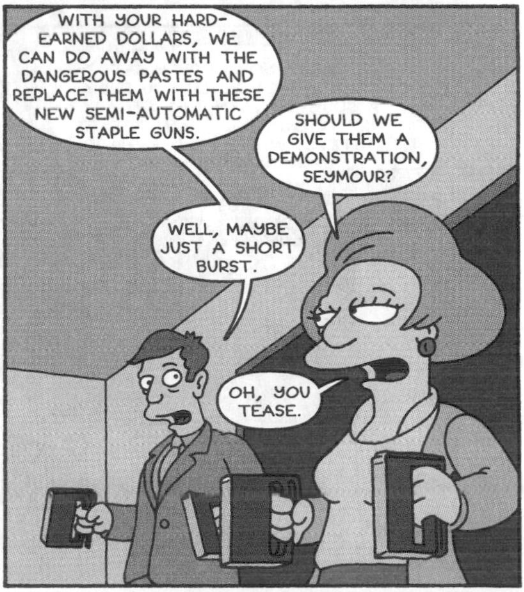
WITH YOUR HARD-EARNED DOLLARS, WE CAN DO AWAY WITH THE DANGEROUS PASTES AND REPLACE THEM WITH THESE NEW SEMI-AUTOMATIC STAPLE GUNS.
SHOULD WE GIVE THEM A DEMONSTRATION, SEYMOUR?
WELL, MAYBE JUST A SHORT BURST.
OH, YOU TEASE.

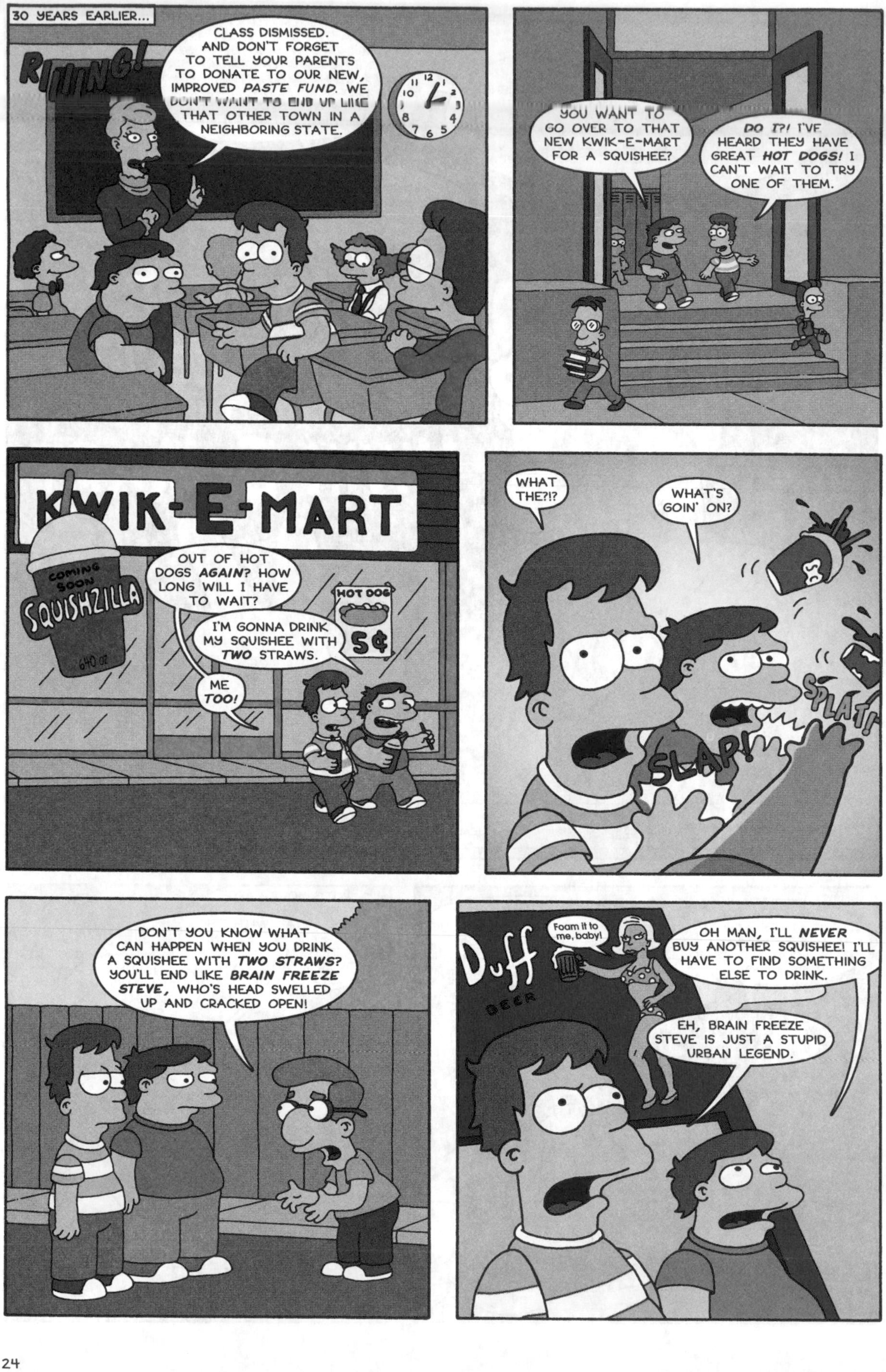

30 YEARS EARLIER...
RIIIING!
CLASS DISMISSED. AND DON'T FORGET TO TELL YOUR PARENTS TO DONATE TO OUR NEW, IMPROVED *PASTE FUND.* WE DON'T WANT TO END UP LIKE THAT OTHER TOWN IN A NEIGHBORING STATE.
YOU WANT TO GO OVER TO THAT NEW KWIK-E-MART FOR A SQUISHEE?
DO I?! I'VE HEARD THEY HAVE GREAT ***HOT DOGS!*** I CAN'T WAIT TO TRY ONE OF THEM.
KWIK-E-MART
COMING SOON SQUISHZILLA 640 OZ
HOT DOG 5¢
OUT OF HOT DOGS ***AGAIN?*** HOW LONG WILL I HAVE TO WAIT?
I'M GONNA DRINK MY SQUISHEE WITH ***TWO*** STRAWS.
ME ***TOO!***
WHAT THE?!?
WHAT'S GOIN' ON?
SLAP!
SPLAT!
DON'T YOU KNOW WHAT CAN HAPPEN WHEN YOU DRINK A SQUISHEE WITH ***TWO STRAWS?*** YOU'LL END LIKE ***BRAIN FREEZE STEVE,*** WHO'S HEAD SWELLED UP AND CRACKED OPEN!
Duff BEER
Foam it to me, baby!
OH MAN, I'LL ***NEVER*** BUY ANOTHER SQUISHEE! I'LL HAVE TO FIND SOMETHING ELSE TO DRINK.
EH, BRAIN FREEZE STEVE IS JUST A STUPID URBAN LEGEND.

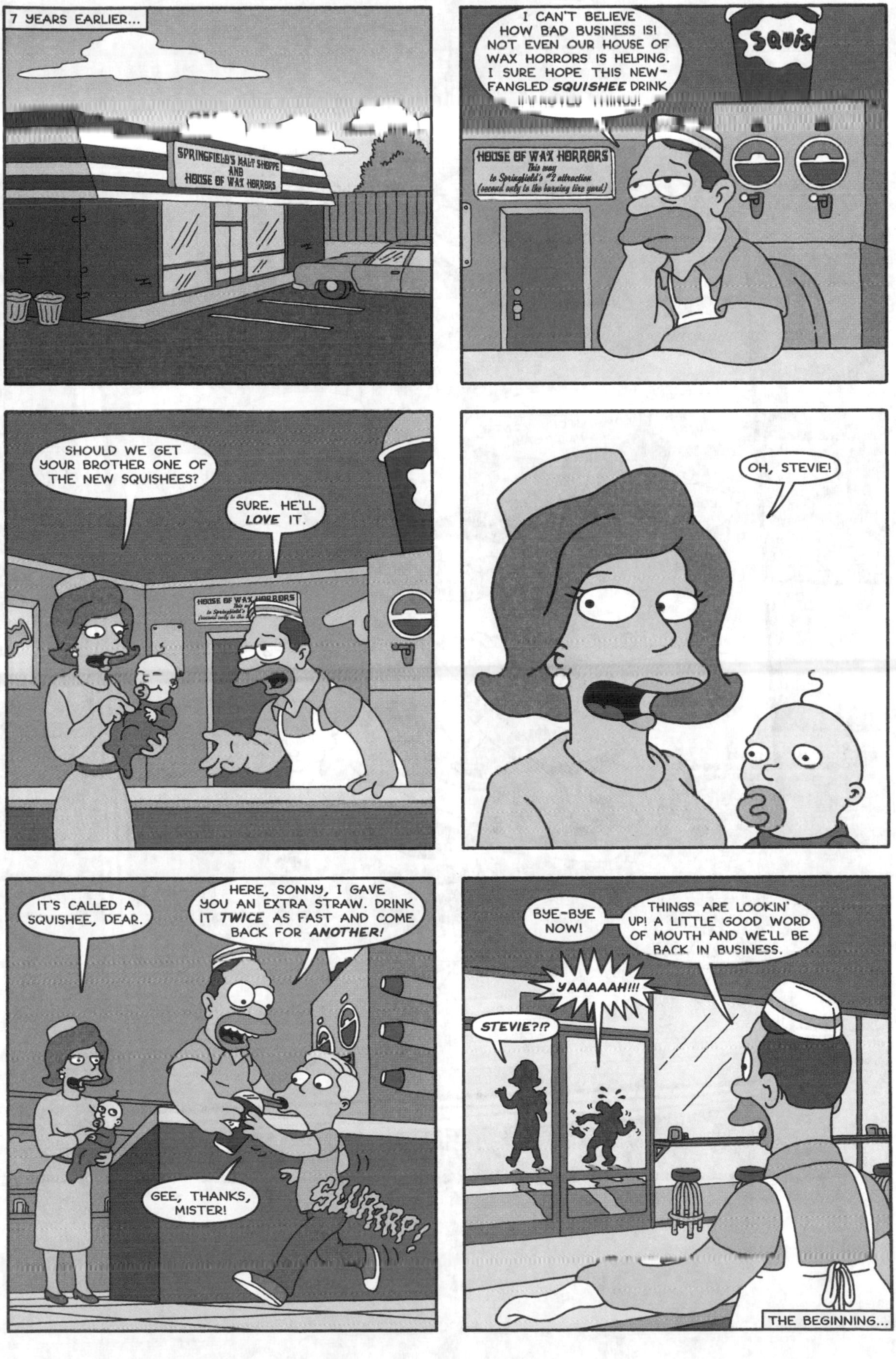
7 YEARS EARLIER...
SPRINGFIELD'S MALT SHOPPE AND HOUSE OF WAX HORRORS
I CAN'T BELIEVE HOW BAD BUSINESS IS! NOT EVEN OUR HOUSE OF WAX HORRORS IS HELPING. I SURE HOPE THIS NEW-FANGLED *SQUISHEE* DRINK
HOUSE OF WAX HORRORS This way to Springfield's #2 attraction (second only to the burning tire yard)
SHOULD WE GET YOUR BROTHER ONE OF THE NEW SQUISHEES?
SURE. HE'LL *LOVE* IT.
OH, STEVIE!
IT'S CALLED A SQUISHEE, DEAR.
HERE, SONNY, I GAVE YOU AN EXTRA STRAW. DRINK IT *TWICE* AS FAST AND COME BACK FOR *ANOTHER!*
GEE, THANKS, MISTER!
SLURRRP!
BYE-BYE NOW!
THINGS ARE LOOKIN' UP! A LITTLE GOOD WORD OF MOUTH AND WE'LL BE BACK IN BUSINESS.
YAAAAAH!!!
STEVIE?!?
THE BEGINNING...

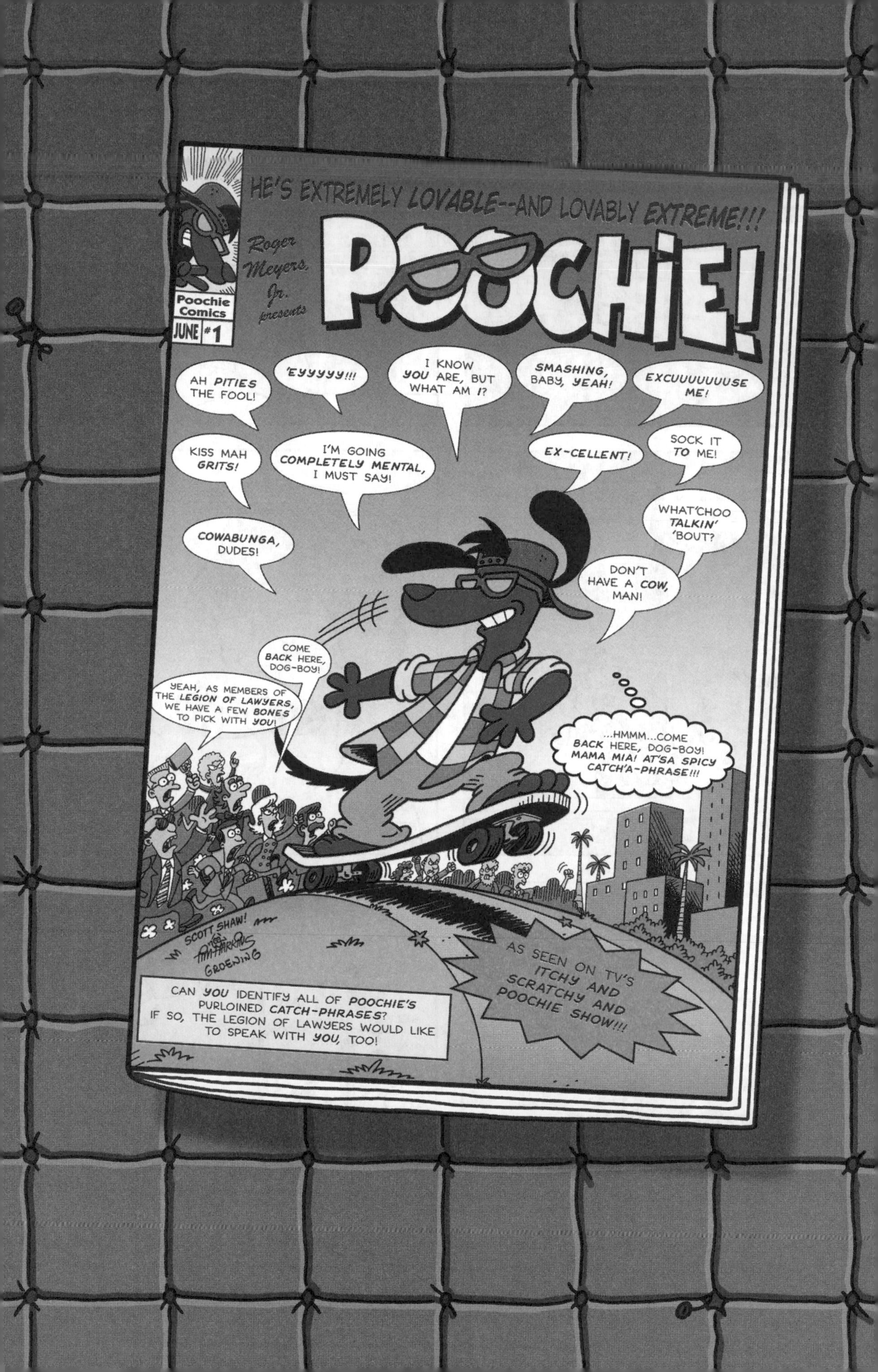

HE'S EXTREMELY LOVABLE--AND LOVABLY EXTREME!!!
Poochie Comics
JUNE #1
Roger Meyers, Jr. presents
POOCHIE!
AH PITIES THE FOOL!
'EYYYYY!!!
I KNOW YOU ARE, BUT WHAT AM I?
SMASHING, BABY, YEAH!
EXCUUUUUUUSE ME!
KISS MAH GRITS!
I'M GOING COMPLETELY MENTAL, I MUST SAY!
EX-CELLENT!
SOCK IT TO ME!
COWABUNGA, DUDES!
WHAT'CHOO TALKIN' 'BOUT?
DON'T HAVE A COW, MAN!
COME BACK HERE, DOG-BOY!
YEAH, AS MEMBERS OF THE LEGION OF LAWYERS, WE HAVE A FEW BONES TO PICK WITH YOU!
...HMMM...COME BACK HERE, DOG-BOY! MAMA MIA! AT'SA SPICY CATCH'A-PHRASE!!!
SCOTT SHAW!
GROENING
AS SEEN ON TV'S ITCHY AND SCRATCHY AND POOCHIE SHOW!!!
CAN YOU IDENTIFY ALL OF POOCHIE'S PURLOINED CATCH-PHRASES? IF SO, THE LEGION OF LAWYERS WOULD LIKE TO SPEAK WITH YOU, TOO!

MEMO FROM THE DESK OF

Barbara Hannigan,

STUDIO MANAGER, ROGER MEYERS, JR. PRODUCTIONS

To: Roger Meyers, Jr.

These old presentation storyboards were recently discovered in the broom closet studio archives. I guess they were drawn up with the expectation that "Poochie" would get his own spin-off cartoon series. (We should've known better, huh, Boss?) Do we toss 'em out, or do you think they're worth anything on the collector's market?

Barb

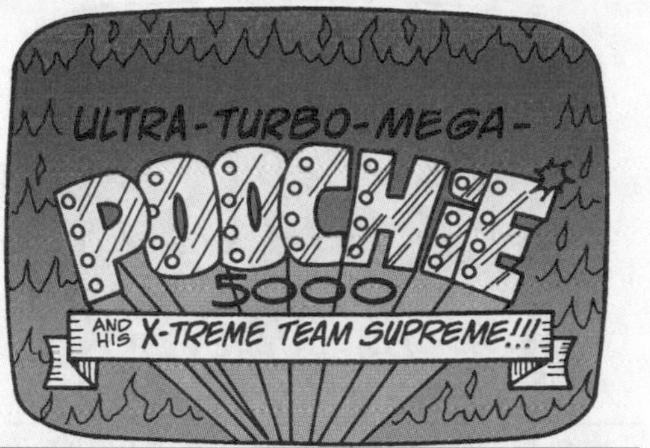
ULTRA-TURBO-MEGA-
POOCHIE
5000
AND HIS X-TREME TEAM SUPREME!!!

Poochie's kickin' tail and takin' dog tags in this **all-new**, in-yer-face animated series that's chock-full of the kind of white-knuckle action that **you**, the new breed of viewer, request, nay, **demand**!!!

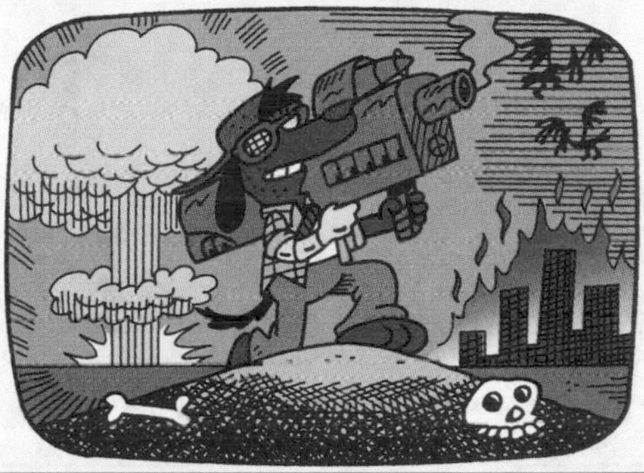

America's favorite cartoon canine cut-up is **trapped** in a post-apocalyptic **future-world** he never made! But **Poochie's** not alone...

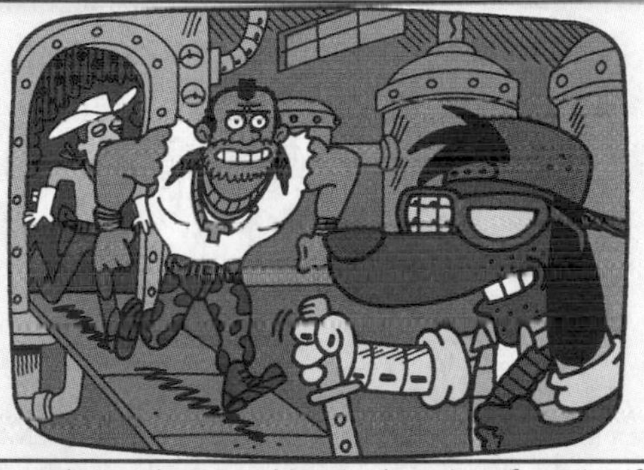

Discovering a **time machine** in the ruins of a scientific research lab, he assembles the greatest **pop cultural personalities** of all time to become his...
X-Treme Team Supreme!

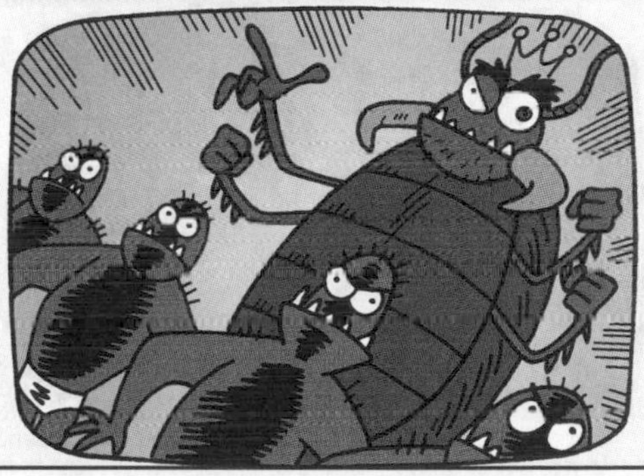

Meanwhile, the **Verminator**, a mutated flea that **rules** this irradiated wasteland, creates his **own** squad of evil underlings (each a major menace in its own right) to enforce his control!

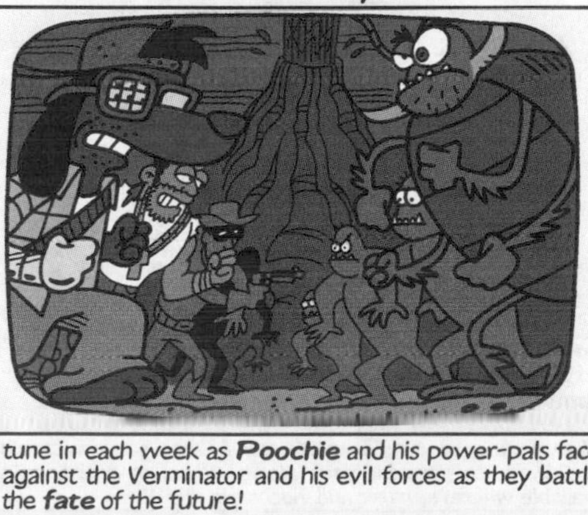

So tune in each week as **Poochie** and his power-pals face off against the Verminator and his evil forces as they battle for the **fate** of the future!

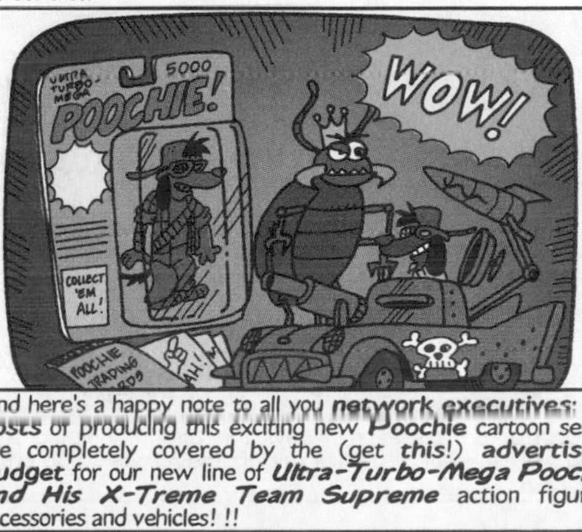
ULTRA TURBO MEGA
5000
POOCHIE!
WOW!
COLLECT 'EM ALL!

And here's a happy note to all you **network executives**: the **costs** of producing this exciting new **Poochie** cartoon series are completely covered by the (get **this**!) **advertising budget** for our new line of ***Ultra-Turbo-Mega Poochie and His X-Treme Team Supreme*** action figures, accessories and vehicles! !!

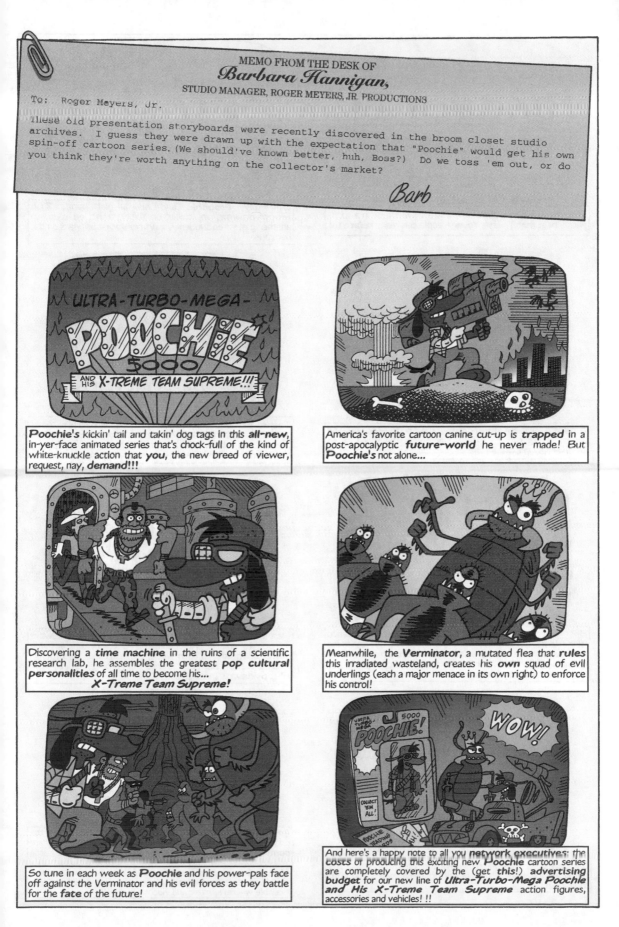

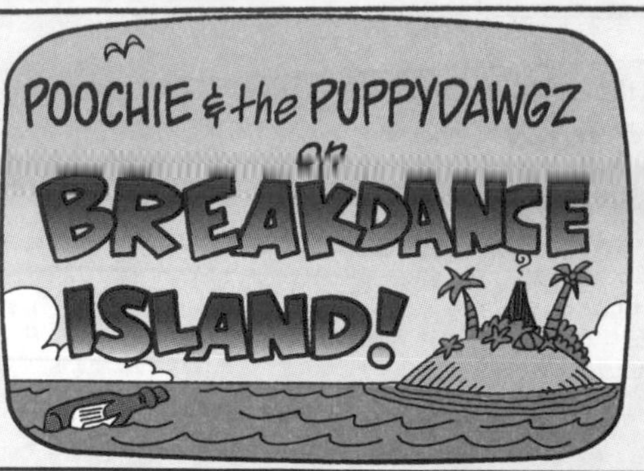
POOCHIE & the PUPPYDAWGZ on
BREAKDANCE ISLAND!

Poochie's a funky dude with a street-wise 'tude in a 'toon with a beat that Today's Young People can really ***relate*** to!

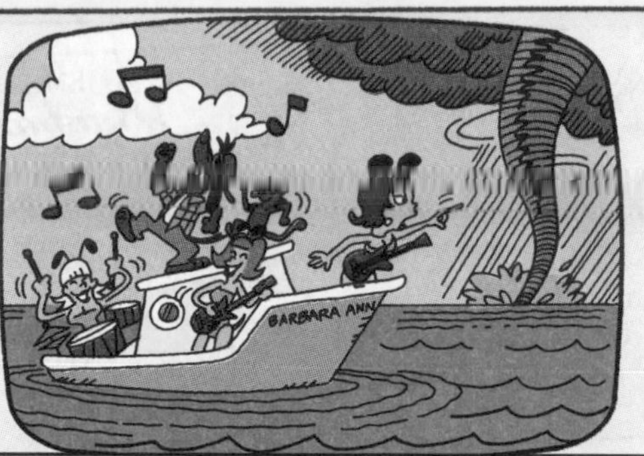
BARBARA ANN

One day, ***Poochie*** and his all-girl band, ***The Puppydawgz***, are chillin' on their ***yacht***, en route to another gig, when suddenly, a ***waterspout*** appears on the horizon!

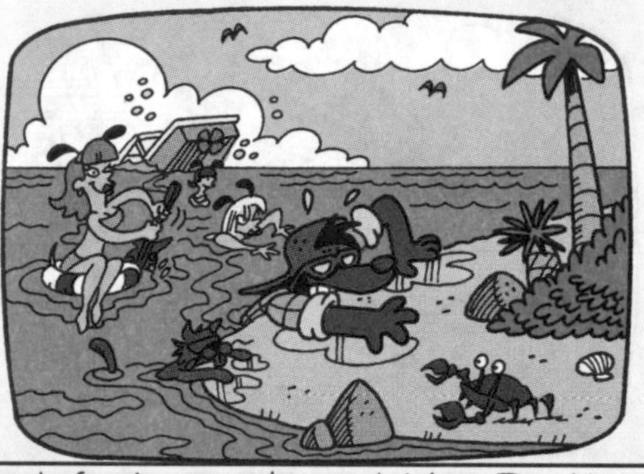

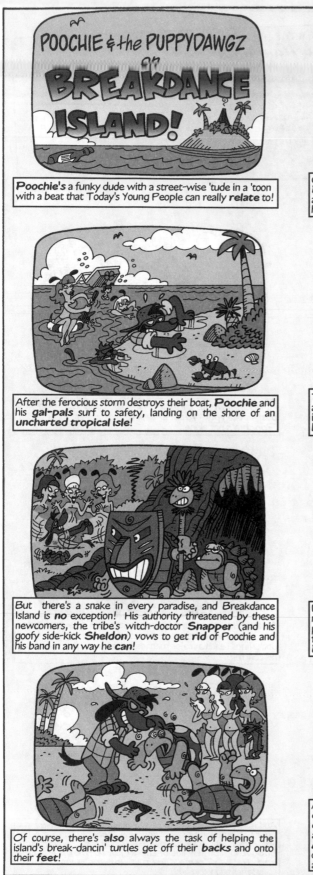

After the ferocious storm destroys their boat, ***Poochie*** and his ***gal-pals*** surf to safety, landing on the shore of an ***uncharted tropical isle***!

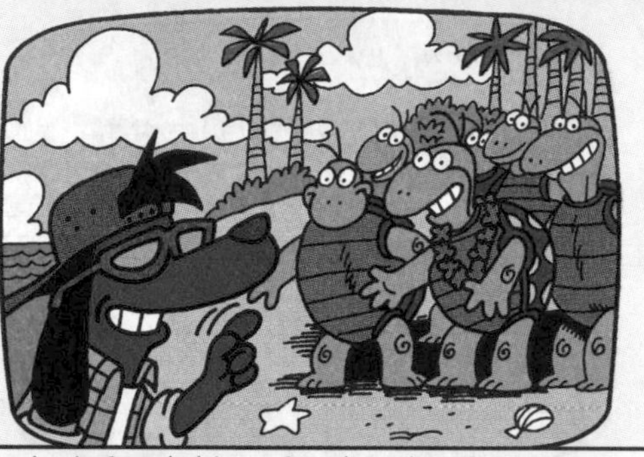

They're befriended by a friendly tribe of ***turtles***! Years ago, a crate of breakdance records washed up on their island, and these naive natives have ***worshipped*** breakdancing ever since!

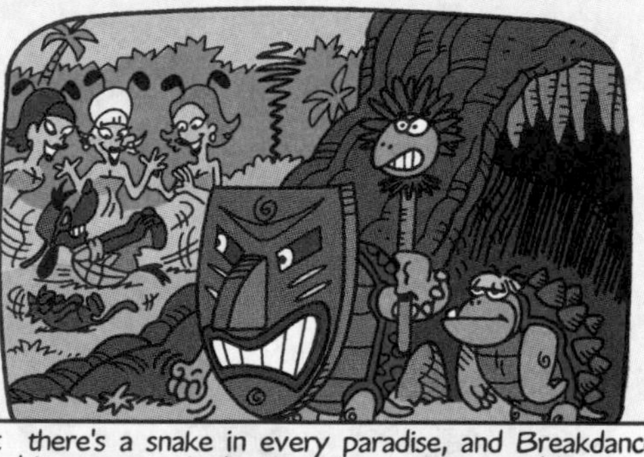

But there's a snake in every paradise, and Breakdance Island is ***no*** exception! His authority threatened by these newcomers, the tribe's witch-doctor ***Snapper*** (and his goofy side-kick ***Sheldon***) vows to get ***rid*** of Poochie and his band in any way he ***can***!

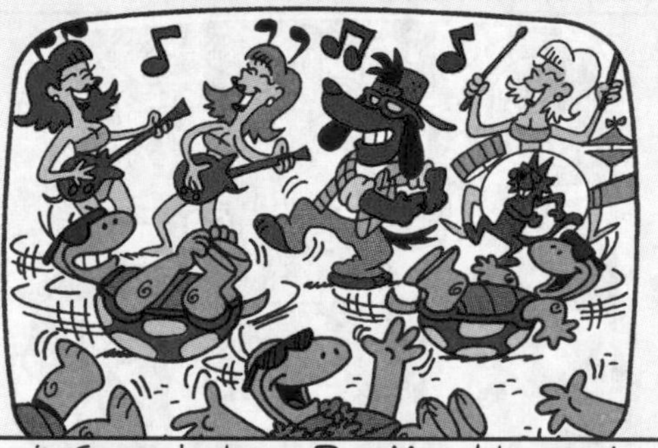

Despite Snapper's schemes, ***Poochie*** and the gang always manage to emerge victorious, thanks to the unstoppable power of ***music***, as each week, we're treated to a funky-fresh slice of hip-hop served up piping hot by the ***Puppydawgs*** themselves!

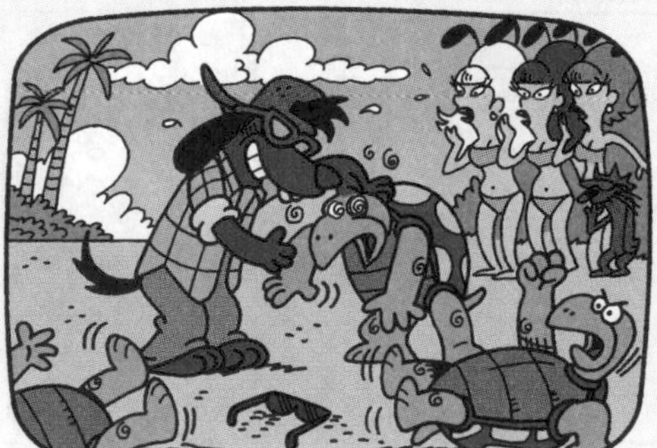

Of course, there's ***also*** always the task of helping the island's break-dancin' turtles get off their ***backs*** and onto their ***feet***!

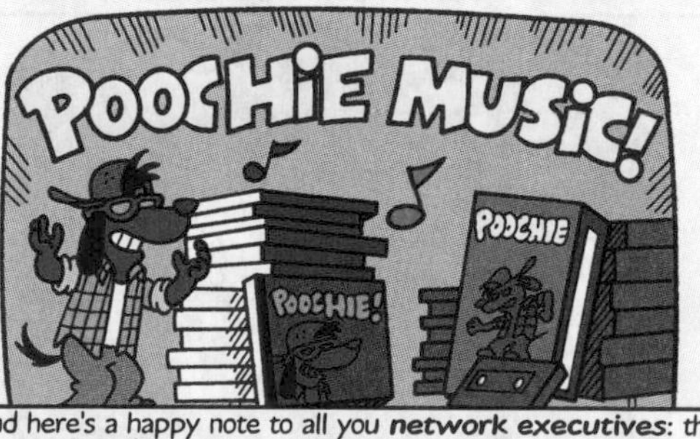
POOCHIE MUSIC!
POOCHIE!
POOCHIE

And here's a happy note to all you ***network executives***: the ***costs*** of producing this exciting new Poochie cartoon series are ***completely*** covered by (yes, it's absolutely true) the ***advertising budget*** for the ***Poochie and the Puppydawgz on Breakdance Island*** soundtrack album on CD and cassette and ***sing-along video***, on VHS and DVD, available wherever music and videos are sold!!!

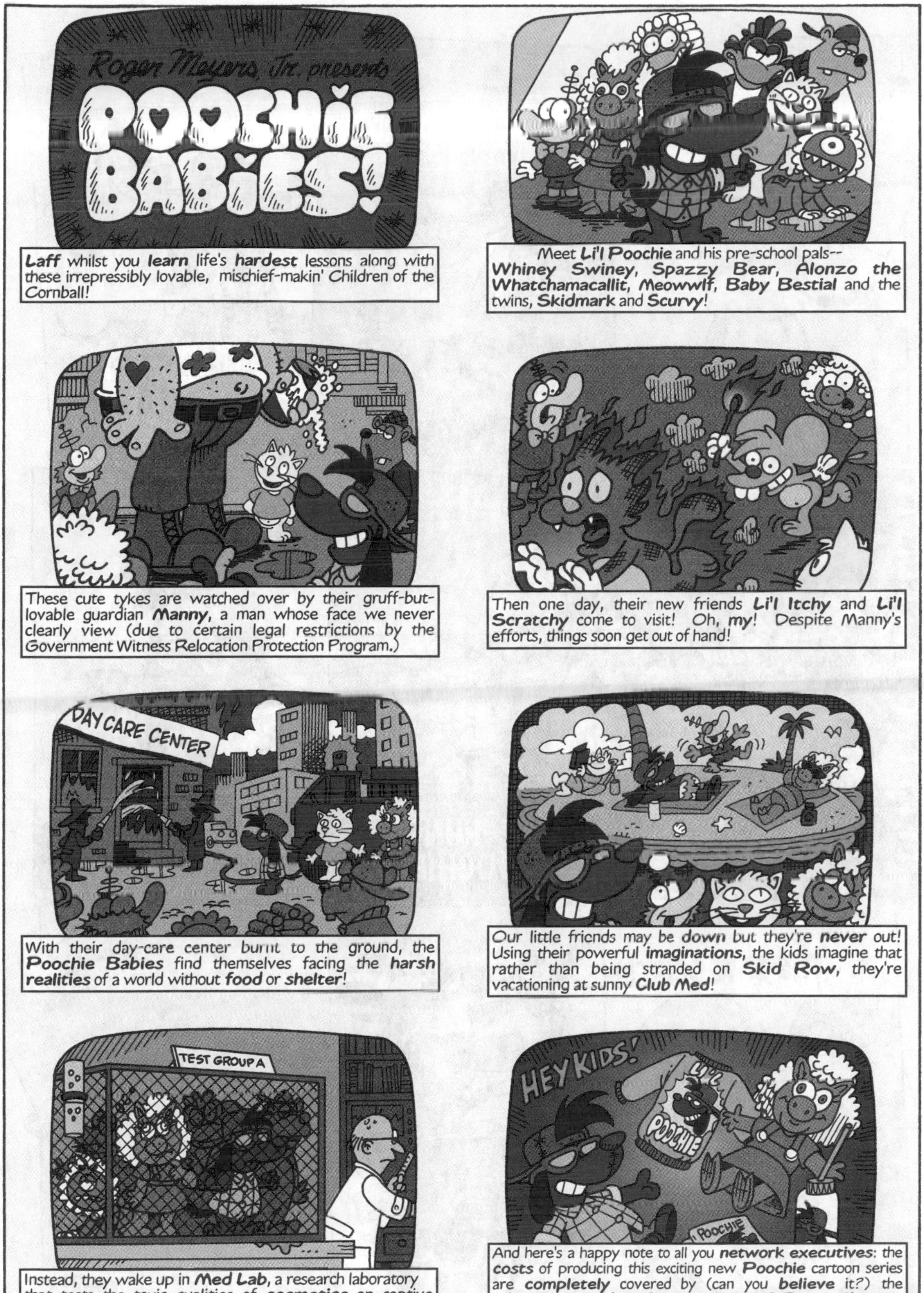
Roger Meyers, Jr. presents
POOCHIE BABIES!
Laff whilst you learn life's hardest lessons along with these irrepressibly lovable, mischief-makin' Children of the Cornball!
Meet Li'l Poochie and his pre-school pals-- Whiney Swiney, Spazzy Bear, Alonzo the Whatchamacallit, Meowwlf, Baby Bestial and the twins, Skidmark and Scurvy!
These cute tykes are watched over by their gruff-but-lovable guardian Manny, a man whose face we never clearly view (due to certain legal restrictions by the Government Witness Relocation Protection Program.)
Then one day, their new friends Li'l Itchy and Li'l Scratchy come to visit! Oh, my! Despite Manny's efforts, things soon get out of hand!
DAY CARE CENTER
With their day-care center burnt to the ground, the Poochie Babies find themselves facing the harsh realities of a world without food or shelter!
Our little friends may be down but they're never out! Using their powerful imaginations, the kids imagine that rather than being stranded on Skid Row, they're vacationing at sunny Club Med!
TEST GROUP A
Instead, they wake up in Med Lab, a research laboratory that tests the toxic qualities of cosmetics on captive animals! Who knows where these plucky toddlers will wind up next?
HEY KIDS!
POOCHIE
POOCHIE
And here's a happy note to all you network executives: the costs of producing this exciting new Poochie cartoon series are completely covered by (can you believe it?) the advertising budget for our new line of Roger Meyers, Jr.s' Poochie Babies cuddle-dolls, activity books and sleepwear!!!

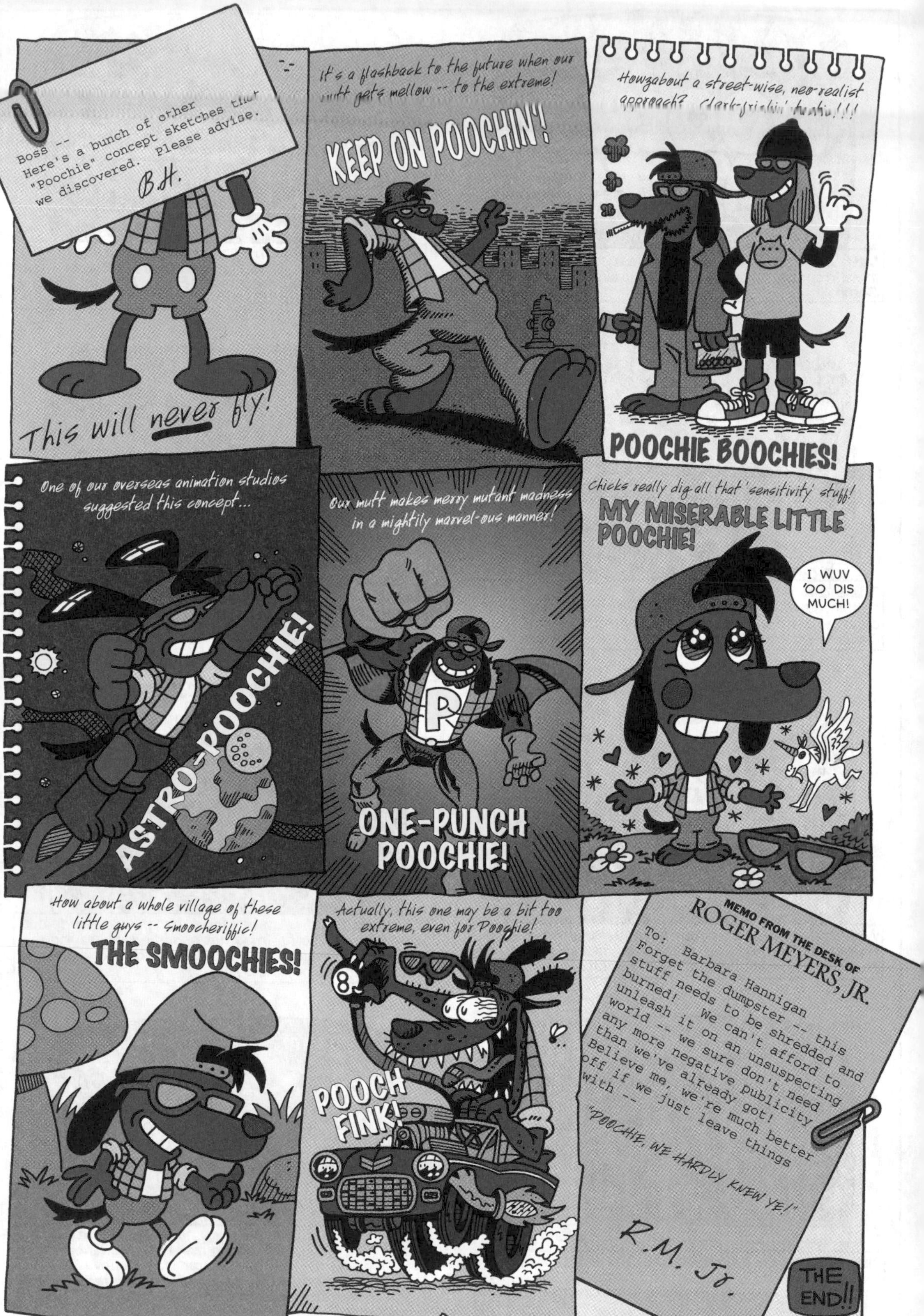
Boss --
Here's a bunch of other "Poochie" concept sketches that we discovered. Please advise.
B.H.
This will never fly!
It's a flashback to the future when our
gets mellow -- to the extreme!
KEEP ON POOCHIN'!
Howzabout a street-wise, neo-realist
approach?
POOCHIE BOOCHIES!
One of our overseas animation studios suggested this concept...
ASTRO-POOCHIE!
Our mutt makes merry mutant madness in a mightily marvel-ous manner!
ONE-PUNCH POOCHIE!
Chicks really dig all that 'sensitivity' stuff!
MY MISERABLE LITTLE POOCHIE!
I WUV 'OO DIS MUCH!
How about a whole village of these little guys -- Smoocheriffic!
THE SMOOCHIES!
Actually, this one may be a bit too extreme, even for Poochie!
POOCH FINK!
MEMO FROM THE DESK OF
ROGER MEYERS, JR.
To: Barbara Hannigan
Forget the dumpster -- this stuff needs to be shredded and burned! We can't afford to unleash it on an unsuspecting world -- we sure don't need any more negative publicity than we've already got! Believe me, we're much better off if we just leave things with --
"POOCHIE, WE HARDLY KNEW YE!"
R.M. Jr.
THE END!!

SCRIPT AND PENCILS SCOTT "BEEN THERE, DONE THAT" SHAW!

INKS TIM "WHERE'S THE REMOTE CONTROL" HARKINS

LETTERS KAREN "CANCEL MY TV GUIDE SUBSCRIPTION" BATES

COLORS NATHAN "BREAK OUT THE EYEDROPS" KANE

EDITOR BILL "WHAT WAS I THINKING" MORRISON

ENDURED BY MATT "KING OF THE VAST WASTELAND" GROENING

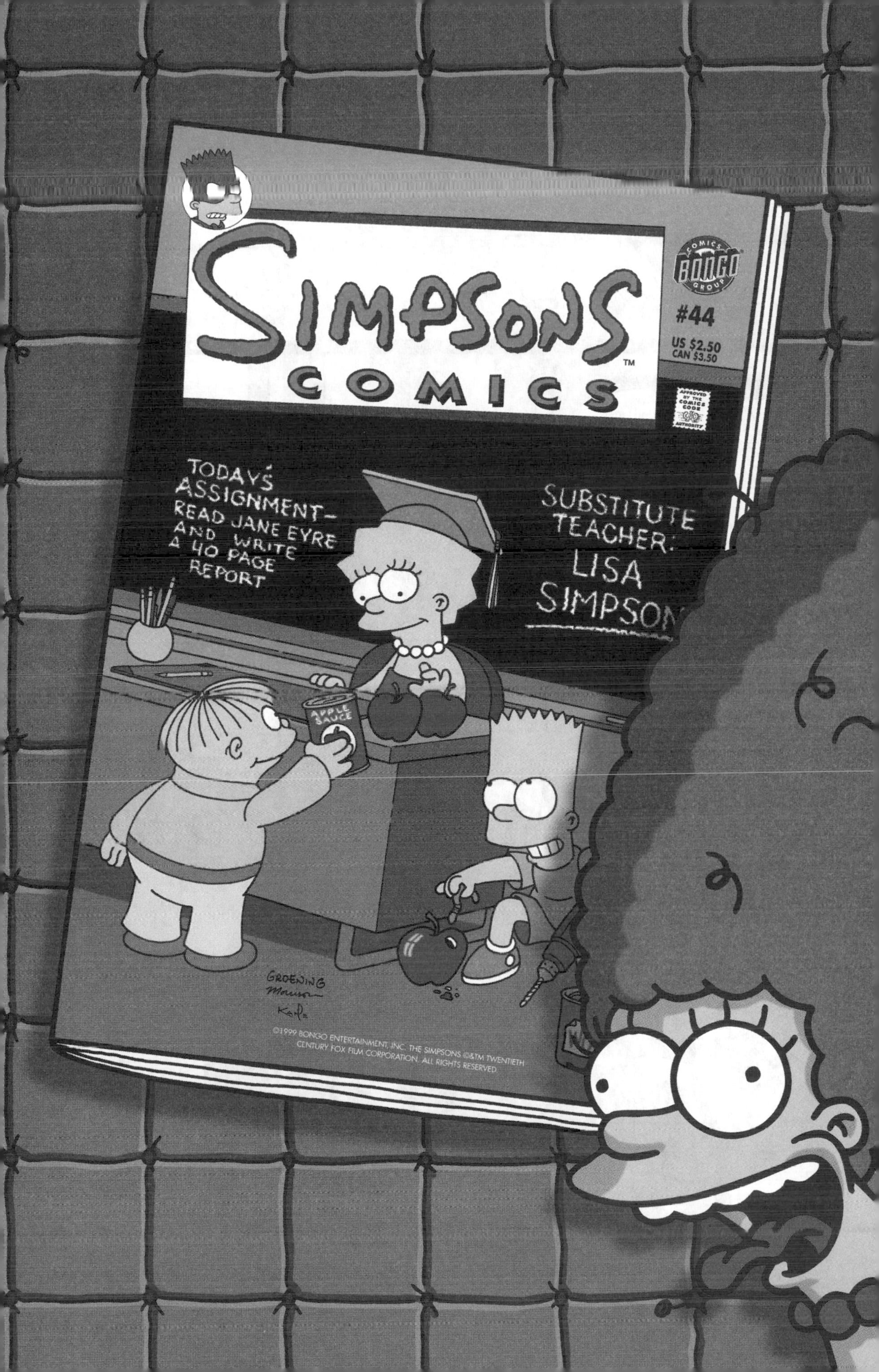
SIMPSONS COMICS™
#44
US $2.50
CAN $3.50
APPROVED BY THE COMICS CODE AUTHORITY
TODAY'S ASSIGNMENT- READ JANE EYRE AND WRITE A 40 PAGE REPORT
SUBSTITUTE TEACHER: LISA SIMPSON
APPLE SAUCE
GROENING
©1999 BONGO ENTERTAINMENT, INC. THE SIMPSONS ©&TM TWENTIETH CENTURY FOX FILM CORPORATION. ALL RIGHTS RESERVED.

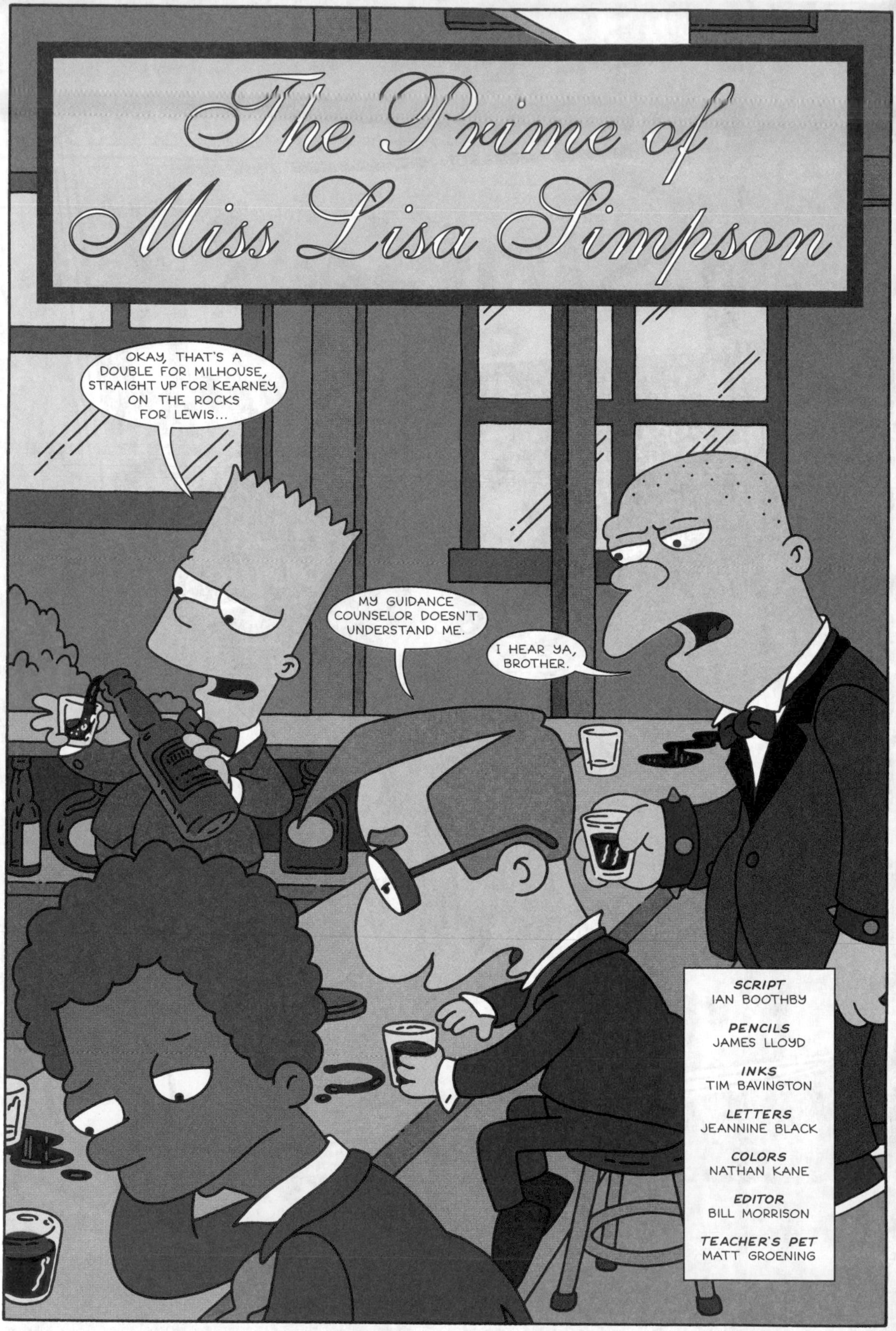
The Prime of Miss Lisa Simpson
OKAY, THAT'S A DOUBLE FOR MILHOUSE, STRAIGHT UP FOR KEARNEY, ON THE ROCKS FOR LEWIS...
MY GUIDANCE COUNSELOR DOESN'T UNDERSTAND ME.
I HEAR YA, BROTHER.
SCRIPT IAN BOOTHBY
PENCILS JAMES LLOYD
INKS TIM BAVINGTON
LETTERS JEANNINE BLACK
COLORS NATHAN KANE
EDITOR BILL MORRISON
TEACHER'S PET MATT GROENING

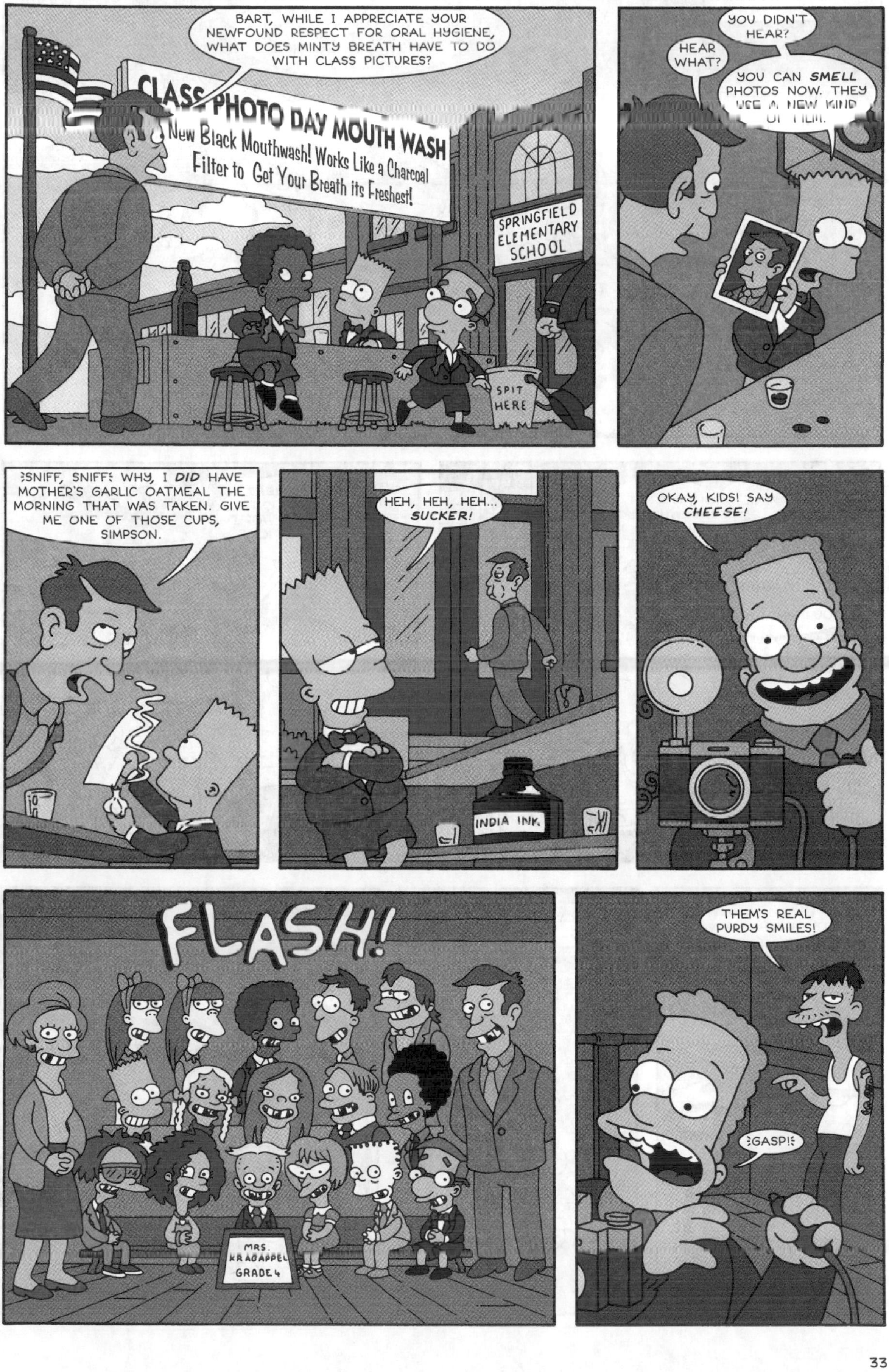
BART, WHILE I APPRECIATE YOUR NEWFOUND RESPECT FOR ORAL HYGIENE, WHAT DOES MINTY BREATH HAVE TO DO WITH CLASS PICTURES?
CLASS PHOTO DAY MOUTH WASH
New Black Mouthwash! Works Like a Charcoal Filter to Get Your Breath its Freshest!
SPRINGFIELD ELEMENTARY SCHOOL
SPIT HERE
YOU DIDN'T HEAR?
HEAR WHAT?
YOU CAN SMELL PHOTOS NOW. THEY USE A NEW KIND OF FILM.
SNIFF, SNIFF WHY, I DID HAVE MOTHER'S GARLIC OATMEAL THE MORNING THAT WAS TAKEN. GIVE ME ONE OF THOSE CUPS, SIMPSON.
HEH, HEH, HEH... SUCKER!
INDIA INK.
OKAY, KIDS! SAY CHEESE!
FLASH!
MRS. KRABAPPEL GRADE 4
THEM'S REAL PURDY SMILES!
GASP!

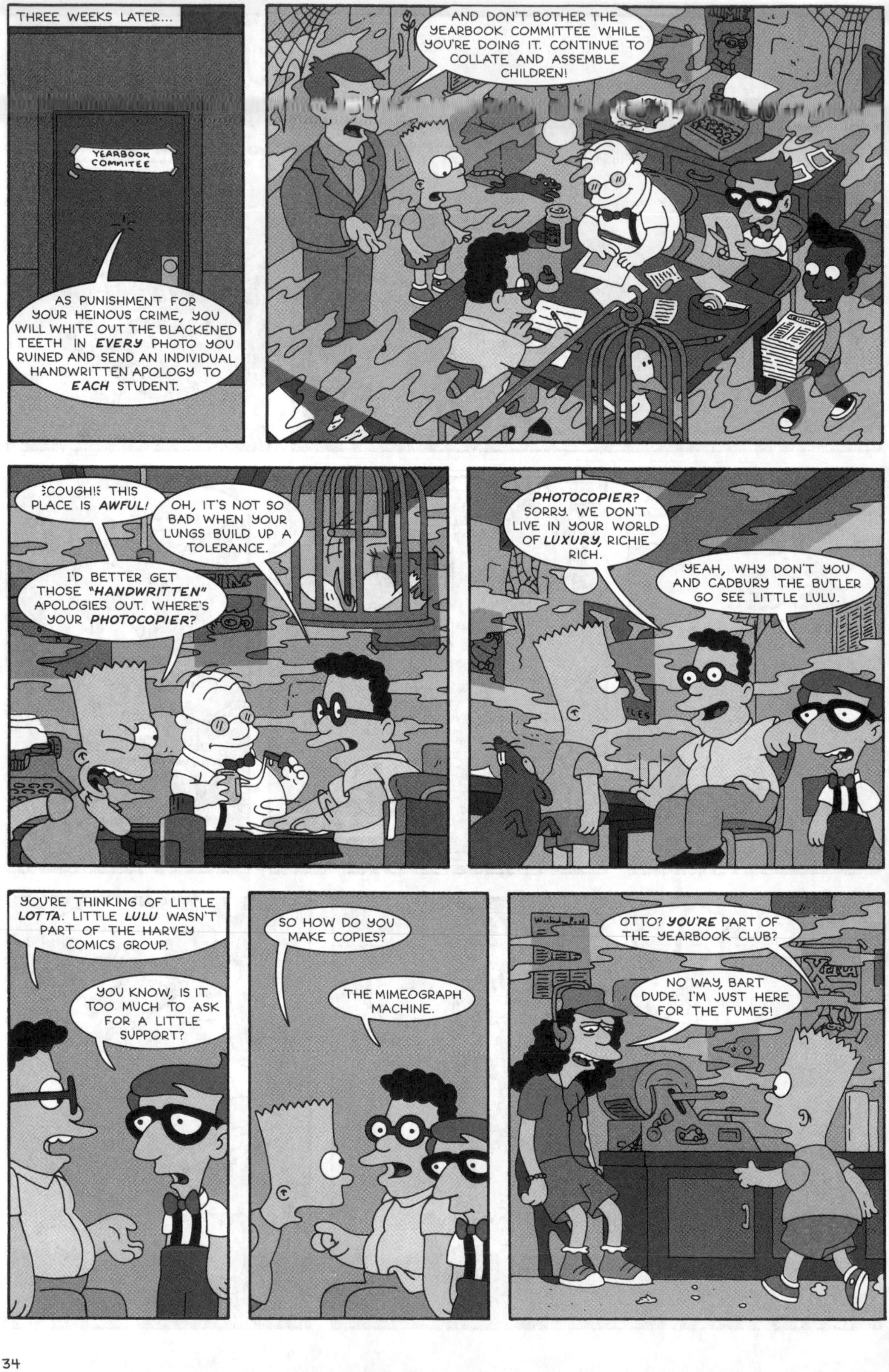
THREE WEEKS LATER...
YEARBOOK COMMITEE
AS PUNISHMENT FOR YOUR HEINOUS CRIME, YOU WILL WHITE OUT THE BLACKENED TEETH IN EVERY PHOTO YOU RUINED AND SEND AN INDIVIDUAL HANDWRITTEN APOLOGY TO EACH STUDENT.
AND DON'T BOTHER THE YEARBOOK COMMITTEE WHILE YOU'RE DOING IT. CONTINUE TO COLLATE AND ASSEMBLE CHILDREN!
COUGH! THIS PLACE IS AWFUL!
OH, IT'S NOT SO BAD WHEN YOUR LUNGS BUILD UP A TOLERANCE.
I'D BETTER GET THOSE "HANDWRITTEN" APOLOGIES OUT. WHERE'S YOUR PHOTOCOPIER?
PHOTOCOPIER? SORRY. WE DON'T LIVE IN YOUR WORLD OF LUXURY, RICHIE RICH.
YEAH, WHY DON'T YOU AND CADBURY THE BUTLER GO SEE LITTLE LULU.
YOU'RE THINKING OF LITTLE LOTTA. LITTLE LULU WASN'T PART OF THE HARVEY COMICS GROUP.
YOU KNOW, IS IT TOO MUCH TO ASK FOR A LITTLE SUPPORT?
SO HOW DO YOU MAKE COPIES?
THE MIMEOGRAPH MACHINE.
OTTO? YOU'RE PART OF THE YEARBOOK CLUB?
NO WAY, BART DUDE. I'M JUST HERE FOR THE FUMES!

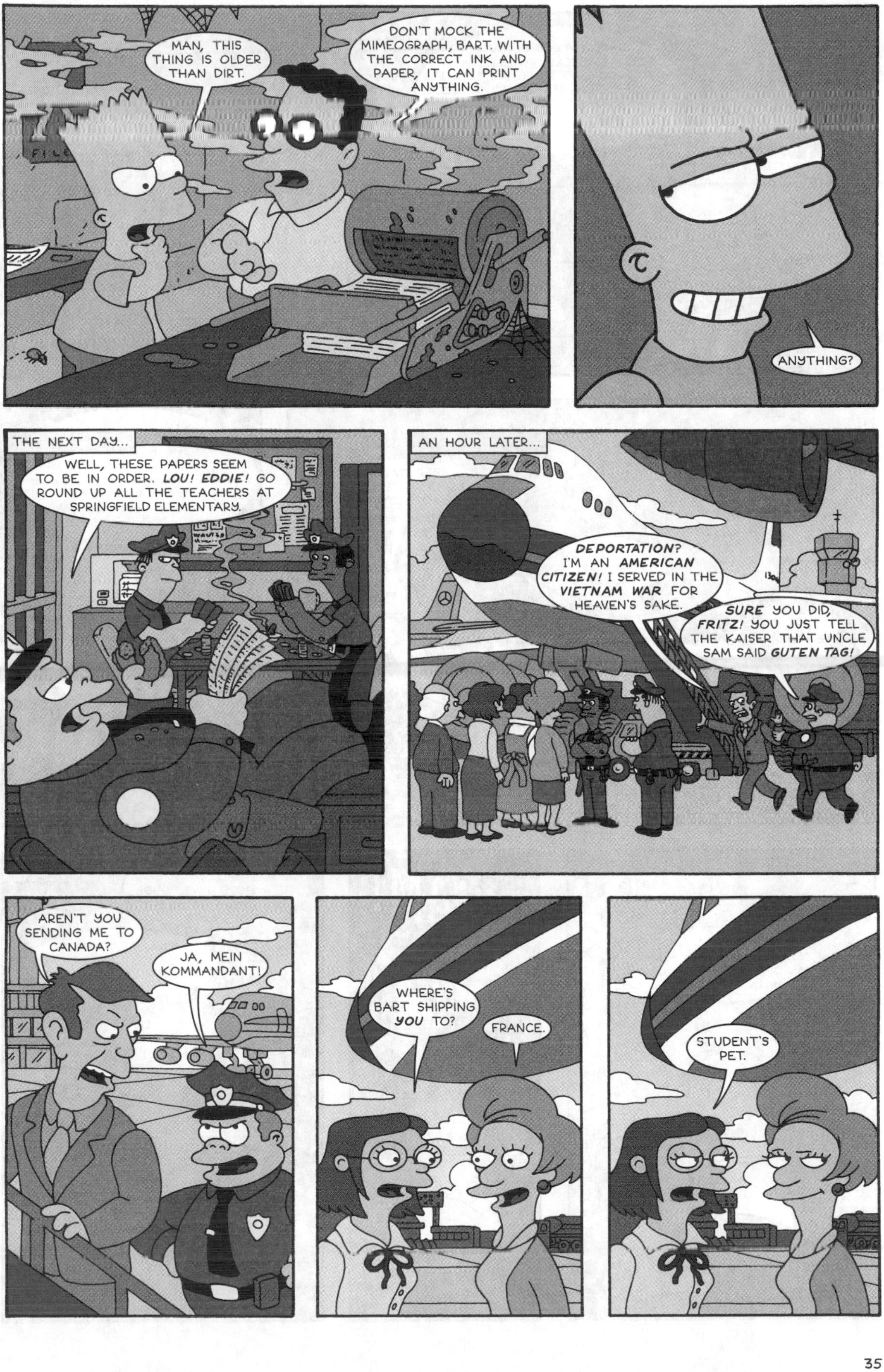

MAN, THIS THING IS OLDER THAN DIRT.
DON'T MOCK THE MIMEOGRAPH, BART. WITH THE CORRECT INK AND PAPER, IT CAN PRINT ANYTHING.
ANYTHING?
THE NEXT DAY...
WELL, THESE PAPERS SEEM TO BE IN ORDER. LOU! EDDIE! GO ROUND UP ALL THE TEACHERS AT SPRINGFIELD ELEMENTARY.
AN HOUR LATER...
DEPORTATION? I'M AN AMERICAN CITIZEN! I SERVED IN THE VIETNAM WAR FOR HEAVEN'S SAKE.
SURE YOU DID, FRITZ! YOU JUST TELL THE KAISER THAT UNCLE SAM SAID GUTEN TAG!
AREN'T YOU SENDING ME TO CANADA?
JA, MEIN KOMMANDANT!
WHERE'S BART SHIPPING YOU TO?
FRANCE.
STUDENT'S PET.

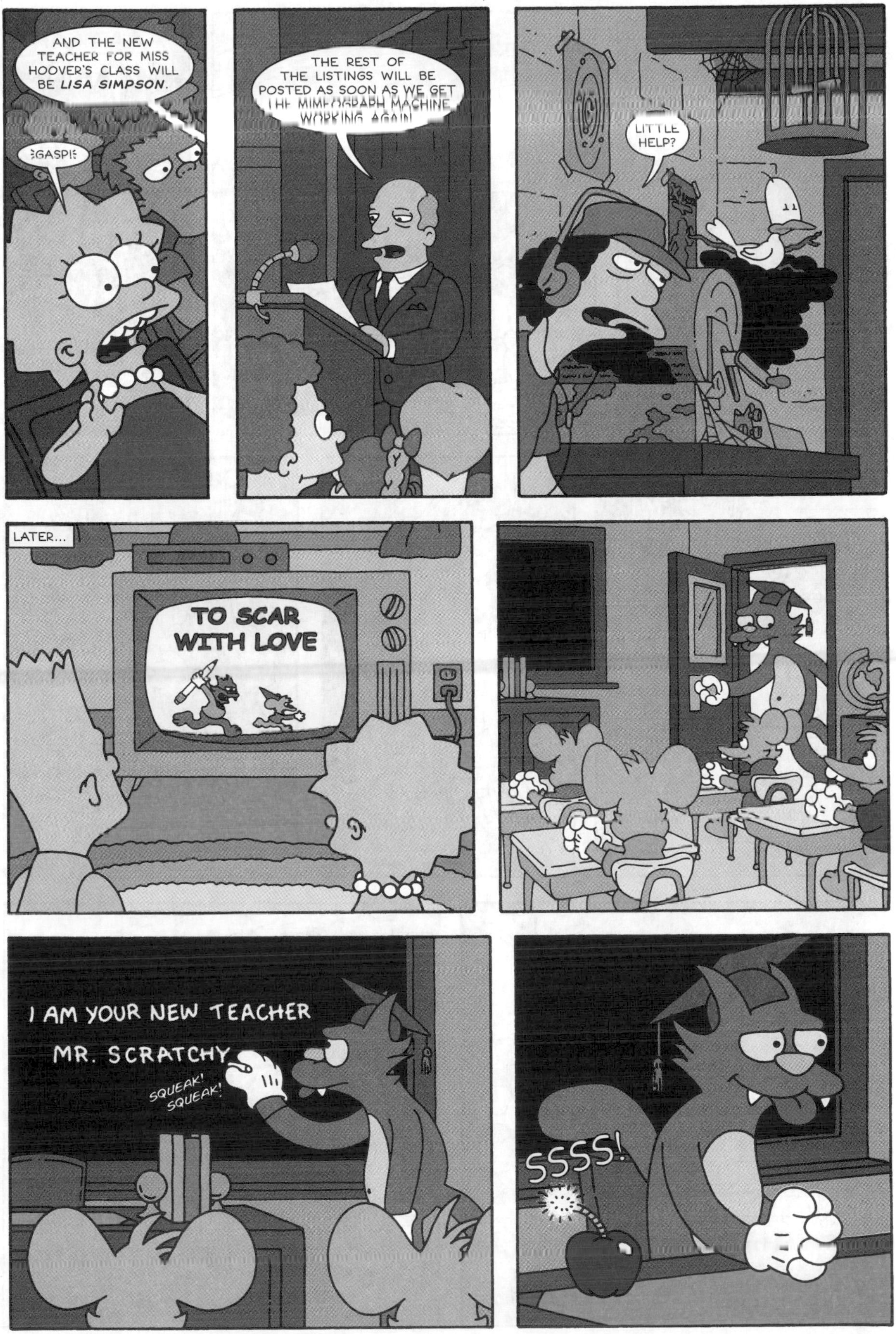
AND THE NEW TEACHER FOR MISS HOOVER'S CLASS WILL BE *LISA SIMPSON*.
GASP!
THE REST OF THE LISTINGS WILL BE POSTED AS SOON AS WE GET THE MIMEOGRAPH MACHINE WORKING AGAIN.
LITTLE HELP?
LATER...
TO SCAR WITH LOVE
I AM YOUR NEW TEACHER
MR. SCRATCHY
SQUEAK! SQUEAK!
SSSS!

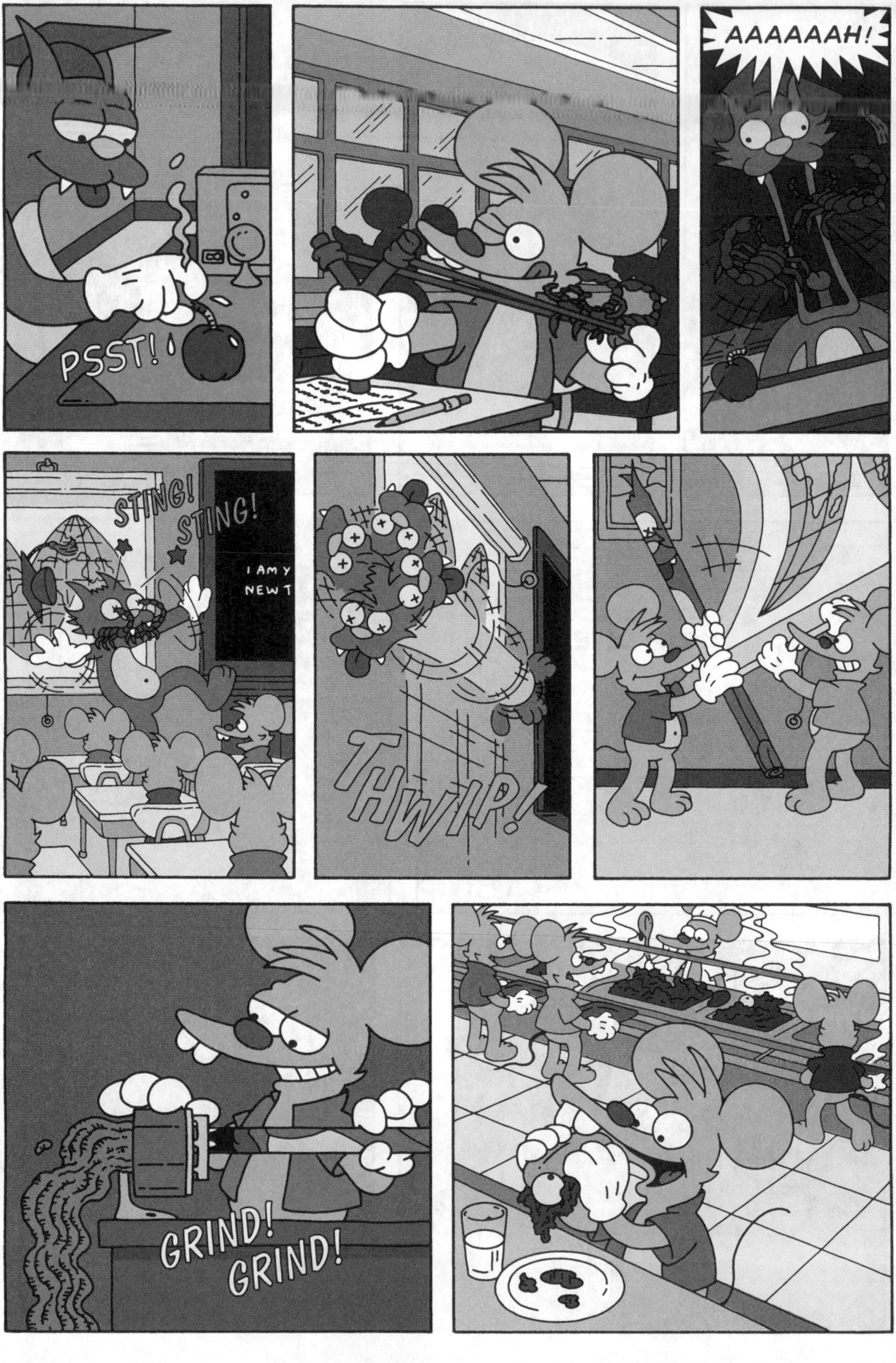
PSST!
AAAAAAH!
STING!
STING!
I AM Y
NEW T
THWIP!
GRIND!
GRIND!

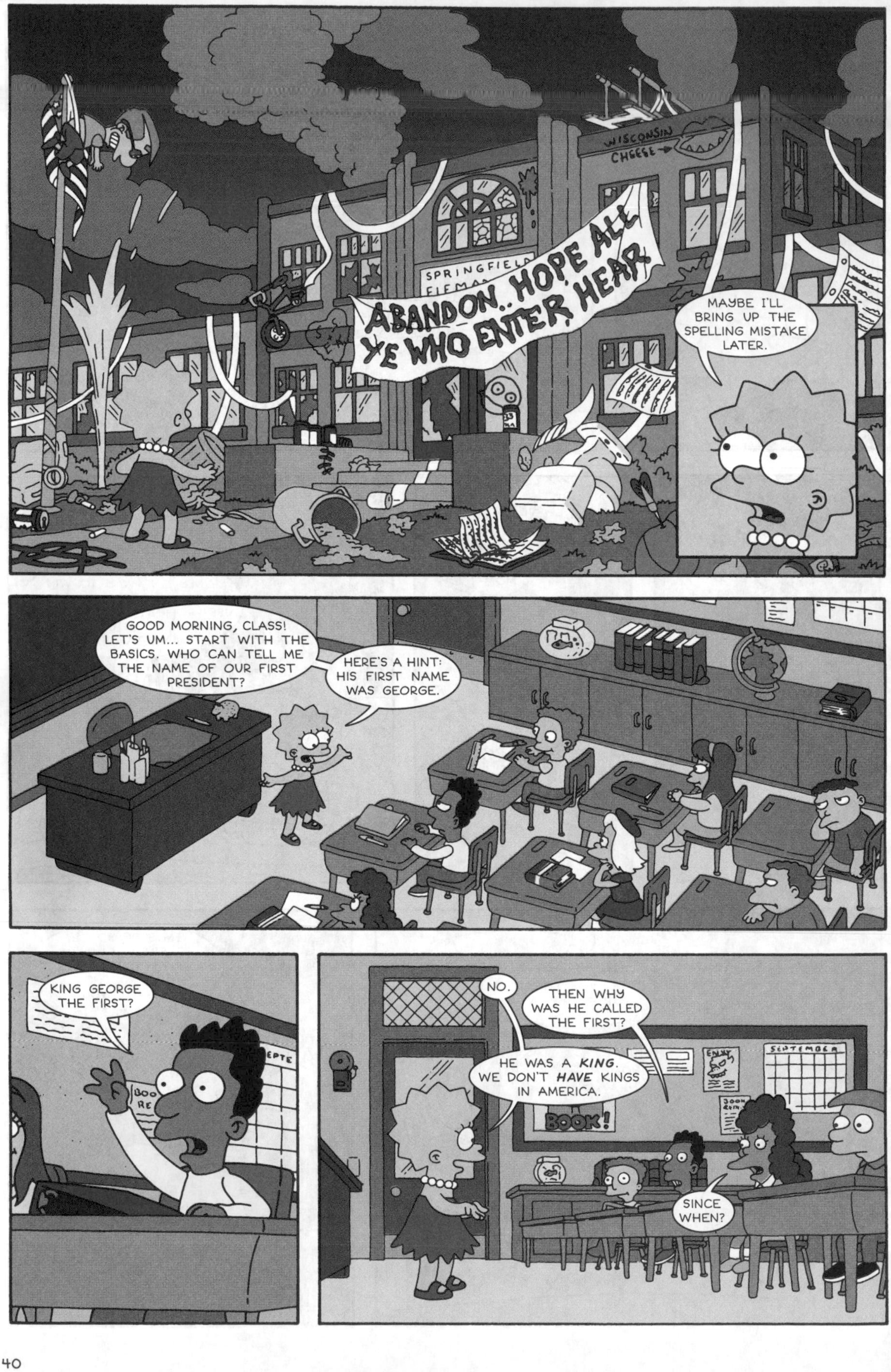

WISCONSIN
CHEESE
SPRINGFIELD
ABANDON.. HOPE ALL YE WHO ENTER HEAR
MAYBE I'LL BRING UP THE SPELLING MISTAKE LATER.
GOOD MORNING, CLASS! LET'S UM... START WITH THE BASICS. WHO CAN TELL ME THE NAME OF OUR FIRST PRESIDENT?
HERE'S A HINT: HIS FIRST NAME WAS GEORGE.
KING GEORGE THE FIRST?
NO.
THEN WHY WAS HE CALLED THE FIRST?
HE WAS A *KING*. WE DON'T *HAVE* KINGS IN AMERICA.
SEPTEMBER
BOOK!
SINCE WHEN?

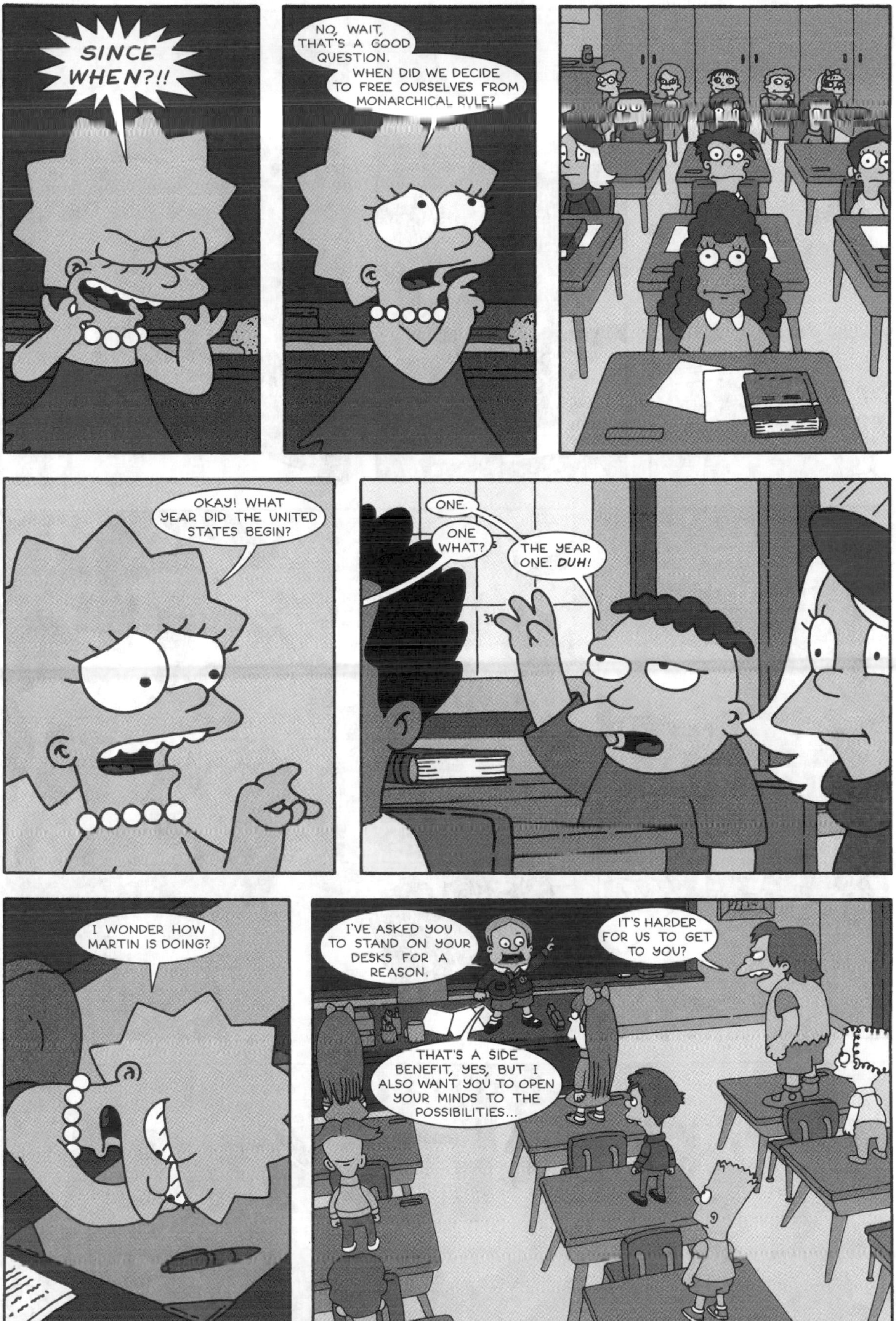
SINCE WHEN?!!
NO, WAIT, THAT'S A GOOD QUESTION.
WHEN DID WE DECIDE TO FREE OURSELVES FROM MONARCHICAL RULE?
OKAY! WHAT YEAR DID THE UNITED STATES BEGIN?
ONE.
ONE WHAT?
THE YEAR ONE. DUH!
I WONDER HOW MARTIN IS DOING?
I'VE ASKED YOU TO STAND ON YOUR DESKS FOR A REASON.
IT'S HARDER FOR US TO GET TO YOU?
THAT'S A SIDE BENEFIT, YES, BUT I ALSO WANT YOU TO OPEN YOUR MINDS TO THE POSSIBILITIES...

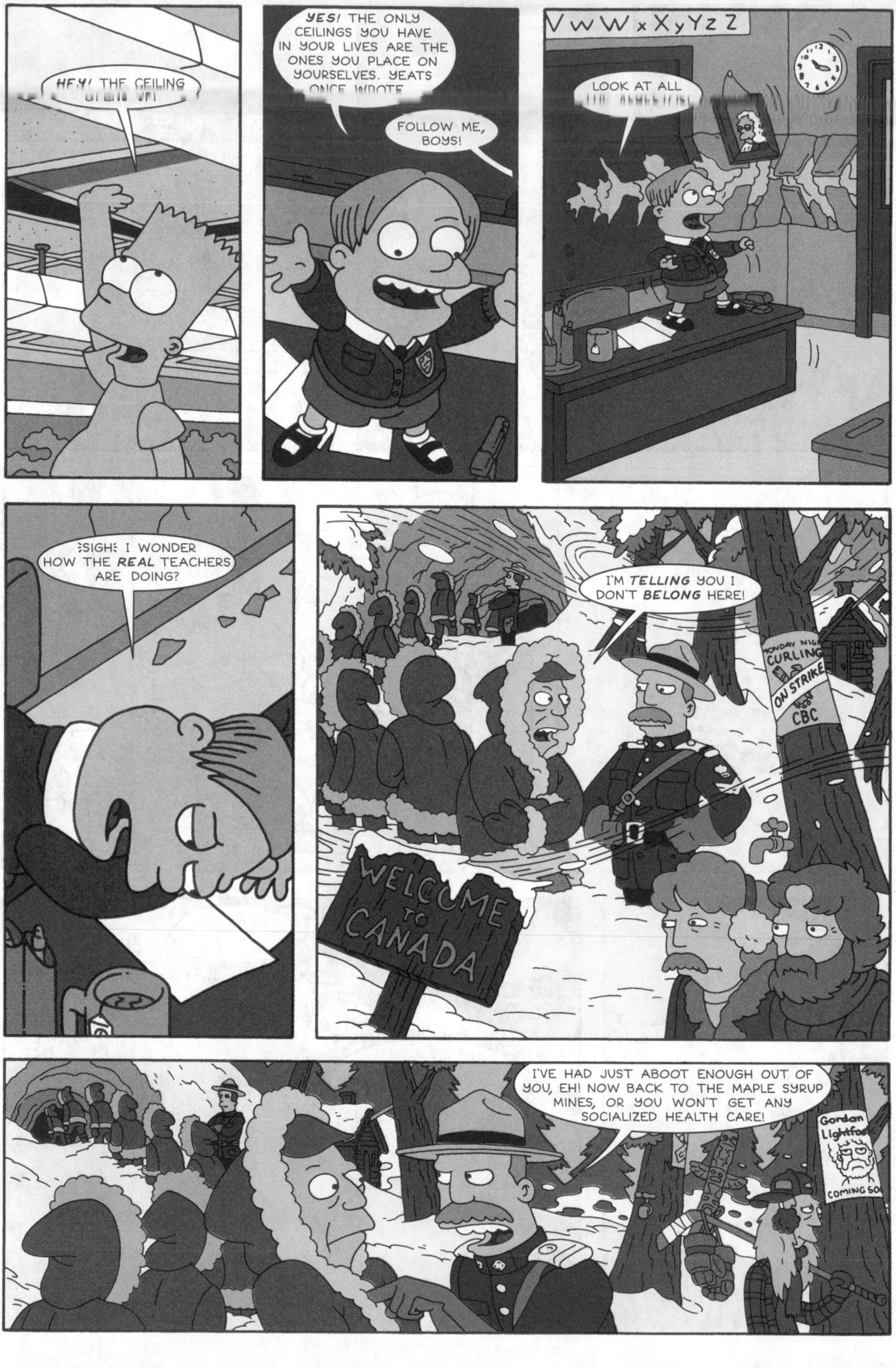

HEY! THE CEILING
YES! THE ONLY CEILINGS YOU HAVE IN YOUR LIVES ARE THE ONES YOU PLACE ON YOURSELVES. YEATS ONCE WROTE
FOLLOW ME, BOYS!
VwWxXyYzZ
LOOK AT ALL
SIGH I WONDER HOW THE REAL TEACHERS ARE DOING?
I'M TELLING YOU I DON'T BELONG HERE!
MONDAY NIGHT CURLING
ON STRIKE
CBC
WELCOME TO CANADA
I'VE HAD JUST ABOOT ENOUGH OUT OF YOU, EH! NOW BACK TO THE MAPLE SYRUP MINES, OR YOU WON'T GET ANY SOCIALIZED HEALTH CARE!
Gordon Lightfoot
COMING SOON

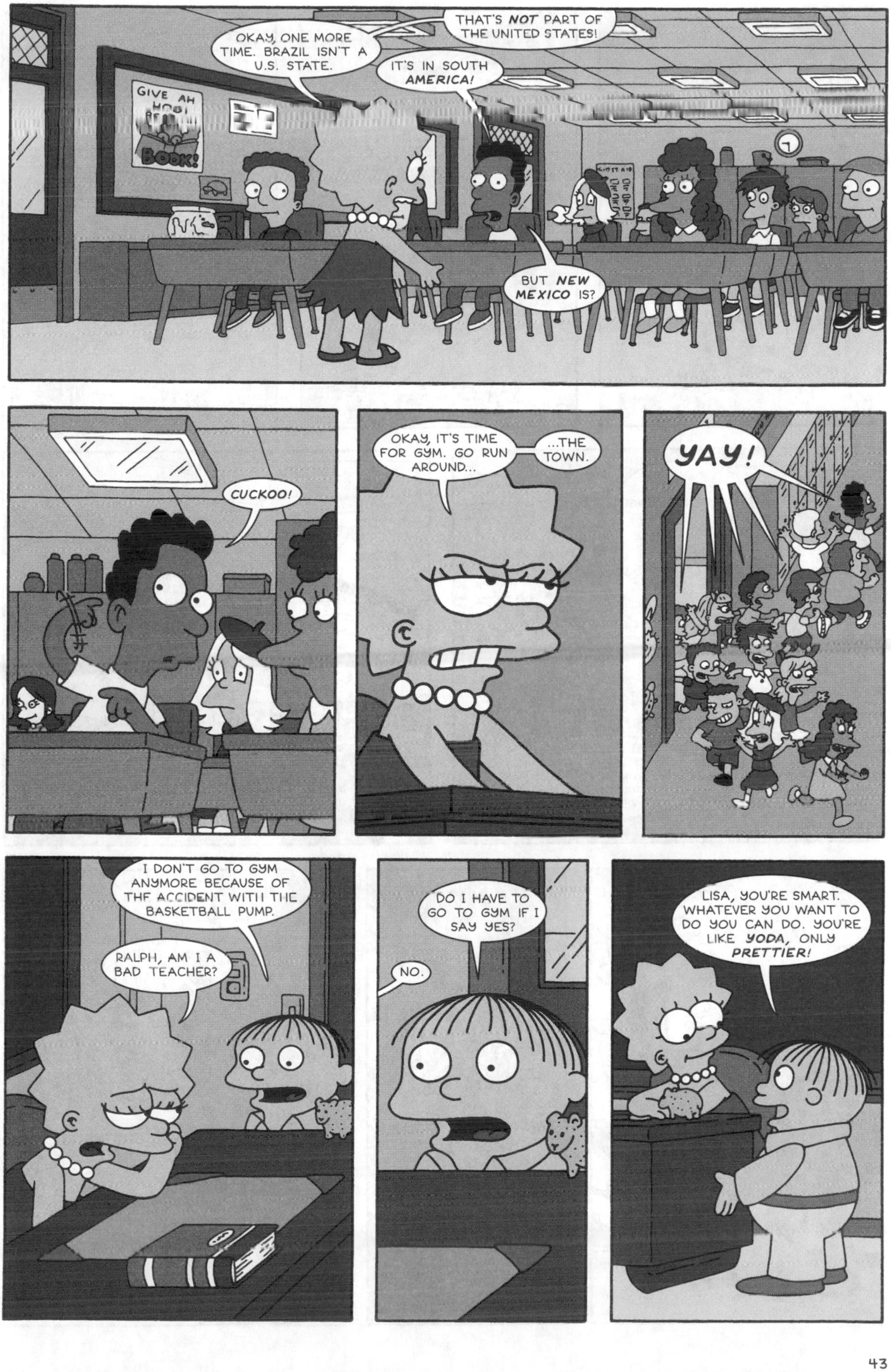
OKAY, ONE MORE TIME. BRAZIL ISN'T A U.S. STATE.
THAT'S NOT PART OF THE UNITED STATES!
IT'S IN SOUTH AMERICA!
BUT NEW MEXICO IS?
GIVE AH HOOT READ A BOOK!
CUCKOO!
OKAY, IT'S TIME FOR GYM. GO RUN AROUND...
...THE TOWN.
YAY!
I DON'T GO TO GYM ANYMORE BECAUSE OF THE ACCIDENT WITH THE BASKETBALL PUMP.
RALPH, AM I A BAD TEACHER?
DO I HAVE TO GO TO GYM IF I SAY YES?
NO.
LISA, YOU'RE SMART. WHATEVER YOU WANT TO DO YOU CAN DO. YOU'RE LIKE YODA, ONLY PRETTIER!

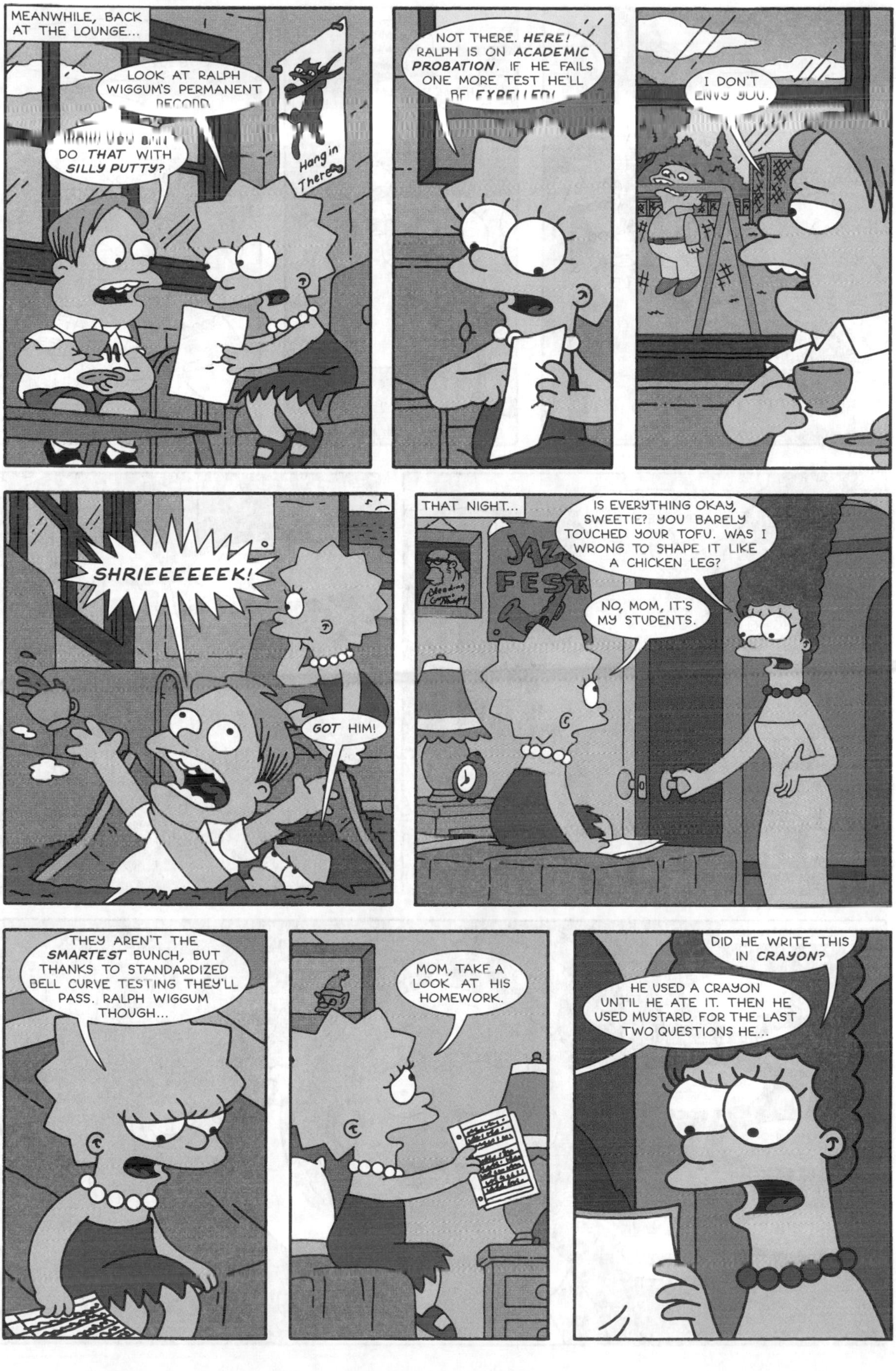

MEANWHILE, BACK AT THE LOUNGE...
LOOK AT RALPH WIGGUM'S PERMANENT RECORD.
DO THAT WITH SILLY PUTTY?
Hang in There
NOT THERE. HERE! RALPH IS ON ACADEMIC PROBATION. IF HE FAILS ONE MORE TEST HE'LL BE EXPELLED!
I DON'T ENVY YOU.
SHRIEEEEEEK!
GOT HIM!
THAT NIGHT...
IS EVERYTHING OKAY, SWEETIE? YOU BARELY TOUCHED YOUR TOFU. WAS I WRONG TO SHAPE IT LIKE A CHICKEN LEG?
NO, MOM, IT'S MY STUDENTS.
THEY AREN'T THE SMARTEST BUNCH, BUT THANKS TO STANDARDIZED BELL CURVE TESTING THEY'LL PASS. RALPH WIGGUM THOUGH...
MOM, TAKE A LOOK AT HIS HOMEWORK.
DID HE WRITE THIS IN CRAYON?
HE USED A CRAYON UNTIL HE ATE IT. THEN HE USED MUSTARD. FOR THE LAST TWO QUESTIONS HE...

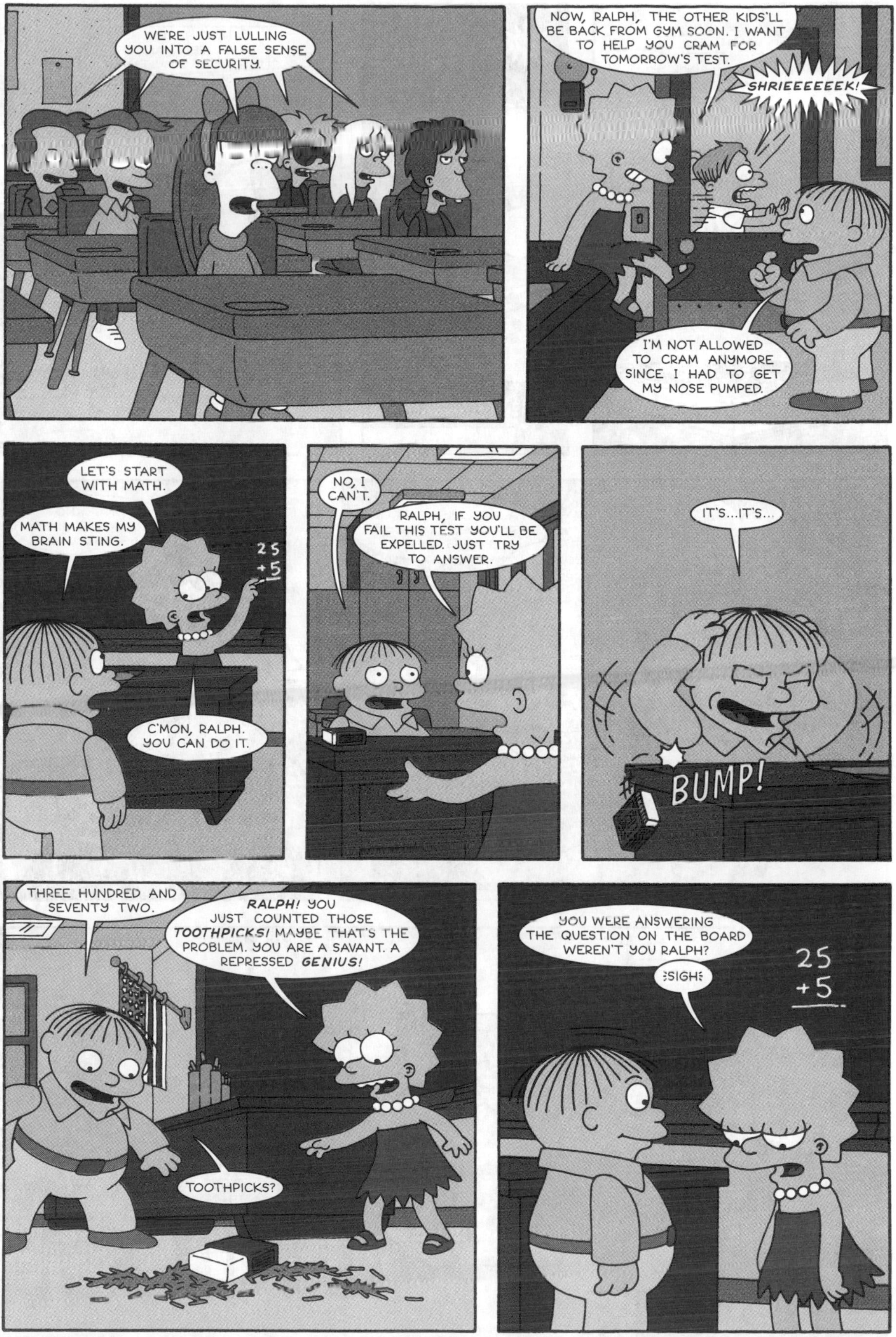
WE'RE JUST LULLING YOU INTO A FALSE SENSE OF SECURITY.
NOW, RALPH, THE OTHER KIDS'LL BE BACK FROM GYM SOON. I WANT TO HELP YOU CRAM FOR TOMORROW'S TEST.
SHRIEEEEEEK!
I'M NOT ALLOWED TO CRAM ANYMORE SINCE I HAD TO GET MY NOSE PUMPED.
LET'S START WITH MATH.
MATH MAKES MY BRAIN STING.
25 +5
C'MON, RALPH. YOU CAN DO IT.
NO, I CAN'T.
RALPH, IF YOU FAIL THIS TEST YOU'LL BE EXPELLED. JUST TRY TO ANSWER.
IT'S...IT'S...
BUMP!
THREE HUNDRED AND SEVENTY TWO.
RALPH! YOU JUST COUNTED THOSE TOOTHPICKS! MAYBE THAT'S THE PROBLEM. YOU ARE A SAVANT. A REPRESSED GENIUS!
TOOTHPICKS?
YOU WERE ANSWERING THE QUESTION ON THE BOARD WEREN'T YOU RALPH?
:SIGH:
25 +5

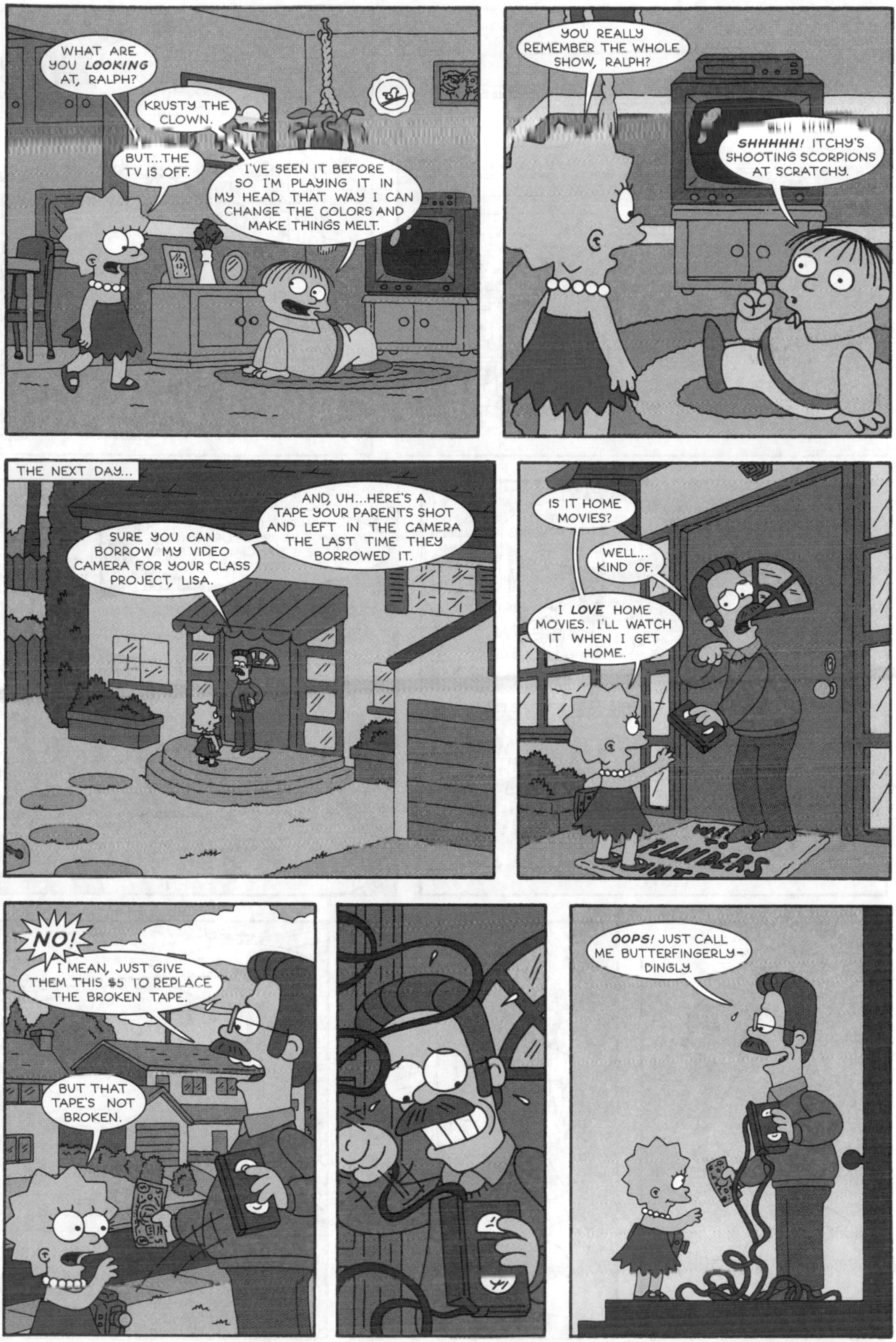
WHAT ARE YOU *LOOKING* AT, RALPH?
KRUSTY THE CLOWN.
BUT...THE TV IS OFF.
I'VE SEEN IT BEFORE SO I'M PLAYING IT IN MY HEAD. THAT WAY I CAN CHANGE THE COLORS AND MAKE THINGS MELT.
YOU REALLY REMEMBER THE WHOLE SHOW, RALPH?
SHHHHH! ITCHY'S SHOOTING SCORPIONS AT SCRATCHY.
THE NEXT DAY...
SURE YOU CAN BORROW MY VIDEO CAMERA FOR YOUR CLASS PROJECT, LISA.
AND, UH...HERE'S A TAPE YOUR PARENTS SHOT AND LEFT IN THE CAMERA THE LAST TIME THEY BORROWED IT.
IS IT HOME MOVIES?
WELL... KIND OF.
I *LOVE* HOME MOVIES. I'LL WATCH IT WHEN I GET HOME.
FLANDERS
NO!
I MEAN, JUST GIVE THEM THIS $5 TO REPLACE THE BROKEN TAPE.
BUT THAT TAPE'S NOT BROKEN.
OOPS! JUST CALL ME BUTTERFINGERLY-DINGLY.

51

BARTMAN IN IDENTITY CRISIS

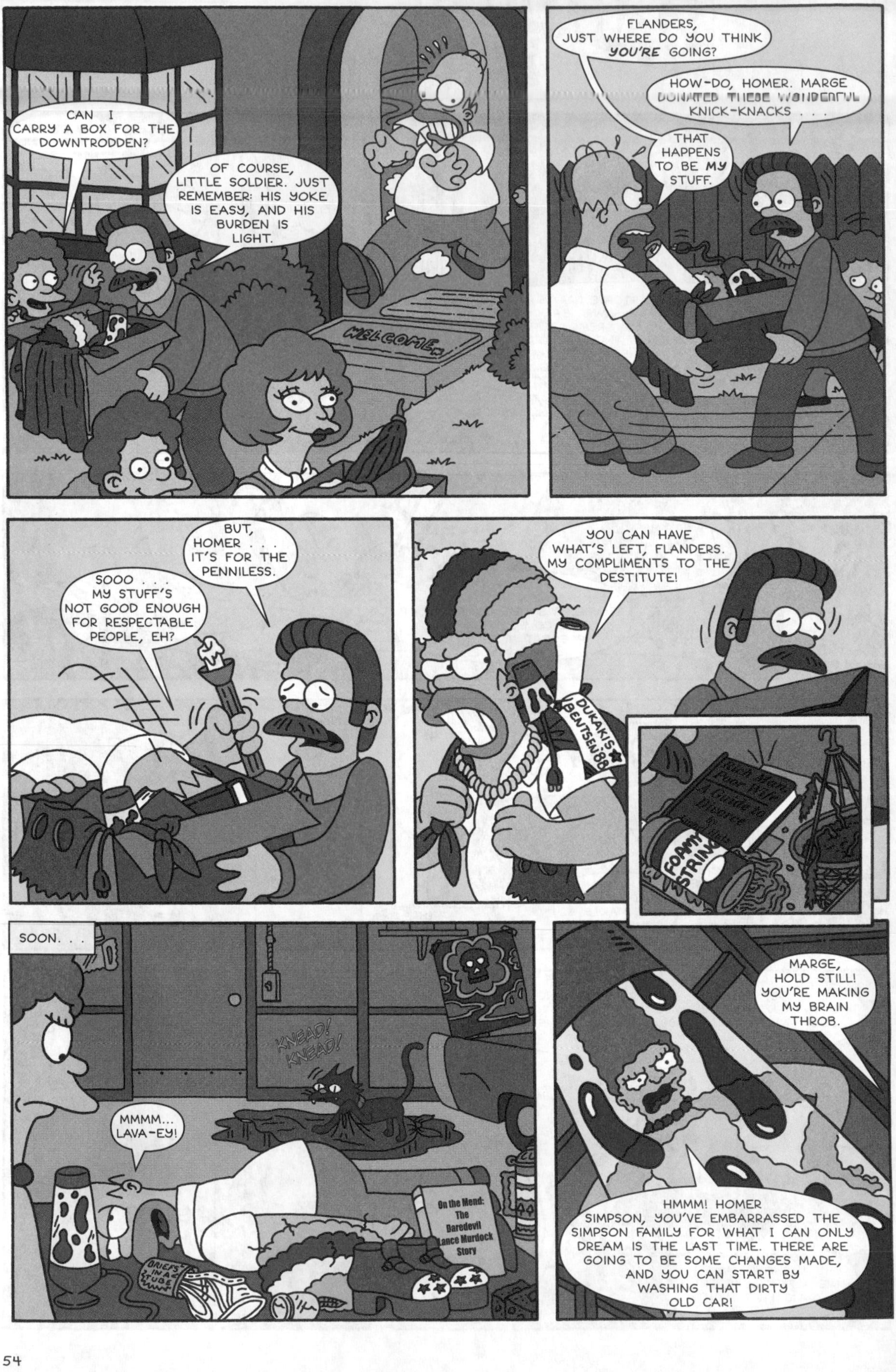
CAN I CARRY A BOX FOR THE DOWNTRODDEN?
OF COURSE, LITTLE SOLDIER. JUST REMEMBER: HIS YOKE IS EASY, AND HIS BURDEN IS LIGHT.
WELCOME
FLANDERS, JUST WHERE DO YOU THINK YOU'RE GOING?
HOW-DO, HOMER. MARGE DONATED THESE WONDERFUL KNICK-KNACKS . . .
THAT HAPPENS TO BE MY STUFF.
SOOO . . . MY STUFF'S NOT GOOD ENOUGH FOR RESPECTABLE PEOPLE, EH?
BUT, HOMER . . . IT'S FOR THE PENNILESS.
YOU CAN HAVE WHAT'S LEFT, FLANDERS. MY COMPLIMENTS TO THE DESTITUTE!
DUKAKIS BENTSEN '88
FOAMY STRING
SOON. . .
KNEAD! KNEAD!
MMMM... LAVA-EY!
BRIEFS IN A TUBE
On the Mend: The Daredevil Lance Murdock Story
MARGE, HOLD STILL! YOU'RE MAKING MY BRAIN THROB.
HMMM! HOMER SIMPSON, YOU'VE EMBARRASSED THE SIMPSON FAMILY FOR WHAT I CAN ONLY DREAM IS THE LAST TIME. THERE ARE GOING TO BE SOME CHANGES MADE, AND YOU CAN START BY WASHING THAT DIRTY OLD CAR!

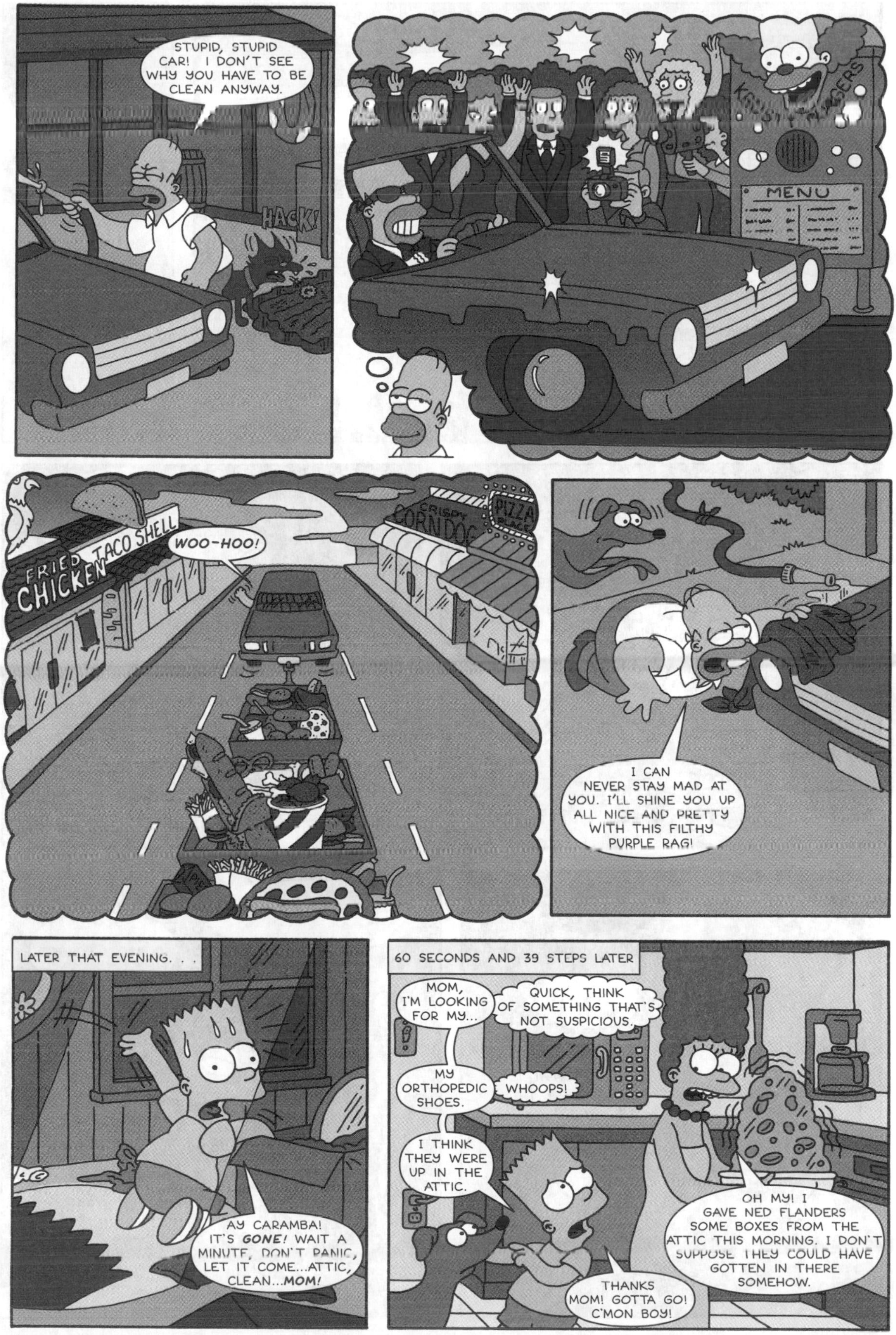
STUPID, STUPID CAR! I DON'T SEE WHY YOU HAVE TO BE CLEAN ANYWAY.
HACK!
MENU
FRIED CHICKEN
TACO SHELL
CRISPY CORN DOG
PIZZA PLACE
WOO-HOO!
I CAN NEVER STAY MAD AT YOU. I'LL SHINE YOU UP ALL NICE AND PRETTY WITH THIS FILTHY PURPLE RAG!
LATER THAT EVENING. . .
AY CARAMBA! IT'S GONE! WAIT A MINUTE, DON'T PANIC, LET IT COME...ATTIC, CLEAN...MOM!
60 SECONDS AND 39 STEPS LATER
MOM, I'M LOOKING FOR MY...
QUICK, THINK OF SOMETHING THAT'S NOT SUSPICIOUS.
MY ORTHOPEDIC SHOES.
WHOOPS!
I THINK THEY WERE UP IN THE ATTIC.
OH MY! I GAVE NED FLANDERS SOME BOXES FROM THE ATTIC THIS MORNING. I DON'T SUPPOSE THEY COULD HAVE GOTTEN IN THERE SOMEHOW.
THANKS MOM! GOTTA GO! C'MON BOY!

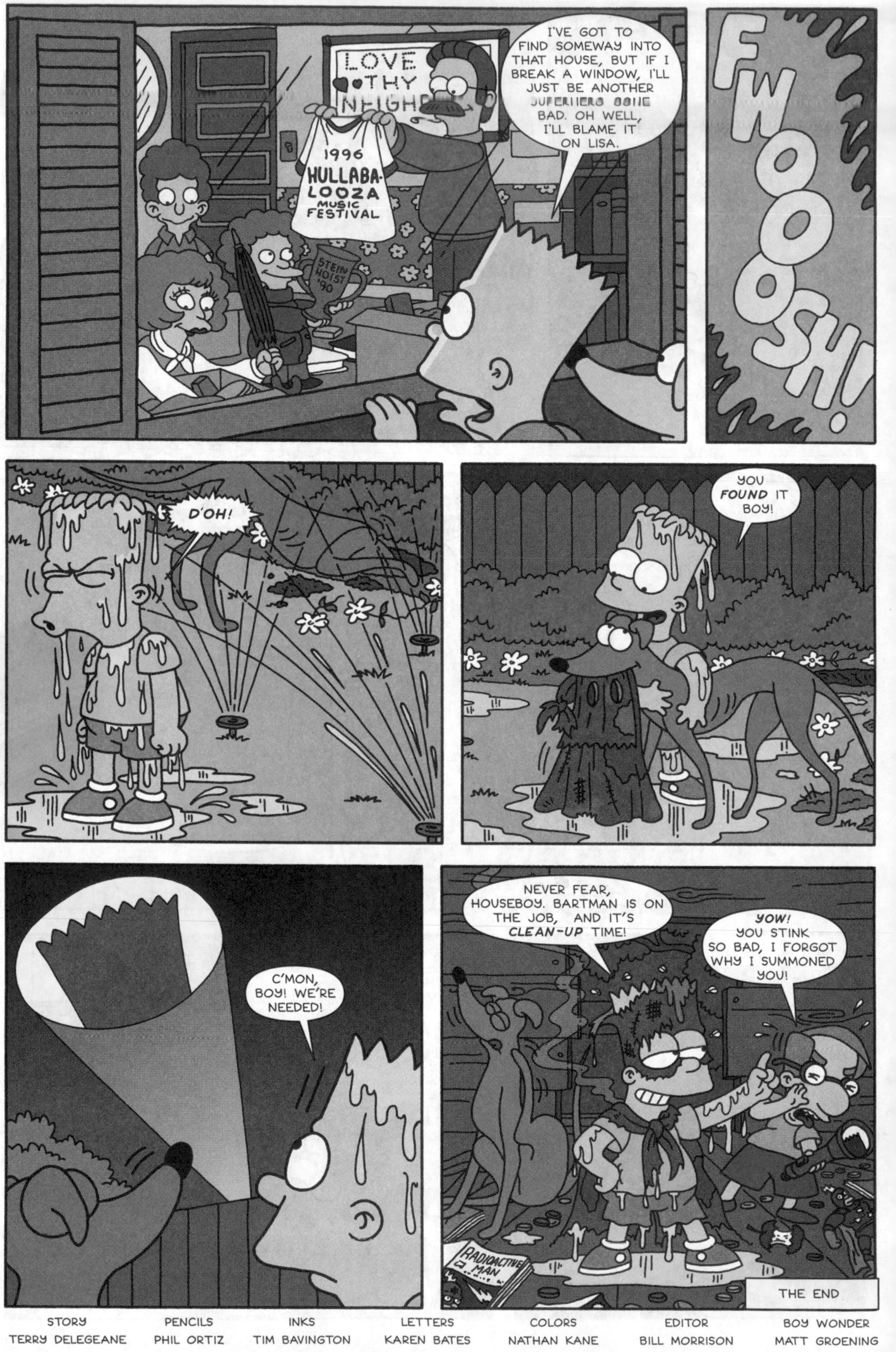
LOVE THY NEIGHB
1996 HULLABA-LOOZA MUSIC FESTIVAL
STEIN HOIST '90
I'VE GOT TO FIND SOMEWAY INTO THAT HOUSE, BUT IF I BREAK A WINDOW, I'LL JUST BE ANOTHER
BAD. OH WELL, I'LL BLAME IT ON LISA.
FWOOOSH!
D'OH!
YOU FOUND IT BOY!
C'MON, BOY! WE'RE NEEDED!
NEVER FEAR, HOUSEBOY. BARTMAN IS ON THE JOB, AND IT'S CLEAN-UP TIME!
YOW! YOU STINK SO BAD, I FORGOT WHY I SUMMONED YOU!
RADIOACTIVE MAN
THE END

STORY TERRY DELEGEANE · PENCILS PHIL ORTIZ · INKS TIM BAVINGTON · LETTERS KAREN BATES · COLORS NATHAN KANE · EDITOR BILL MORRISON · BOY WONDER MATT GROENING

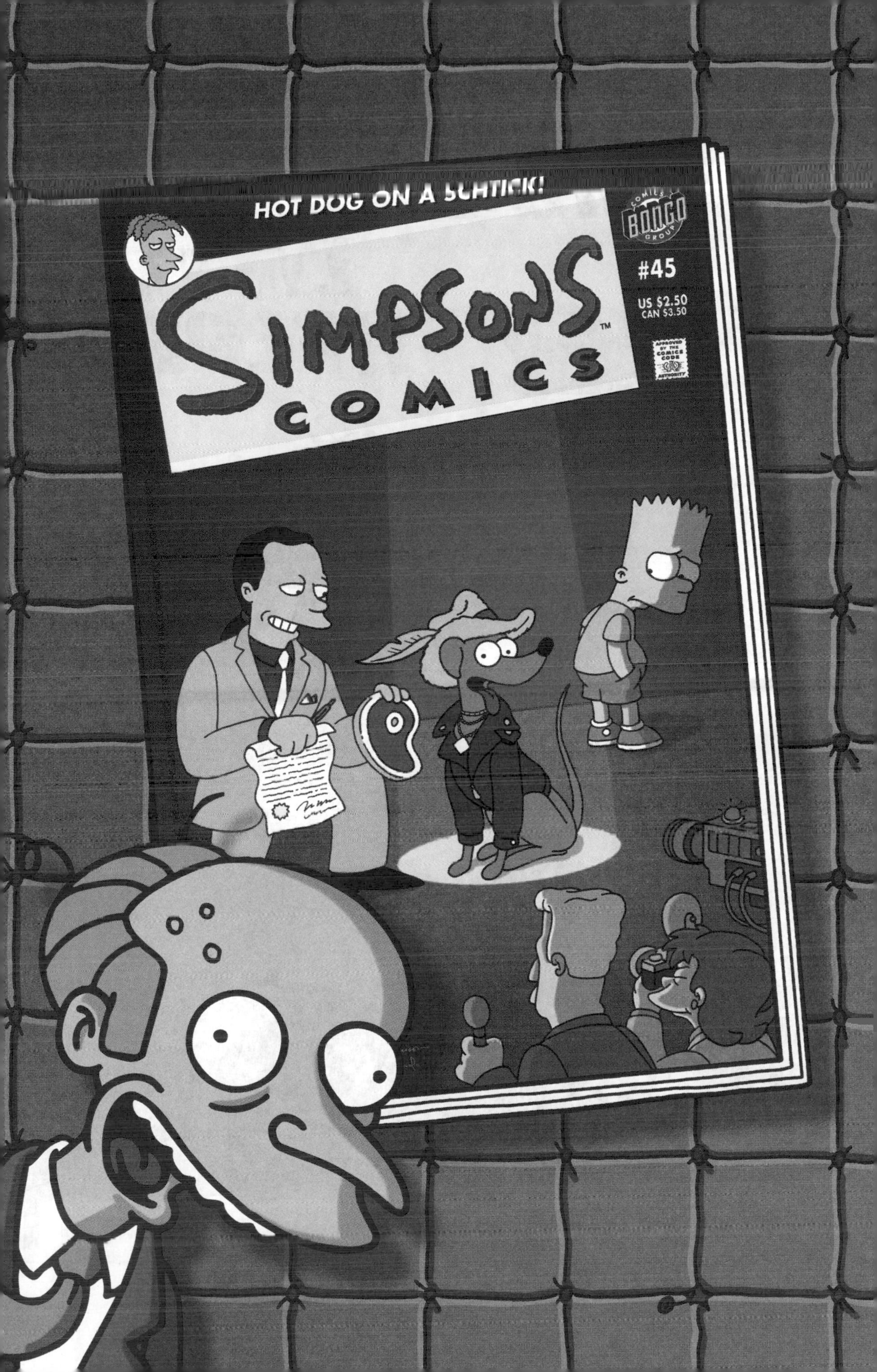
HOT DOG ON A SCHTICK!
SIMPSONS COMICS
#45
US $2.50
CAN $3.50

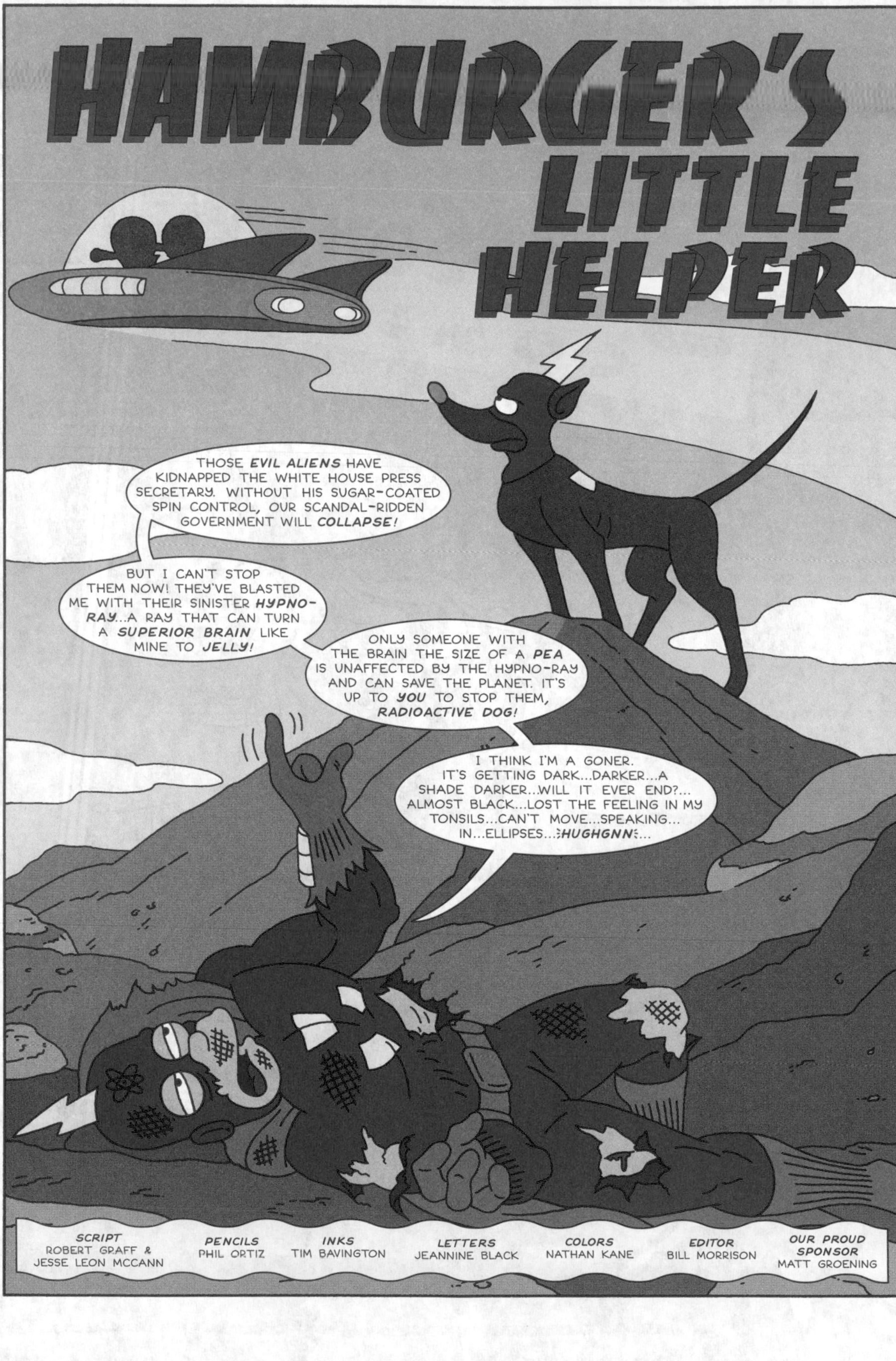
HAMBURGER'S LITTLE HELPER
THOSE EVIL ALIENS HAVE KIDNAPPED THE WHITE HOUSE PRESS SECRETARY. WITHOUT HIS SUGAR-COATED SPIN CONTROL, OUR SCANDAL-RIDDEN GOVERNMENT WILL COLLAPSE!
BUT I CAN'T STOP THEM NOW! THEY'VE BLASTED ME WITH THEIR SINISTER HYPNO-RAY...A RAY THAT CAN TURN A SUPERIOR BRAIN LIKE MINE TO JELLY!
ONLY SOMEONE WITH THE BRAIN THE SIZE OF A PEA IS UNAFFECTED BY THE HYPNO-RAY AND CAN SAVE THE PLANET. IT'S UP TO YOU TO STOP THEM, RADIOACTIVE DOG!
I THINK I'M A GONER. IT'S GETTING DARK...DARKER...A SHADE DARKER...WILL IT EVER END?... ALMOST BLACK...LOST THE FEELING IN MY TONSILS...CAN'T MOVE...SPEAKING... IN...ELLIPSES...HUGHGNN...
SCRIPT ROBERT GRAFF & JESSE LEON MCCANN
PENCILS PHIL ORTIZ
INKS TIM BAVINGTON
LETTERS JEANNINE BLACK
COLORS NATHAN KANE
EDITOR BILL MORRISON
OUR PROUD SPONSOR MATT GROENING

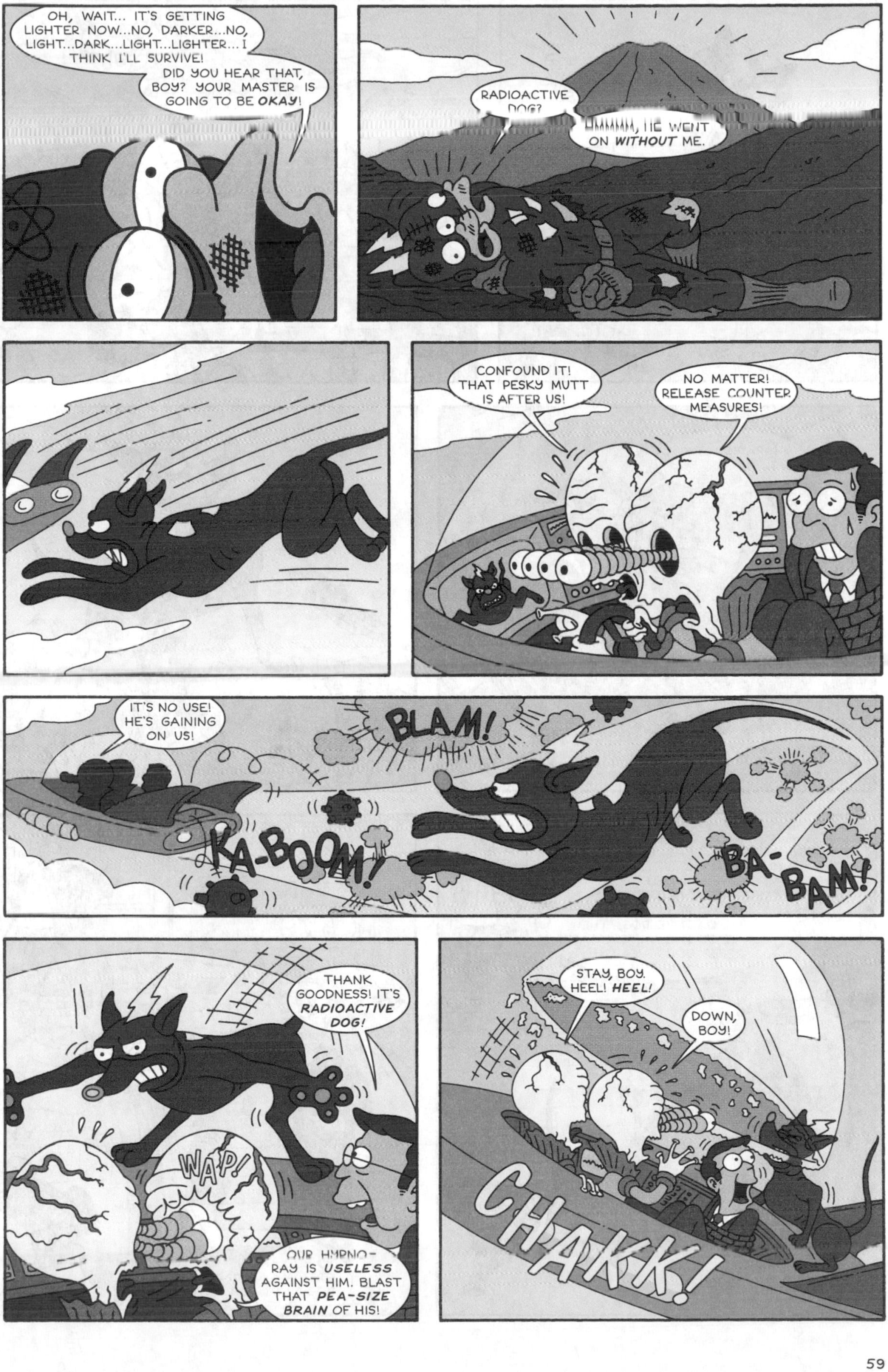

OH, WAIT... IT'S GETTING LIGHTER NOW...NO, DARKER...NO, LIGHT...DARK...LIGHT...LIGHTER... I THINK I'LL SURVIVE!
DID YOU HEAR THAT, BOY? YOUR MASTER IS GOING TO BE OKAY!
RADIOACTIVE DOG?
ON WITHOUT ME.
CONFOUND IT! THAT PESKY MUTT IS AFTER US!
NO MATTER! RELEASE COUNTER MEASURES!
IT'S NO USE! HE'S GAINING ON US!
BLAM!
KA-BOOM!
BA-BAM!
THANK GOODNESS! IT'S RADIOACTIVE DOG!
WAP!
OUR HYPNO-RAY IS USELESS AGAINST HIM. BLAST THAT PEA-SIZE BRAIN OF HIS!
STAY, BOY. HEEL! HEEL!
DOWN, BOY!
CHAKK!

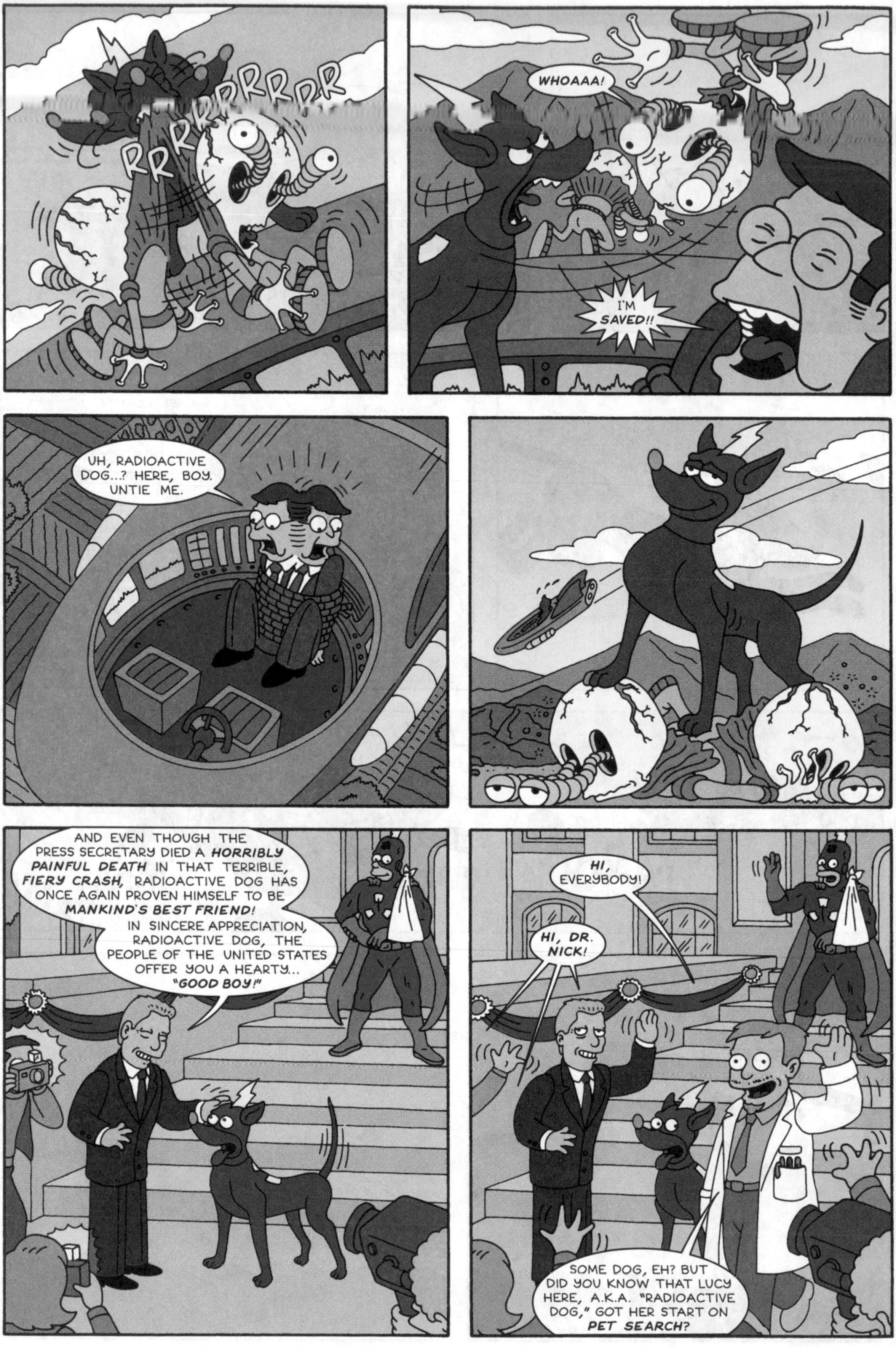
RRRRRRRRR
WHOAAA!
I'M SAVED!!
UH, RADIOACTIVE DOG...? HERE, BOY. UNTIE ME.
AND EVEN THOUGH THE PRESS SECRETARY DIED A **HORRIBLY PAINFUL DEATH** IN THAT TERRIBLE, **FIERY CRASH,** RADIOACTIVE DOG HAS ONCE AGAIN PROVEN HIMSELF TO BE **MANKIND'S BEST FRIEND!**
IN SINCERE APPRECIATION, RADIOACTIVE DOG, THE PEOPLE OF THE UNITED STATES OFFER YOU A HEARTY... **"GOOD BOY!"**
HI, EVERYBODY!
HI, DR. NICK!
SOME DOG, EH? BUT DID YOU KNOW THAT LUCY HERE, A.K.A. "RADIOACTIVE DOG," GOT HER START ON **PET SEARCH?**

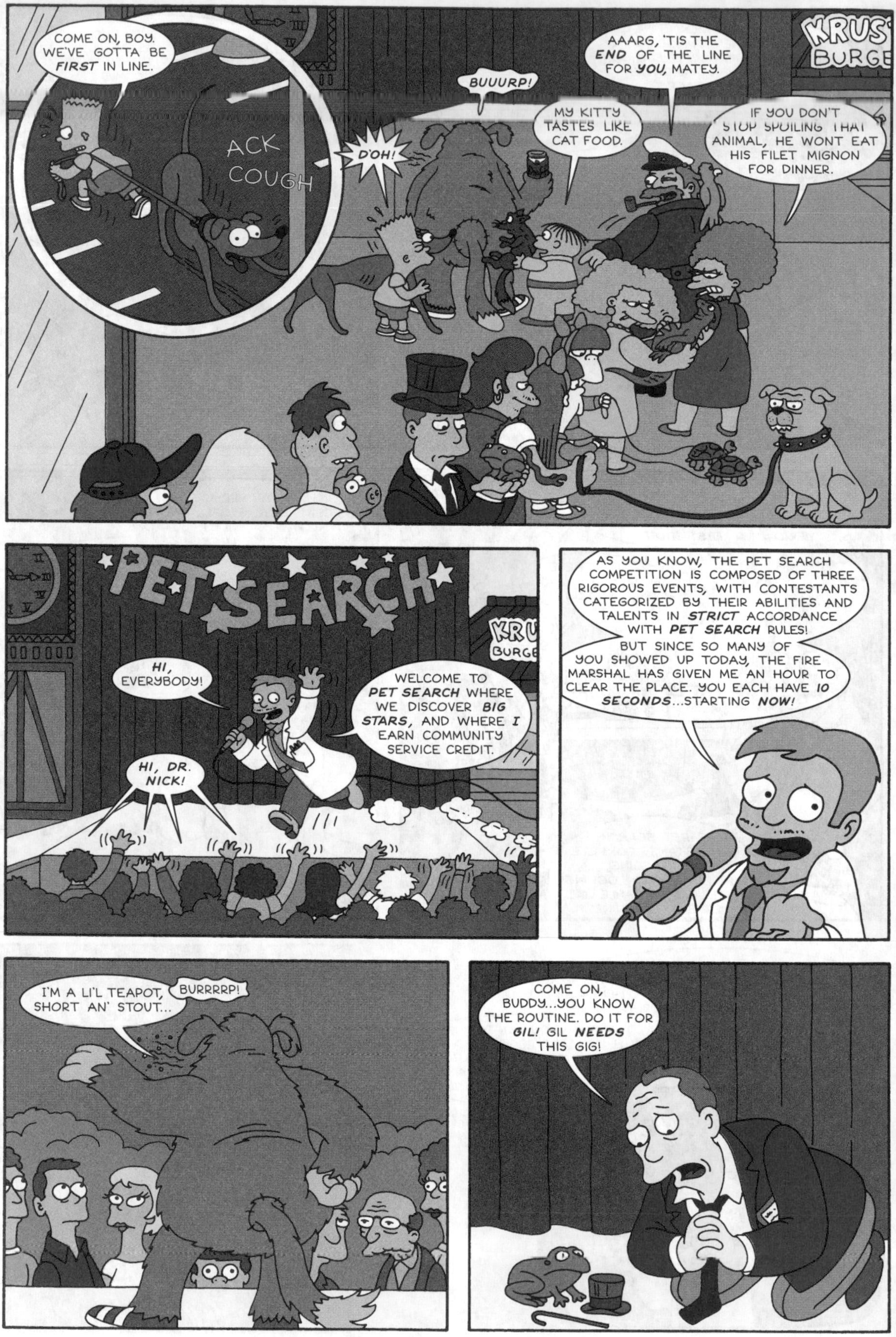
COME ON, BOY. WE'VE GOTTA BE FIRST IN LINE.
ACK COUGH
D'OH!
BUUURP!
MY KITTY TASTES LIKE CAT FOOD.
AAARG, 'TIS THE END OF THE LINE FOR YOU, MATEY.
IF YOU DON'T STOP SPOILING THAT ANIMAL, HE WONT EAT HIS FILET MIGNON FOR DINNER.
KRUS BURGE
PET SEARCH
HI, EVERYBODY!
WELCOME TO PET SEARCH WHERE WE DISCOVER BIG STARS, AND WHERE I EARN COMMUNITY SERVICE CREDIT.
HI, DR. NICK!
AS YOU KNOW, THE PET SEARCH COMPETITION IS COMPOSED OF THREE RIGOROUS EVENTS, WITH CONTESTANTS CATEGORIZED BY THEIR ABILITIES AND TALENTS IN STRICT ACCORDANCE WITH PET SEARCH RULES!
BUT SINCE SO MANY OF YOU SHOWED UP TODAY, THE FIRE MARSHAL HAS GIVEN ME AN HOUR TO CLEAR THE PLACE. YOU EACH HAVE 10 SECONDS...STARTING NOW!
I'M A LI'L TEAPOT, SHORT AN' STOUT...
BURRRRP!
COME ON, BUDDY...YOU KNOW THE ROUTINE. DO IT FOR GIL! GIL NEEDS THIS GIG!

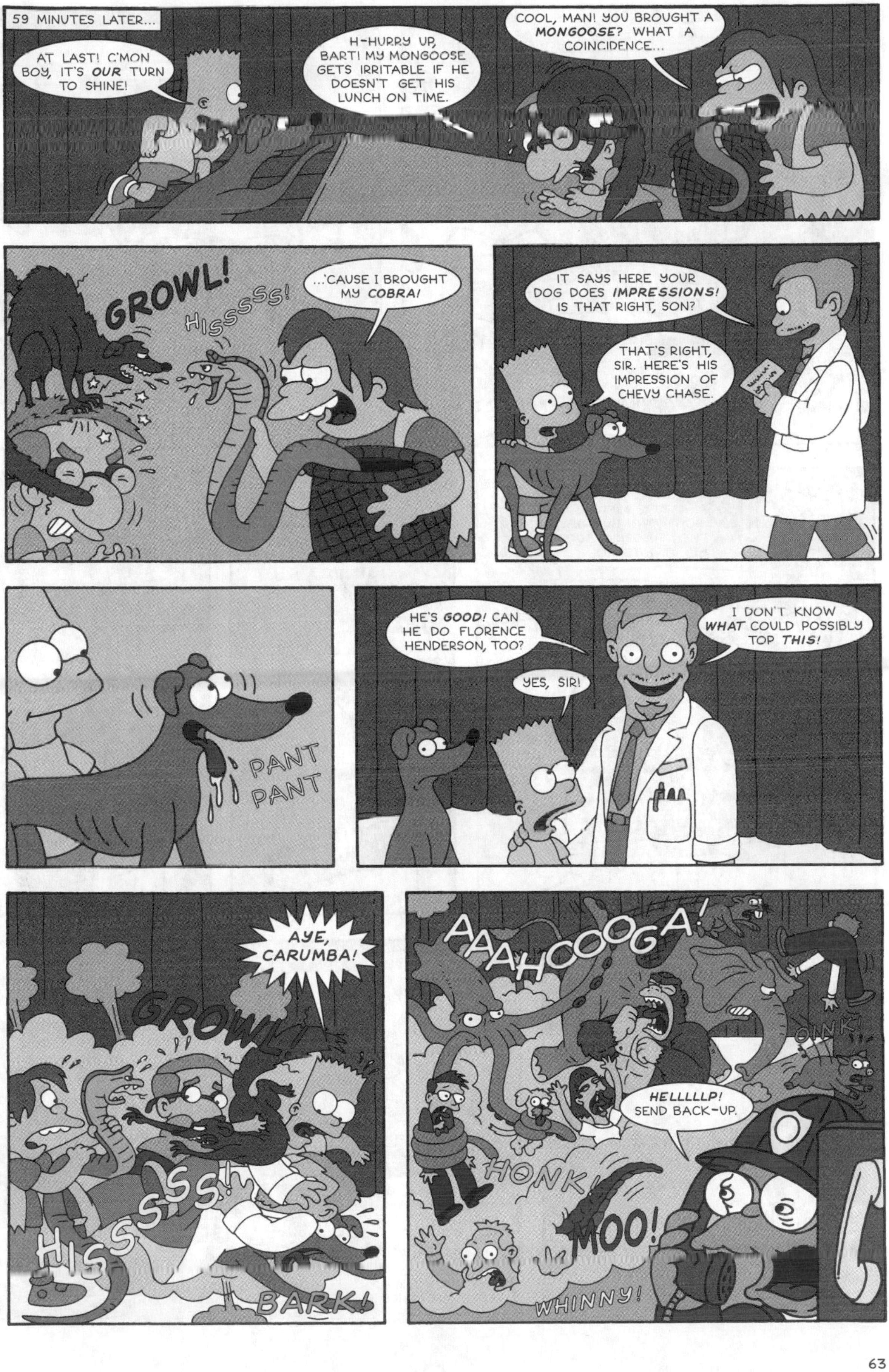
59 MINUTES LATER...
AT LAST! C'MON BOY, IT'S OUR TURN TO SHINE!
H-HURRY UP, BART! MY MONGOOSE GETS IRRITABLE IF HE DOESN'T GET HIS LUNCH ON TIME.
COOL, MAN! YOU BROUGHT A MONGOOSE? WHAT A COINCIDENCE...
GROWL!
HISSSSS!
...'CAUSE I BROUGHT MY COBRA!
IT SAYS HERE YOUR DOG DOES IMPRESSIONS! IS THAT RIGHT, SON?
THAT'S RIGHT, SIR. HERE'S HIS IMPRESSION OF CHEVY CHASE.
PANT PANT
HE'S GOOD! CAN HE DO FLORENCE HENDERSON, TOO?
YES, SIR!
I DON'T KNOW WHAT COULD POSSIBLY TOP THIS!
AYE, CARUMBA!
GROWL!
HISSSSS!
BARK!
AAAHCOOOGA!
OINK!
HELLLLLP! SEND BACK-UP.
HONK!
MOO!
WHINNY!

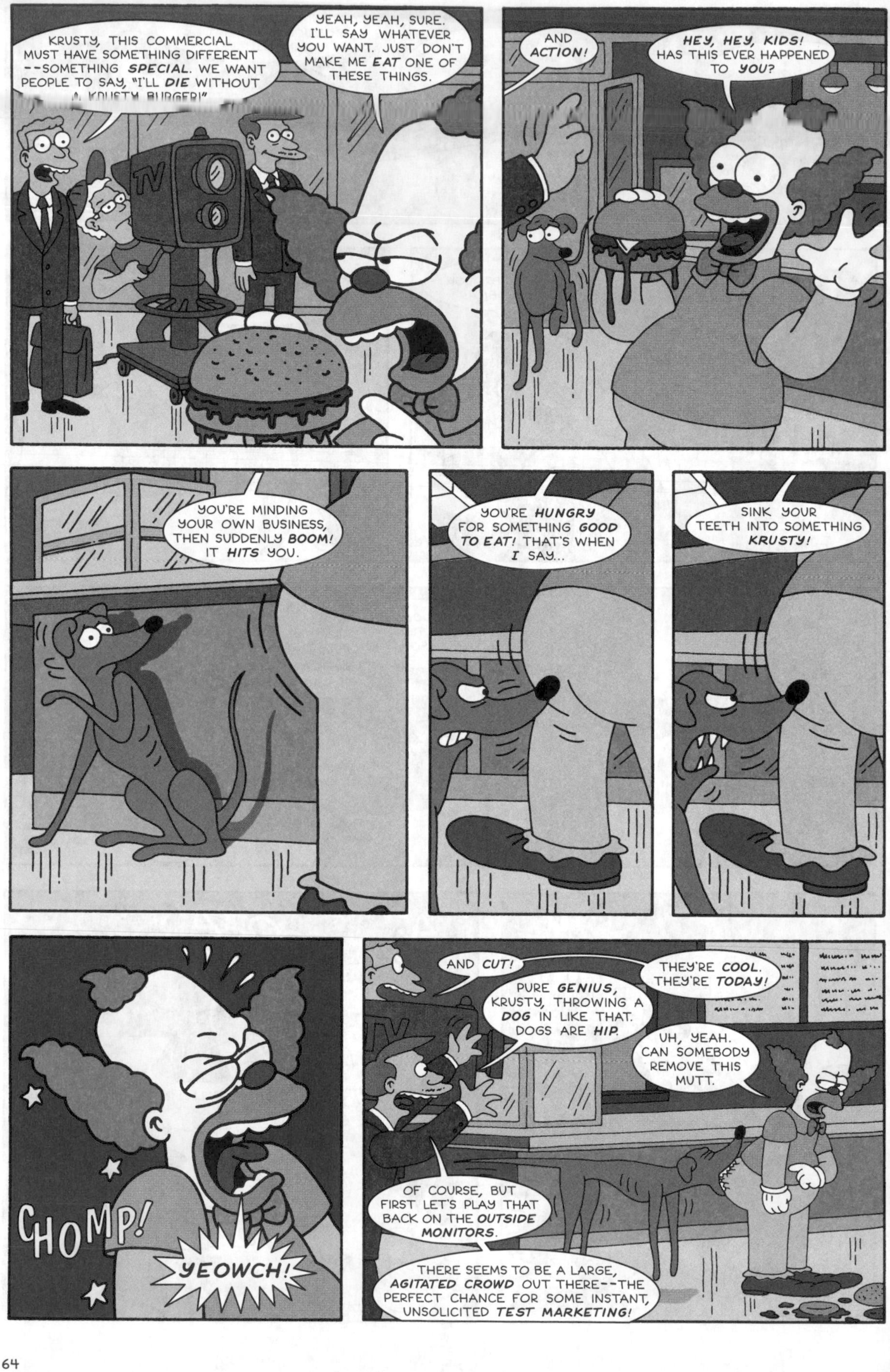
KRUSTY, THIS COMMERCIAL MUST HAVE SOMETHING DIFFERENT --SOMETHING **SPECIAL**. WE WANT PEOPLE TO SAY, "I'LL **DIE** WITHOUT A KRUSTY BURGER!"
YEAH, YEAH, SURE. I'LL SAY WHATEVER YOU WANT. JUST DON'T MAKE ME **EAT** ONE OF THESE THINGS.
TV
AND **ACTION!**
HEY, HEY, KIDS! HAS THIS EVER HAPPENED TO **YOU?**
YOU'RE MINDING YOUR OWN BUSINESS, THEN SUDDENLY **BOOM!** IT **HITS** YOU.
YOU'RE **HUNGRY** FOR SOMETHING **GOOD TO EAT!** THAT'S WHEN **I** SAY...
SINK YOUR TEETH INTO SOMETHING **KRUSTY!**
CHOMP!
YEOWCH!
AND **CUT!**
THEY'RE **COOL**. THEY'RE **TODAY!**
PURE **GENIUS,** KRUSTY, THROWING A **DOG** IN LIKE THAT. DOGS ARE **HIP**.
UH, YEAH. CAN SOMEBODY REMOVE THIS MUTT.
OF COURSE, BUT FIRST LET'S PLAY THAT BACK ON THE **OUTSIDE MONITORS**.
THERE SEEMS TO BE A LARGE, **AGITATED CROWD** OUT THERE--THE PERFECT CHANCE FOR SOME INSTANT, UNSOLICITED **TEST MARKETING!**

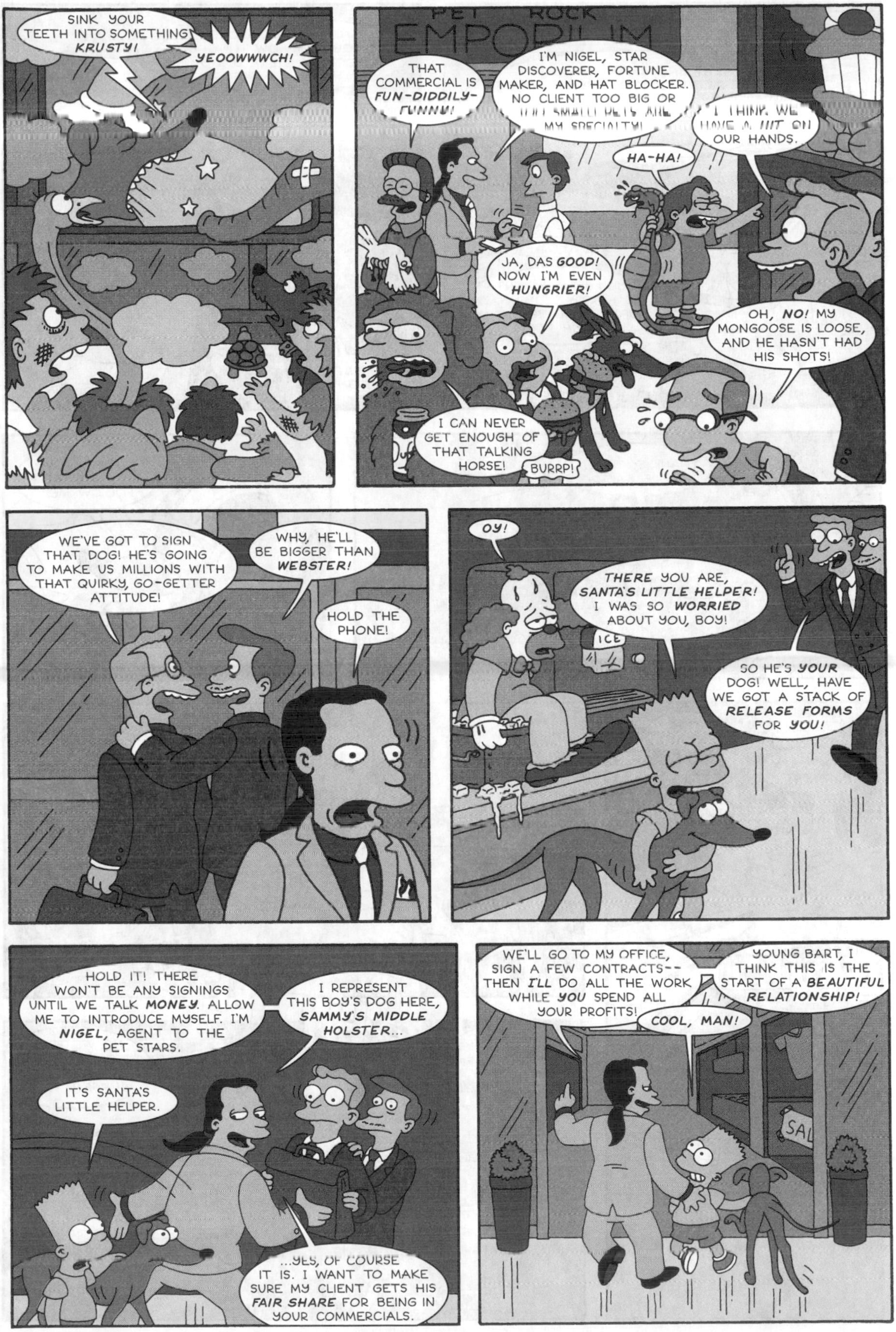
SINK YOUR TEETH INTO SOMETHING KRUSTY!
YEOOWWWCH!
PET ROCK EMPORIUM
THAT COMMERCIAL IS FUN-DIDDILY-FUNNY!
I'M NIGEL, STAR DISCOVERER, FORTUNE MAKER, AND HAT BLOCKER. NO CLIENT TOO BIG OR TOO SMALL! PETS ARE MY SPECIALTY!
I THINK WE HAVE A HIT ON OUR HANDS.
HA-HA!
JA, DAS GOOD! NOW I'M EVEN HUNGRIER!
OH, NO! MY MONGOOSE IS LOOSE, AND HE HASN'T HAD HIS SHOTS!
I CAN NEVER GET ENOUGH OF THAT TALKING HORSE!
BURRP!
WE'VE GOT TO SIGN THAT DOG! HE'S GOING TO MAKE US MILLIONS WITH THAT QUIRKY, GO-GETTER ATTITUDE!
WHY, HE'LL BE BIGGER THAN WEBSTER!
HOLD THE PHONE!
OY!
THERE YOU ARE, SANTA'S LITTLE HELPER! I WAS SO WORRIED ABOUT YOU, BOY!
ICE
SO HE'S YOUR DOG! WELL, HAVE WE GOT A STACK OF RELEASE FORMS FOR YOU!
HOLD IT! THERE WON'T BE ANY SIGNINGS UNTIL WE TALK MONEY. ALLOW ME TO INTRODUCE MYSELF. I'M NIGEL, AGENT TO THE PET STARS.
I REPRESENT THIS BOY'S DOG HERE, SAMMY'S MIDDLE HOLSTER...
IT'S SANTA'S LITTLE HELPER.
...YES, OF COURSE IT IS. I WANT TO MAKE SURE MY CLIENT GETS HIS FAIR SHARE FOR BEING IN YOUR COMMERCIALS.
WE'LL GO TO MY OFFICE, SIGN A FEW CONTRACTS-- THEN I'LL DO ALL THE WORK WHILE YOU SPEND ALL YOUR PROFITS!
YOUNG BART, I THINK THIS IS THE START OF A BEAUTIFUL RELATIONSHIP!
COOL, MAN!

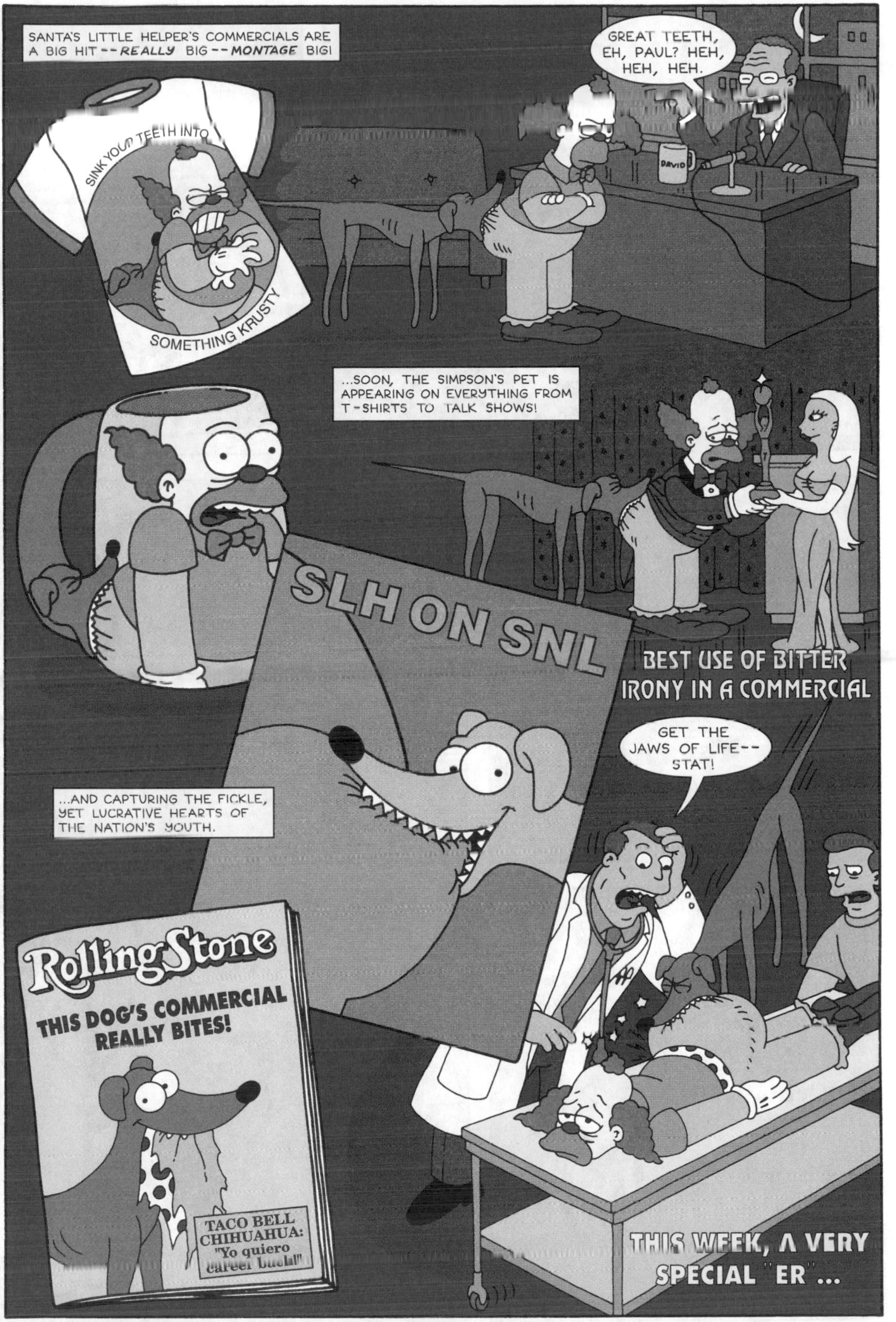
SANTA'S LITTLE HELPER'S COMMERCIALS ARE A BIG HIT--*REALLY* BIG--*MONTAGE* BIG!
SINK YOUR TEETH INTO
SOMETHING KRUSTY
GREAT TEETH, EH, PAUL? HEH, HEH, HEH.
DAVID
...SOON, THE SIMPSON'S PET IS APPEARING ON EVERYTHING FROM T-SHIRTS TO TALK SHOWS!
SLH ON SNL
BEST USE OF BITTER IRONY IN A COMMERCIAL
...AND CAPTURING THE FICKLE, YET LUCRATIVE HEARTS OF THE NATION'S YOUTH.
GET THE JAWS OF LIFE--STAT!
Rolling Stone
THIS DOG'S COMMERCIAL REALLY BITES!
TACO BELL CHIHUAHUA:
"Yo quiero
THIS WEEK, A VERY SPECIAL "ER"...

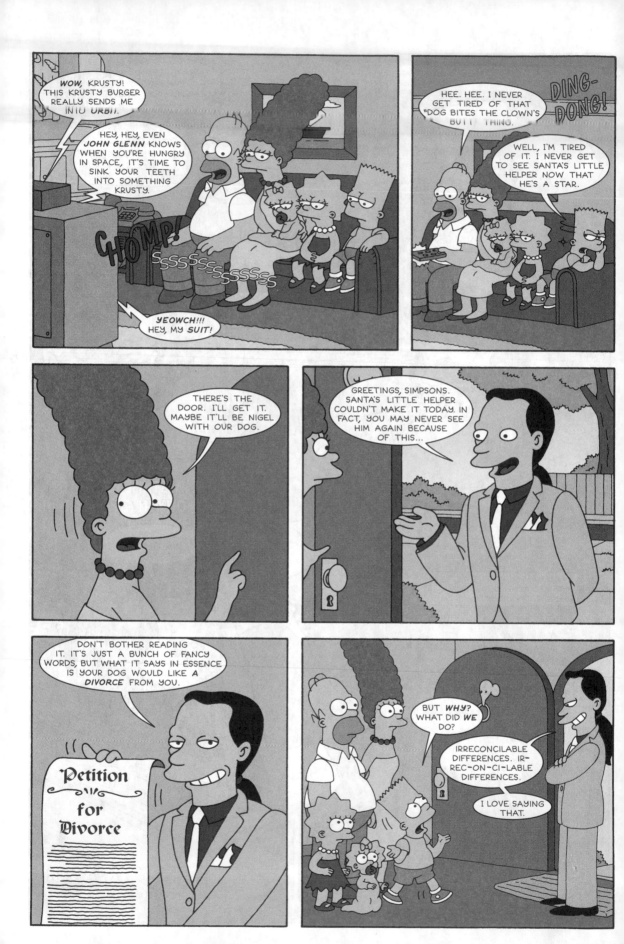

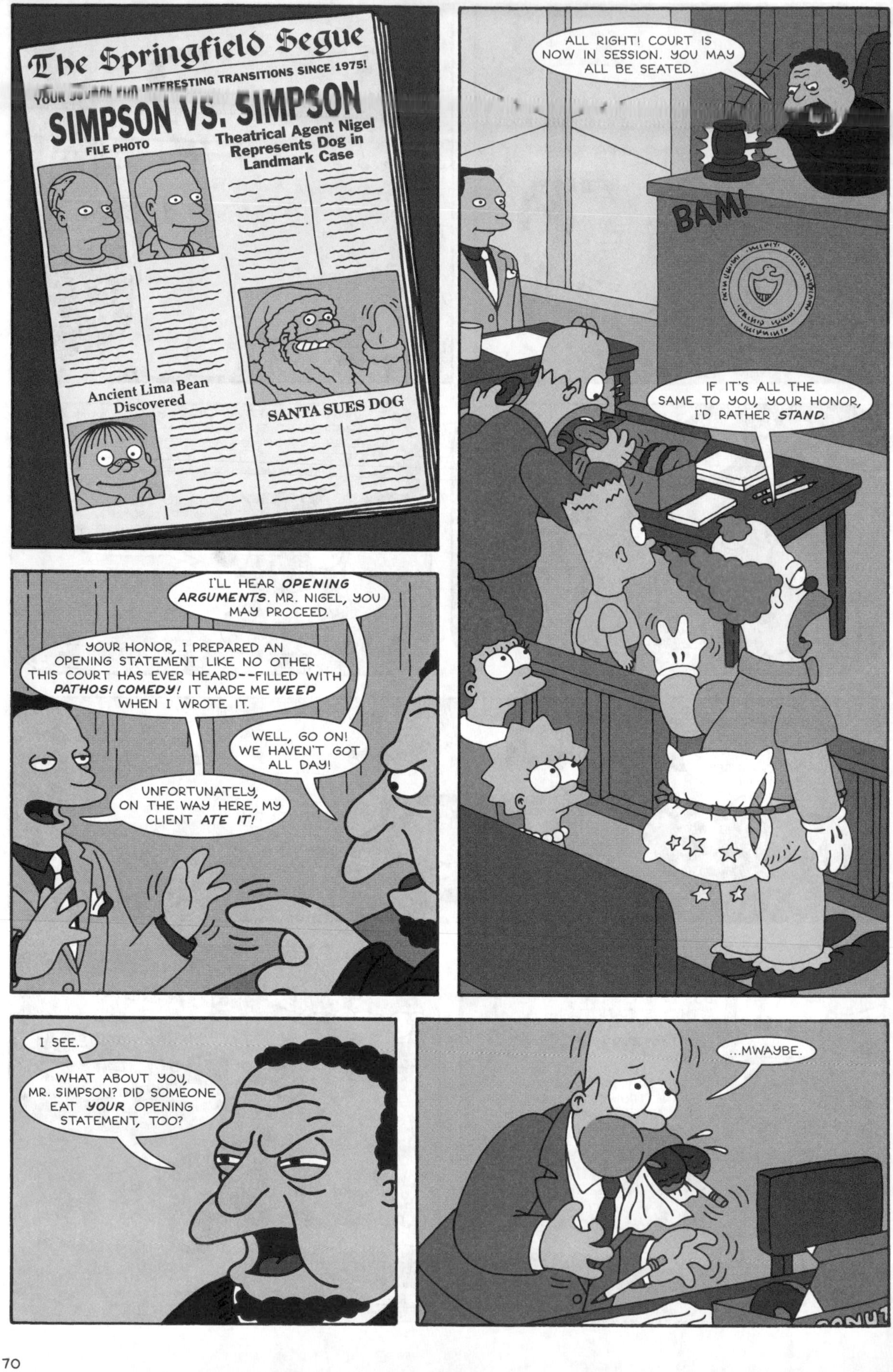
The Springfield Segue
INTERESTING TRANSITIONS SINCE 1975!
SIMPSON VS. SIMPSON
FILE PHOTO
Theatrical Agent Nigel Represents Dog in Landmark Case
Ancient Lima Bean Discovered
SANTA SUES DOG
ALL RIGHT! COURT IS NOW IN SESSION. YOU MAY ALL BE SEATED.
BAM!
IF IT'S ALL THE SAME TO YOU, YOUR HONOR, I'D RATHER STAND.
I'LL HEAR OPENING ARGUMENTS. MR. NIGEL, YOU MAY PROCEED.
YOUR HONOR, I PREPARED AN OPENING STATEMENT LIKE NO OTHER THIS COURT HAS EVER HEARD--FILLED WITH PATHOS! COMEDY! IT MADE ME WEEP WHEN I WROTE IT.
UNFORTUNATELY, ON THE WAY HERE, MY CLIENT ATE IT!
WELL, GO ON! WE HAVEN'T GOT ALL DAY!
I SEE.
WHAT ABOUT YOU, MR. SIMPSON? DID SOMEONE EAT YOUR OPENING STATEMENT, TOO?
...MWAYBE.

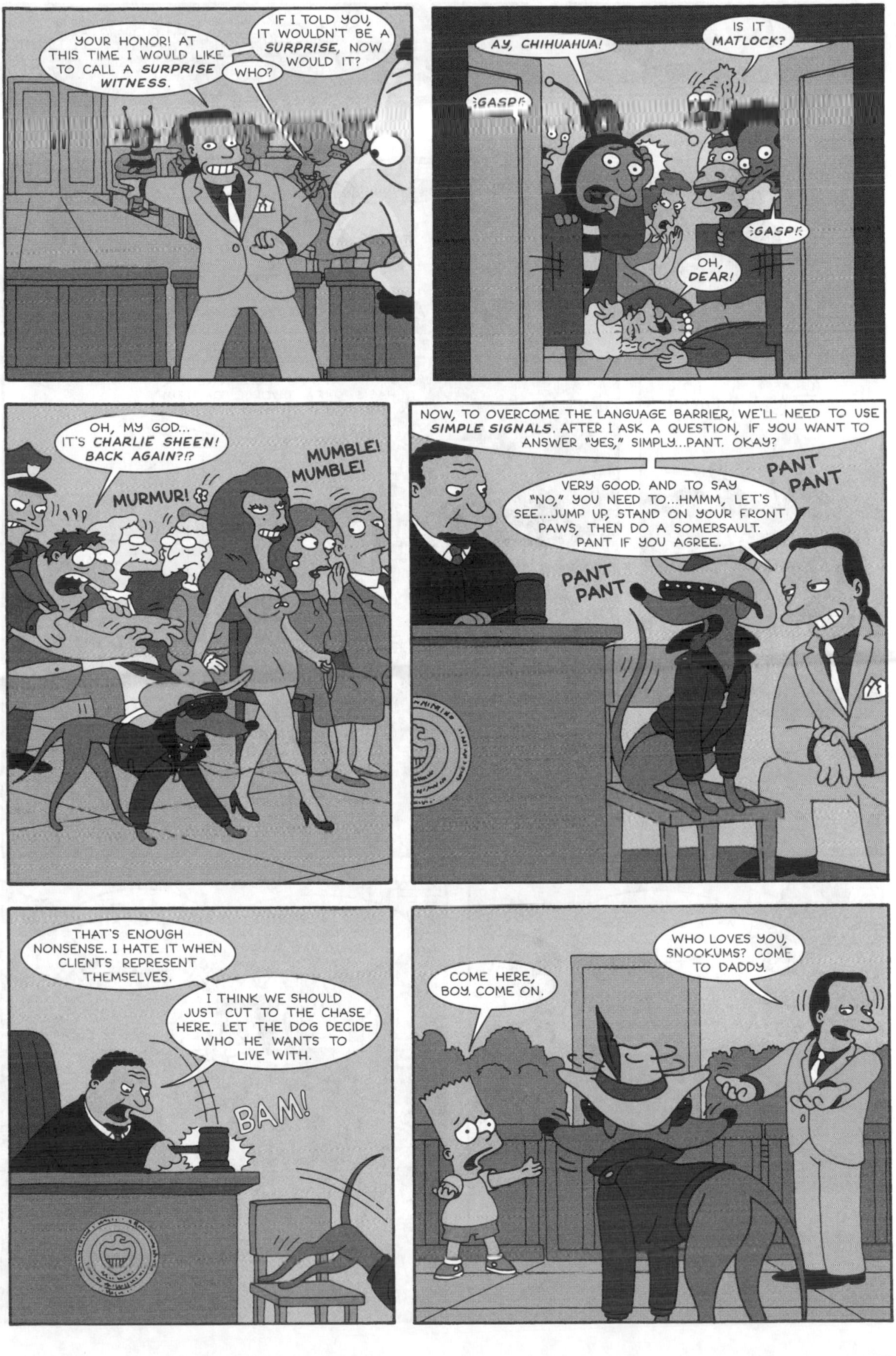

YOUR HONOR! AT THIS TIME I WOULD LIKE TO CALL A SURPRISE WITNESS.
WHO?
IF I TOLD YOU, IT WOULDN'T BE A SURPRISE, NOW WOULD IT?
AY, CHIHUAHUA!
IS IT MATLOCK?
GASP!
GASP!
OH, DEAR!
OH, MY GOD... IT'S CHARLIE SHEEN! BACK AGAIN?!?
MURMUR!
MUMBLE! MUMBLE!
NOW, TO OVERCOME THE LANGUAGE BARRIER, WE'LL NEED TO USE SIMPLE SIGNALS. AFTER I ASK A QUESTION, IF YOU WANT TO ANSWER "YES," SIMPLY...PANT. OKAY?
PANT PANT
VERY GOOD. AND TO SAY "NO," YOU NEED TO...HMMM, LET'S SEE...JUMP UP, STAND ON YOUR FRONT PAWS, THEN DO A SOMERSAULT. PANT IF YOU AGREE.
PANT PANT
THAT'S ENOUGH NONSENSE. I HATE IT WHEN CLIENTS REPRESENT THEMSELVES.
I THINK WE SHOULD JUST CUT TO THE CHASE HERE. LET THE DOG DECIDE WHO HE WANTS TO LIVE WITH.
BAM!
COME HERE, BOY. COME ON.
WHO LOVES YOU, SNOOKUMS? COME TO DADDY.

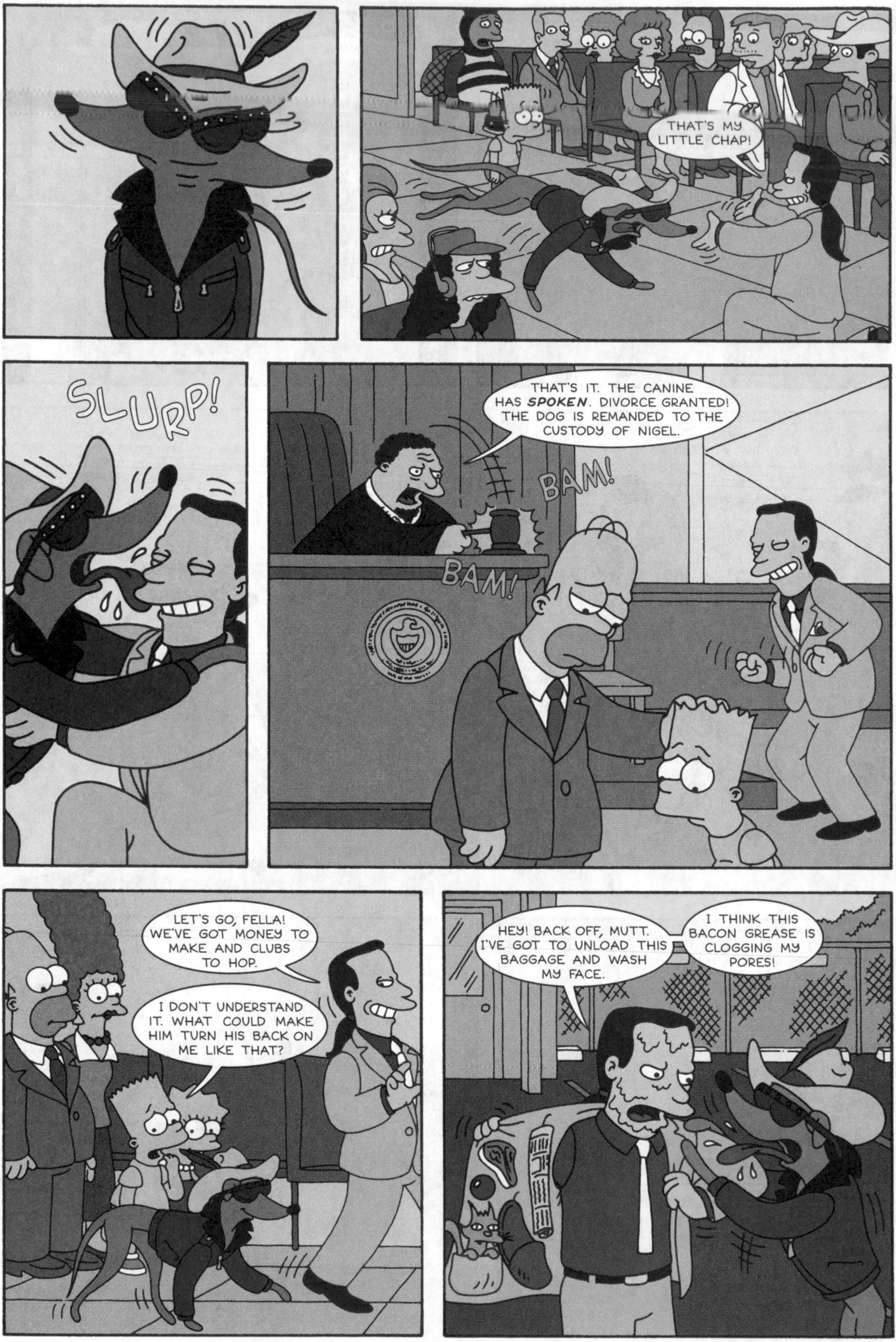
THAT'S MY LITTLE CHAP!
SLURP!
THAT'S IT. THE CANINE HAS SPOKEN. DIVORCE GRANTED! THE DOG IS REMANDED TO THE CUSTODY OF NIGEL.
BAM!
BAM!
LET'S GO, FELLA! WE'VE GOT MONEY TO MAKE AND CLUBS TO HOP.
I DON'T UNDERSTAND IT. WHAT COULD MAKE HIM TURN HIS BACK ON ME LIKE THAT?
HEY! BACK OFF, MUTT. I'VE GOT TO UNLOAD THIS BAGGAGE AND WASH MY FACE.
I THINK THIS BACON GREASE IS CLOGGING MY PORES!

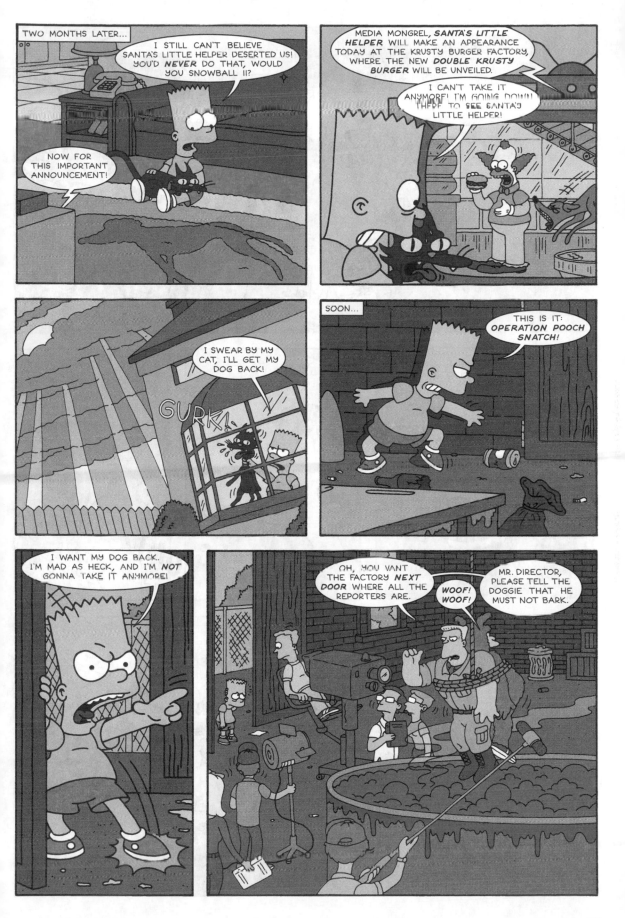

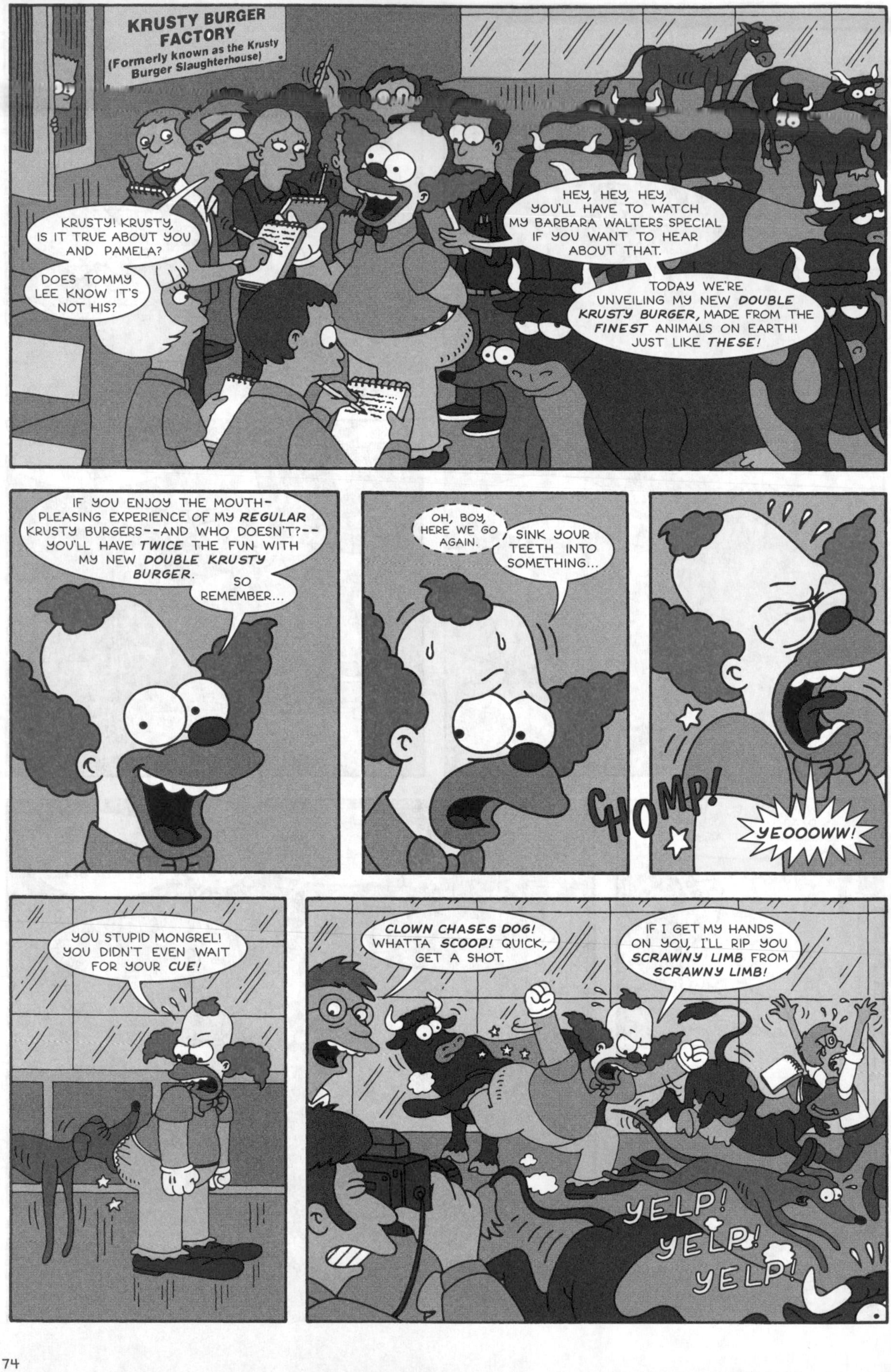
KRUSTY BURGER FACTORY
(Formerly known as the Krusty Burger Slaughterhouse)
KRUSTY! KRUSTY, IS IT TRUE ABOUT YOU AND PAMELA?
DOES TOMMY LEE KNOW IT'S NOT HIS?
HEY, HEY, HEY, YOU'LL HAVE TO WATCH MY BARBARA WALTERS SPECIAL IF YOU WANT TO HEAR ABOUT THAT.
TODAY WE'RE UNVEILING MY NEW DOUBLE KRUSTY BURGER, MADE FROM THE FINEST ANIMALS ON EARTH! JUST LIKE THESE!
IF YOU ENJOY THE MOUTH-PLEASING EXPERIENCE OF MY REGULAR KRUSTY BURGERS--AND WHO DOESN'T?--YOU'LL HAVE TWICE THE FUN WITH MY NEW DOUBLE KRUSTY BURGER.
SO REMEMBER...
OH, BOY, HERE WE GO AGAIN.
SINK YOUR TEETH INTO SOMETHING...
CHOMP!
YEOOOWW!
YOU STUPID MONGREL! YOU DIDN'T EVEN WAIT FOR YOUR CUE!
CLOWN CHASES DOG! WHATTA SCOOP! QUICK, GET A SHOT.
IF I GET MY HANDS ON YOU, I'LL RIP YOU SCRAWNY LIMB FROM SCRAWNY LIMB!
YELP!
YELP!
YELP!

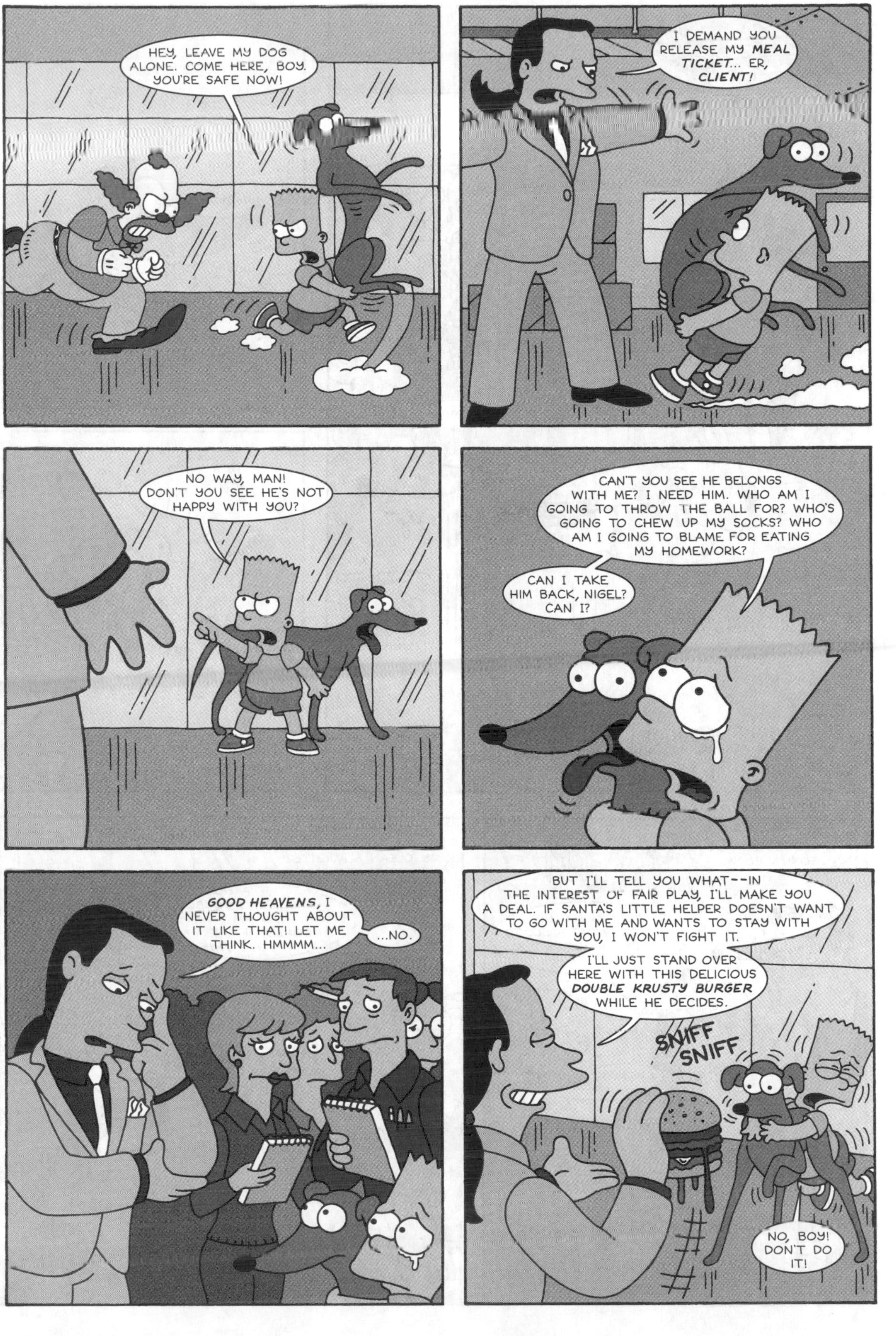
HEY, LEAVE MY DOG ALONE. COME HERE, BOY. YOU'RE SAFE NOW!
I DEMAND YOU RELEASE MY MEAL TICKET... ER, CLIENT!
NO WAY, MAN! DON'T YOU SEE HE'S NOT HAPPY WITH YOU?
CAN'T YOU SEE HE BELONGS WITH ME? I NEED HIM. WHO AM I GOING TO THROW THE BALL FOR? WHO'S GOING TO CHEW UP MY SOCKS? WHO AM I GOING TO BLAME FOR EATING MY HOMEWORK?
CAN I TAKE HIM BACK, NIGEL? CAN I?
GOOD HEAVENS, I NEVER THOUGHT ABOUT IT LIKE THAT! LET ME THINK. HMMMM...
...NO.
BUT I'LL TELL YOU WHAT--IN THE INTEREST OF FAIR PLAY, I'LL MAKE YOU A DEAL. IF SANTA'S LITTLE HELPER DOESN'T WANT TO GO WITH ME AND WANTS TO STAY WITH YOU, I WON'T FIGHT IT.
I'LL JUST STAND OVER HERE WITH THIS DELICIOUS DOUBLE KRUSTY BURGER WHILE HE DECIDES.
SNIFF SNIFF
NO, BOY! DON'T DO IT!

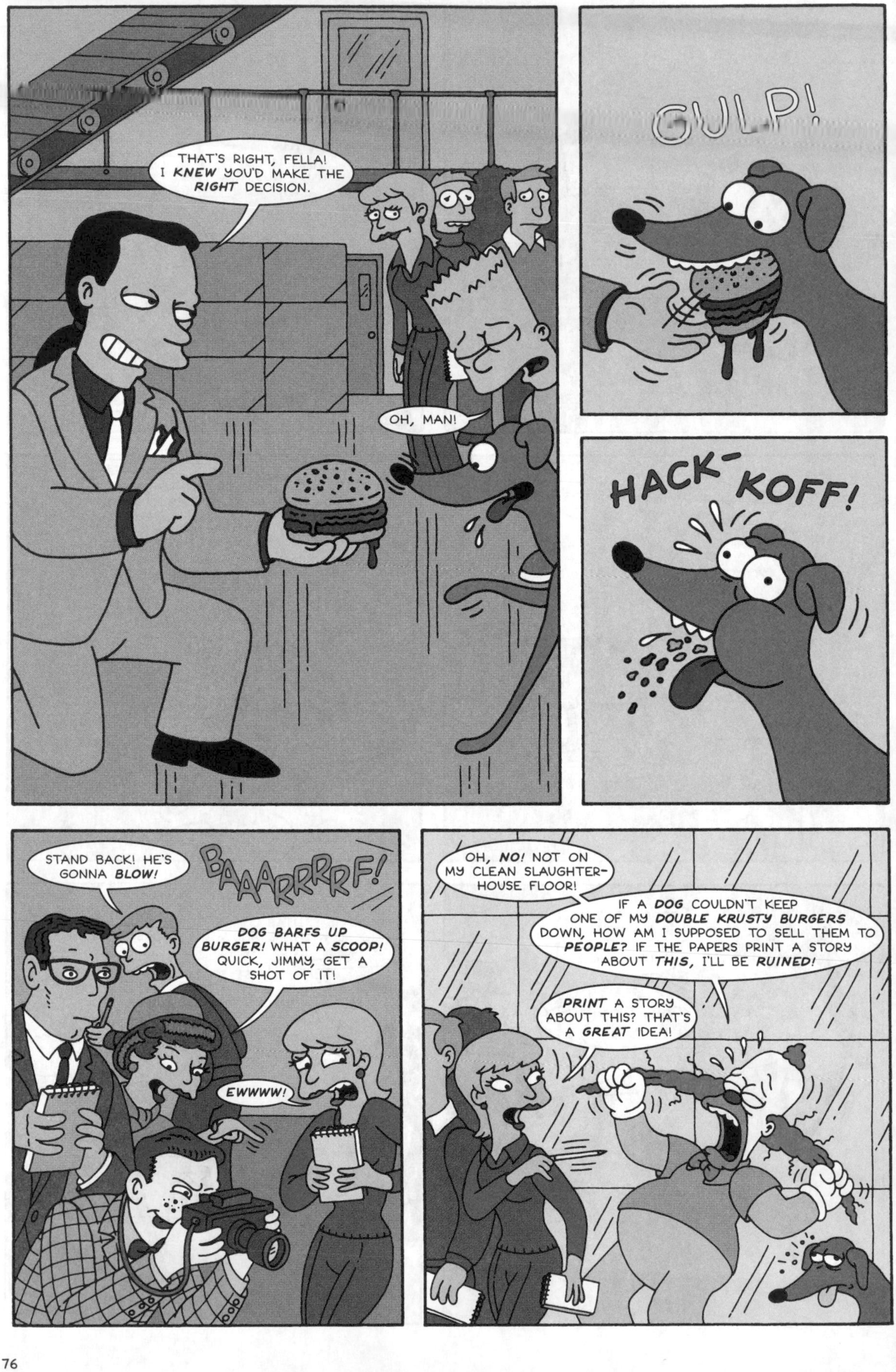
THAT'S RIGHT, FELLA! I KNEW YOU'D MAKE THE RIGHT DECISION.
OH, MAN!
GULP!
HACK-KOFF!
STAND BACK! HE'S GONNA BLOW!
BAAARRRRF!
DOG BARFS UP BURGER! WHAT A SCOOP! QUICK, JIMMY, GET A SHOT OF IT!
EWWWW!
OH, NO! NOT ON MY CLEAN SLAUGHTER-HOUSE FLOOR!
IF A DOG COULDN'T KEEP ONE OF MY DOUBLE KRUSTY BURGERS DOWN, HOW AM I SUPPOSED TO SELL THEM TO PEOPLE? IF THE PAPERS PRINT A STORY ABOUT THIS, I'LL BE RUINED!
PRINT A STORY ABOUT THIS? THAT'S A GREAT IDEA!

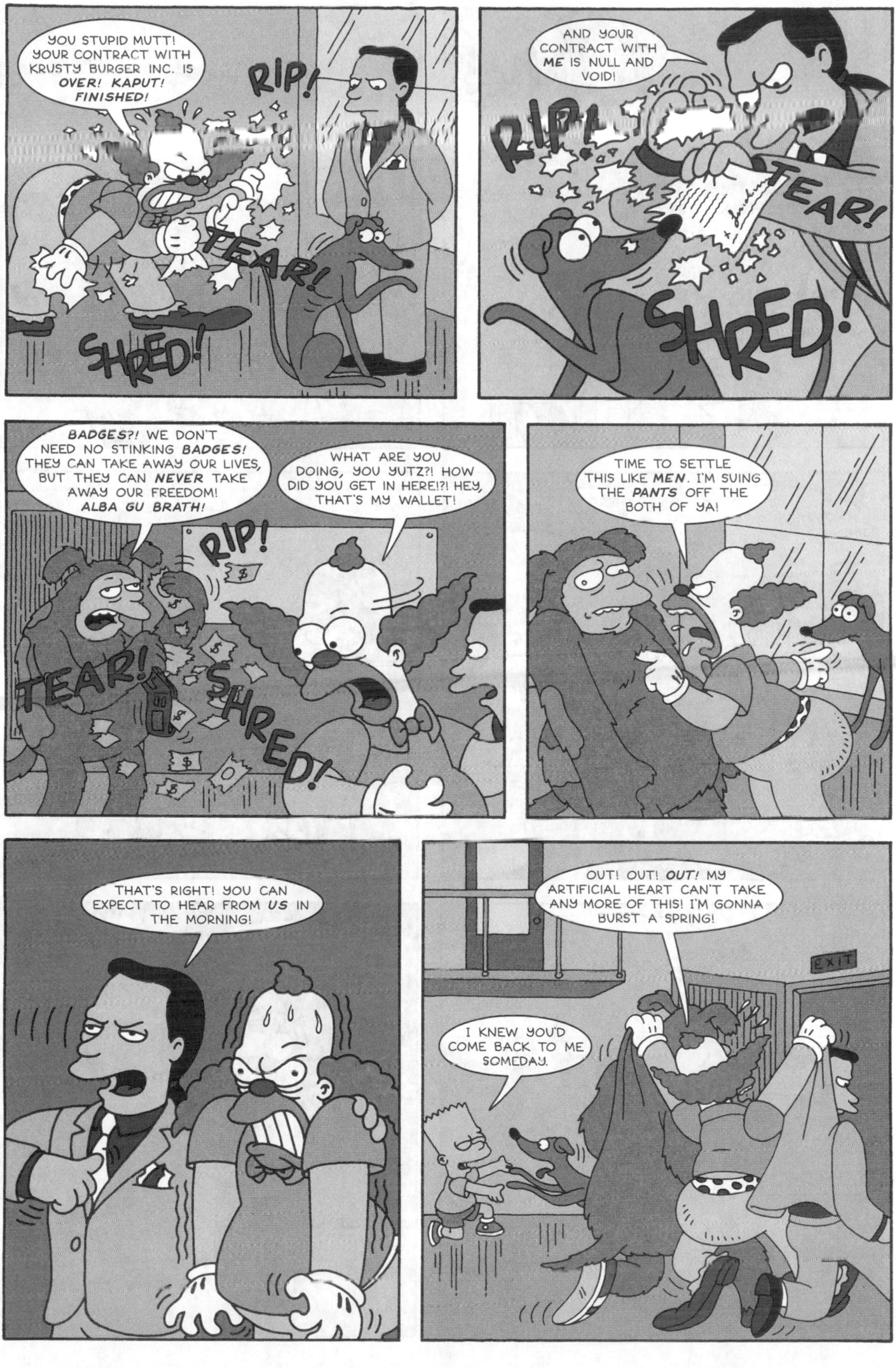
YOU STUPID MUTT! YOUR CONTRACT WITH KRUSTY BURGER INC. IS OVER! KAPUT! FINISHED!
RIP!
TEAR!
SHRED!
AND YOUR CONTRACT WITH ME IS NULL AND VOID!
RIP!
TEAR!
SHRED!
BADGES?! WE DON'T NEED NO STINKING BADGES! THEY CAN TAKE AWAY OUR LIVES, BUT THEY CAN NEVER TAKE AWAY OUR FREEDOM! ALBA GU BRATH!
WHAT ARE YOU DOING, YOU YUTZ?! HOW DID YOU GET IN HERE!?! HEY, THAT'S MY WALLET!
RIP!
TEAR!
SHRED!
TIME TO SETTLE THIS LIKE MEN. I'M SUING THE PANTS OFF THE BOTH OF YA!
THAT'S RIGHT! YOU CAN EXPECT TO HEAR FROM US IN THE MORNING!
OUT! OUT! OUT! MY ARTIFICIAL HEART CAN'T TAKE ANY MORE OF THIS! I'M GONNA BURST A SPRING!
EXIT
I KNEW YOU'D COME BACK TO ME SOMEDAY.

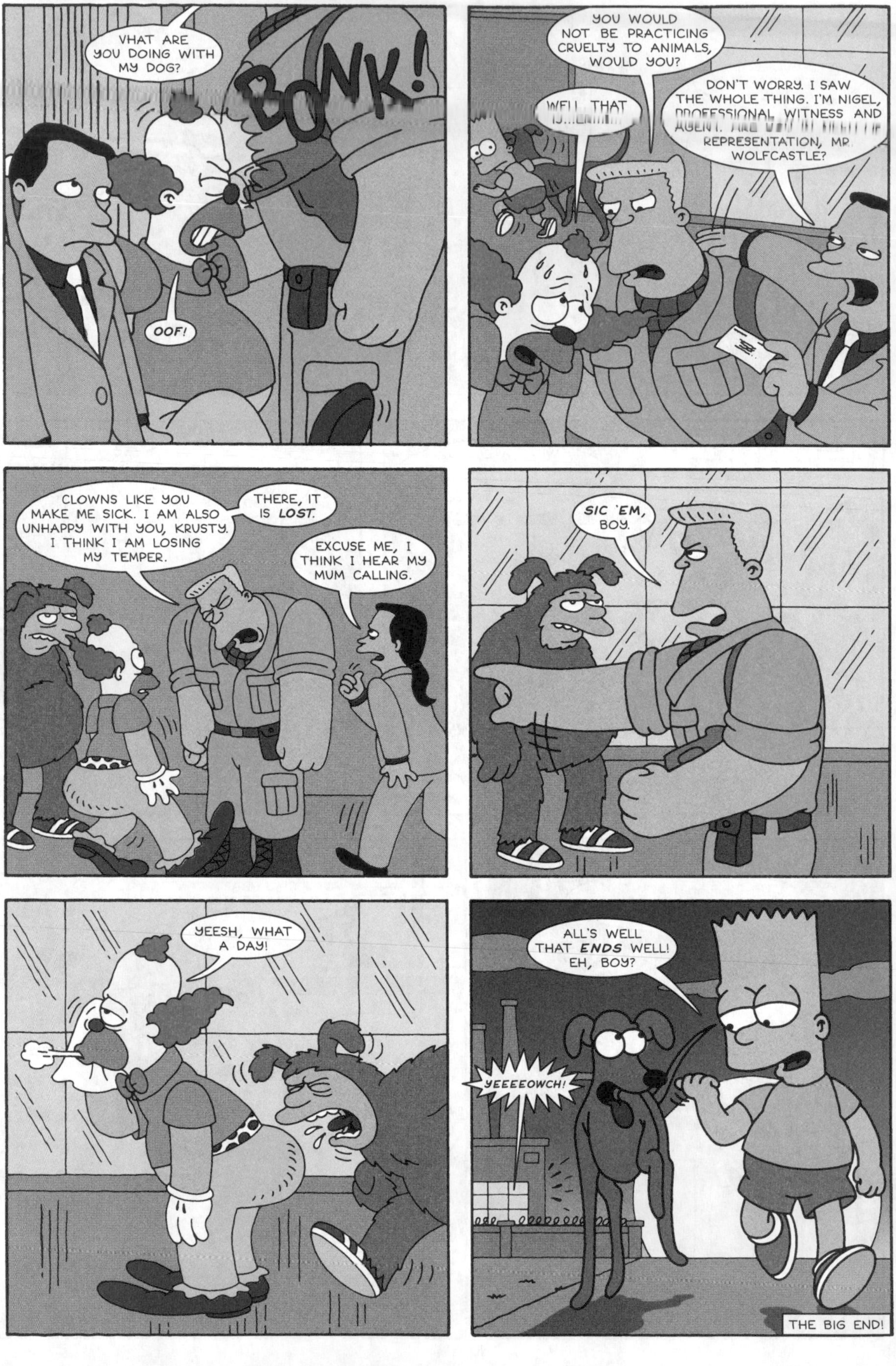
VHAT ARE YOU DOING WITH MY DOG?
BONK!
OOF!
YOU WOULD NOT BE PRACTICING CRUELTY TO ANIMALS, WOULD YOU?
WELL, THAT
DON'T WORRY. I SAW THE WHOLE THING. I'M NIGEL, PROFESSIONAL WITNESS AND AGENT.
REPRESENTATION, MR. WOLFCASTLE?
CLOWNS LIKE YOU MAKE ME SICK. I AM ALSO UNHAPPY WITH YOU, KRUSTY. I THINK I AM LOSING MY TEMPER.
THERE, IT IS LOST.
EXCUSE ME, I THINK I HEAR MY MUM CALLING.
SIC 'EM, BOY.
YEESH, WHAT A DAY!
ALL'S WELL THAT ENDS WELL! EH, BOY?
YEEEEOWCH!
THE BIG END!

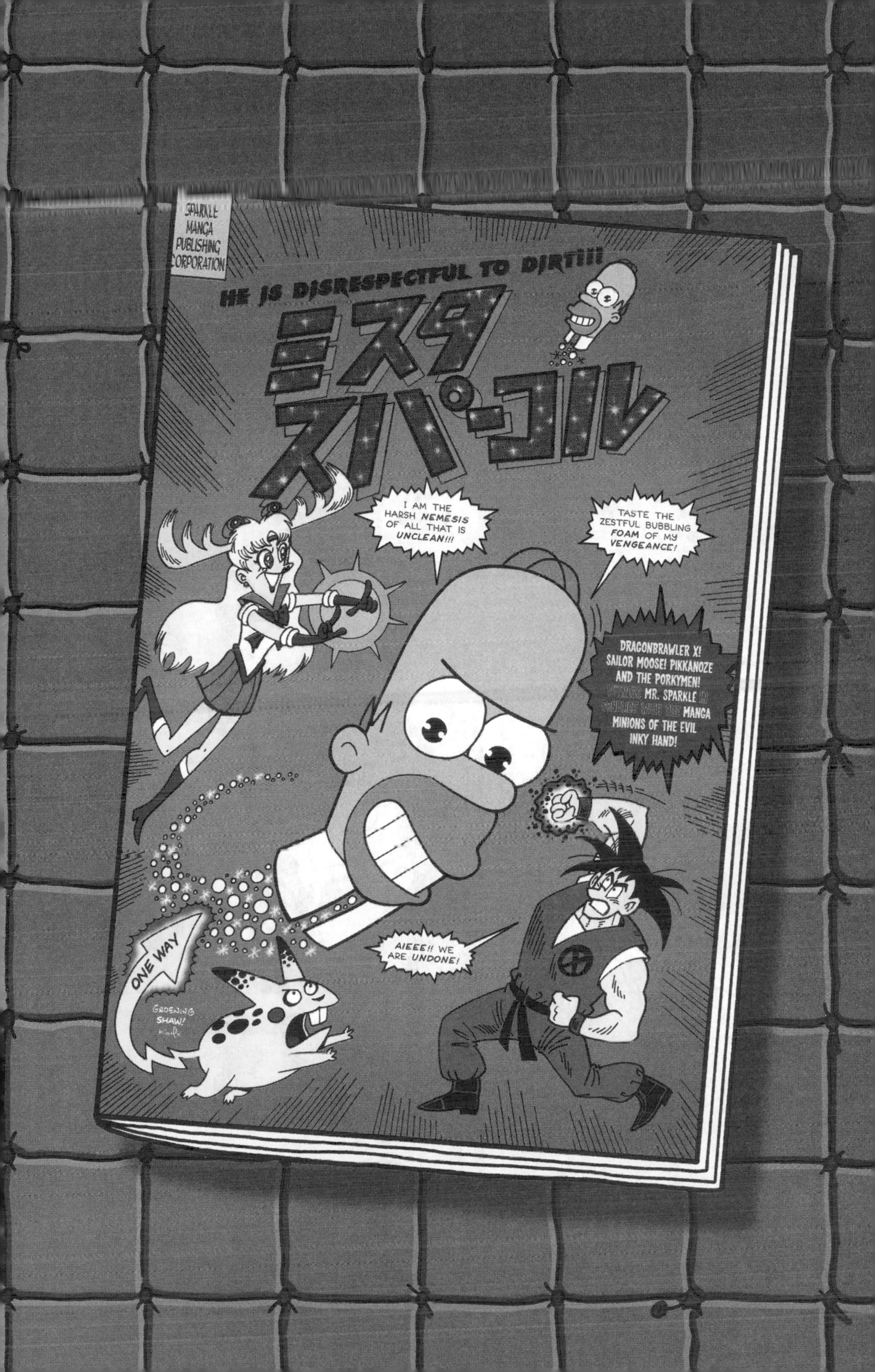
SPARKLE MANGA PUBLISHING CORPORATION
HE IS DISRESPECTFUL TO DIRT!!!
ミスタ スパーコル
I AM THE HARSH NEMESIS OF ALL THAT IS UNCLEAN!!!
TASTE THE ZESTFUL BUBBLING FOAM OF MY VENGEANCE!
DRAGONBRAWLER X! SAILOR MOOSE! PIKKANOZE AND THE PORKYMEN!
MR. SPARKLE
MANGA MINIONS OF THE EVIL INKY HAND!
AIEEE!! WE ARE UNDONE!
ONE WAY
GROENING SHAW!

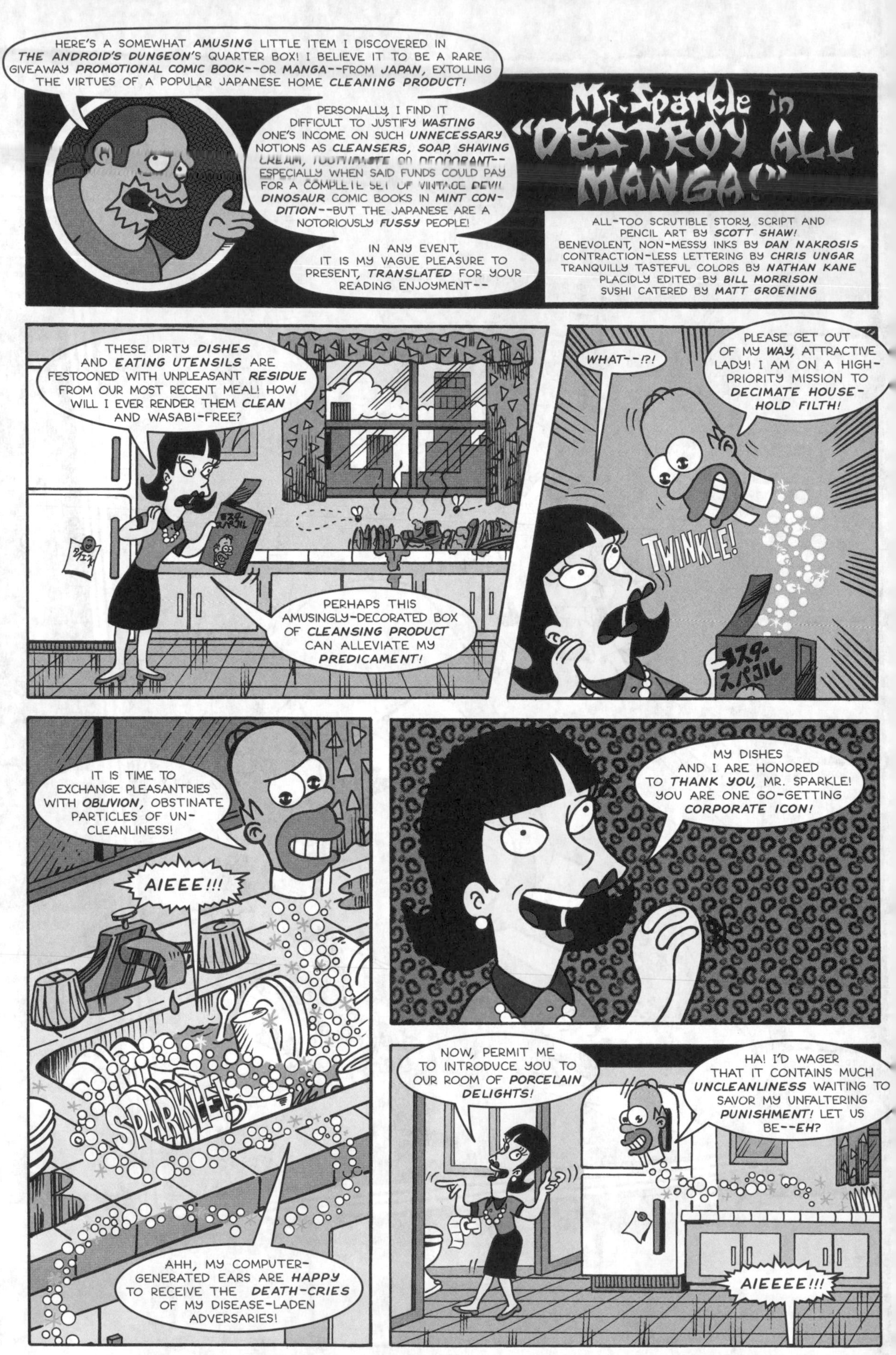
HERE'S A SOMEWHAT AMUSING LITTLE ITEM I DISCOVERED IN THE ANDROID'S DUNGEON'S QUARTER BOX! I BELIEVE IT TO BE A RARE GIVEAWAY PROMOTIONAL COMIC BOOK--OR MANGA--FROM JAPAN, EXTOLLING THE VIRTUES OF A POPULAR JAPANESE HOME CLEANING PRODUCT!
PERSONALLY, I FIND IT DIFFICULT TO JUSTIFY WASTING ONE'S INCOME ON SUCH UNNECESSARY NOTIONS AS CLEANSERS, SOAP, SHAVING CREAM, TOOTHPASTE OR DEODORANT--ESPECIALLY WHEN SAID FUNDS COULD PAY FOR A COMPLETE SET OF VINTAGE DEVIL DINOSAUR COMIC BOOKS IN MINT CONDITION--BUT THE JAPANESE ARE A NOTORIOUSLY FUSSY PEOPLE!
IN ANY EVENT, IT IS MY VAGUE PLEASURE TO PRESENT, TRANSLATED FOR YOUR READING ENJOYMENT--
Mr. Sparkle in "DESTROY ALL MANGA!"
ALL-TOO SCRUTIBLE STORY, SCRIPT AND PENCIL ART BY SCOTT SHAW!
BENEVOLENT, NON-MESSY INKS BY DAN NAKROSIS
CONTRACTION-LESS LETTERING BY CHRIS UNGAR
TRANQUILLY TASTEFUL COLORS BY NATHAN KANE
PLACIDLY EDITED BY BILL MORRISON
SUSHI CATERED BY MATT GROENING
THESE DIRTY DISHES AND EATING UTENSILS ARE FESTOONED WITH UNPLEASANT RESIDUE FROM OUR MOST RECENT MEAL! HOW WILL I EVER RENDER THEM CLEAN AND WASABI-FREE?
PERHAPS THIS AMUSINGLY-DECORATED BOX OF CLEANSING PRODUCT CAN ALLEVIATE MY PREDICAMENT!
WHAT--!?!
PLEASE GET OUT OF MY WAY, ATTRACTIVE LADY! I AM ON A HIGH-PRIORITY MISSION TO DECIMATE HOUSEHOLD FILTH!
TWINKLE!
IT IS TIME TO EXCHANGE PLEASANTRIES WITH OBLIVION, OBSTINATE PARTICLES OF UNCLEANLINESS!
AIEEE!!!
SPARKLE!
AHH, MY COMPUTER-GENERATED EARS ARE HAPPY TO RECEIVE THE DEATH-CRIES OF MY DISEASE-LADEN ADVERSARIES!
MY DISHES AND I ARE HONORED TO THANK YOU, MR. SPARKLE! YOU ARE ONE GO-GETTING CORPORATE ICON!
NOW, PERMIT ME TO INTRODUCE YOU TO OUR ROOM OF PORCELAIN DELIGHTS!
HA! I'D WAGER THAT IT CONTAINS MUCH UNCLEANLINESS WAITING TO SAVOR MY UNFALTERING PUNISHMENT! LET US BE--EH?
AIEEEE!!!

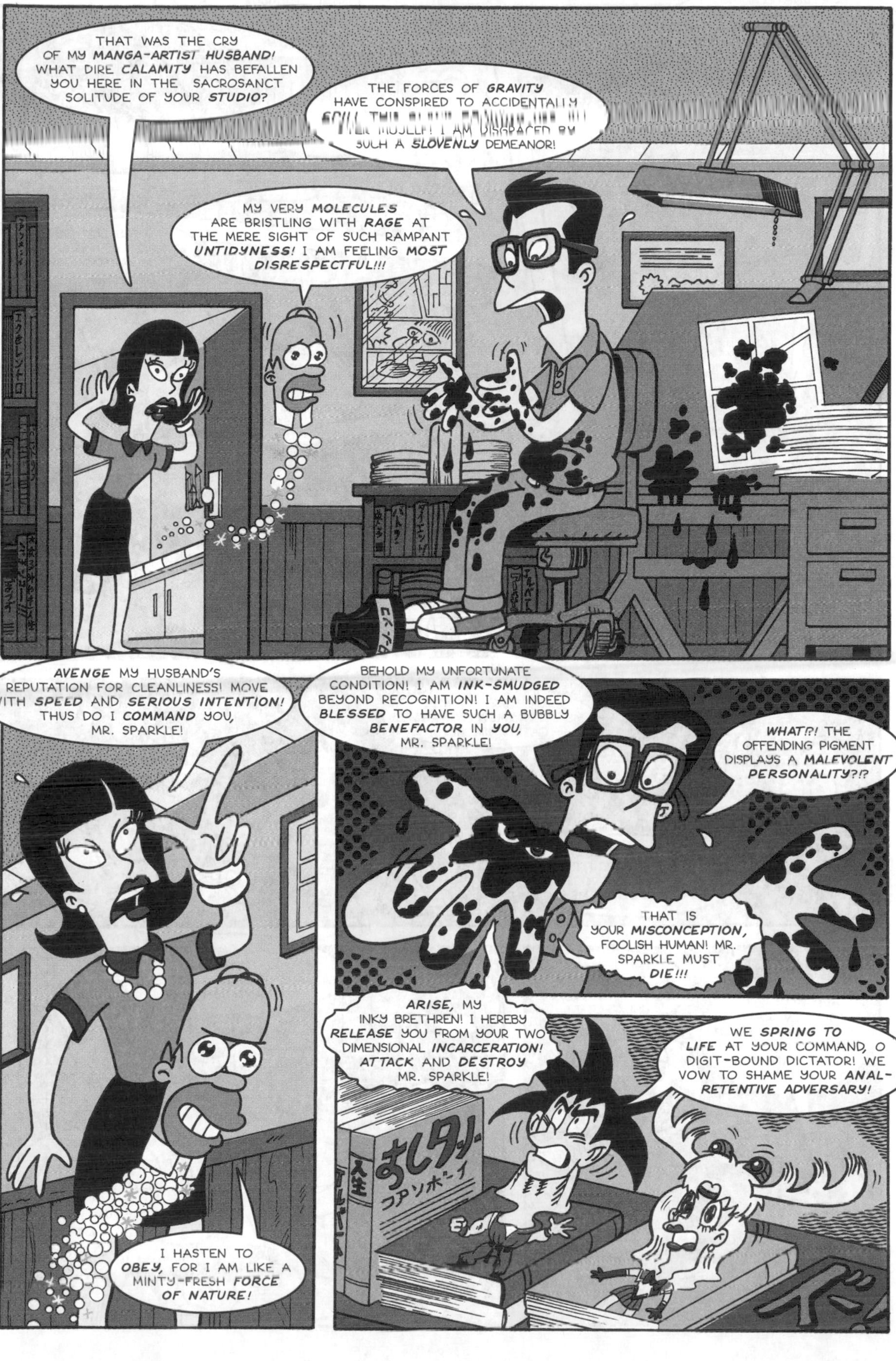

THAT WAS THE CRY OF MY **MANGA-ARTIST HUSBAND!** WHAT DIRE **CALAMITY** HAS BEFALLEN YOU HERE IN THE SACROSANCT SOLITUDE OF YOUR **STUDIO?**
THE FORCES OF **GRAVITY** HAVE CONSPIRED TO ACCIDENTALLY
I AM DISGRACED BY SUCH A **SLOVENLY** DEMEANOR!
MY VERY **MOLECULES** ARE BRISTLING WITH **RAGE** AT THE MERE SIGHT OF SUCH RAMPANT **UNTIDYNESS!** I AM FEELING **MOST DISRESPECTFUL!!!**
AVENGE MY HUSBAND'S REPUTATION FOR CLEANLINESS! MOVE WITH **SPEED** AND **SERIOUS INTENTION!** THUS DO I **COMMAND** YOU, MR. SPARKLE!
I HASTEN TO **OBEY,** FOR I AM LIKE A MINTY-FRESH **FORCE OF NATURE!**
BEHOLD MY UNFORTUNATE CONDITION! I AM **INK-SMUDGED** BEYOND RECOGNITION! I AM INDEED **BLESSED** TO HAVE SUCH A BUBBLY **BENEFACTOR** IN **YOU,** MR. SPARKLE!
WHAT?! THE OFFENDING PIGMENT DISPLAYS A **MALEVOLENT PERSONALITY?!?**
THAT IS YOUR **MISCONCEPTION,** FOOLISH HUMAN! MR. SPARKLE MUST **DIE!!!**
ARISE, MY INKY BRETHREN! I HEREBY **RELEASE** YOU FROM YOUR TWO DIMENSIONAL **INCARCERATION! ATTACK** AND **DESTROY** MR. SPARKLE!
WE **SPRING TO LIFE** AT YOUR COMMAND, O DIGIT-BOUND DICTATOR! WE VOW TO SHAME YOUR **ANAL-RETENTIVE ADVERSARY!**

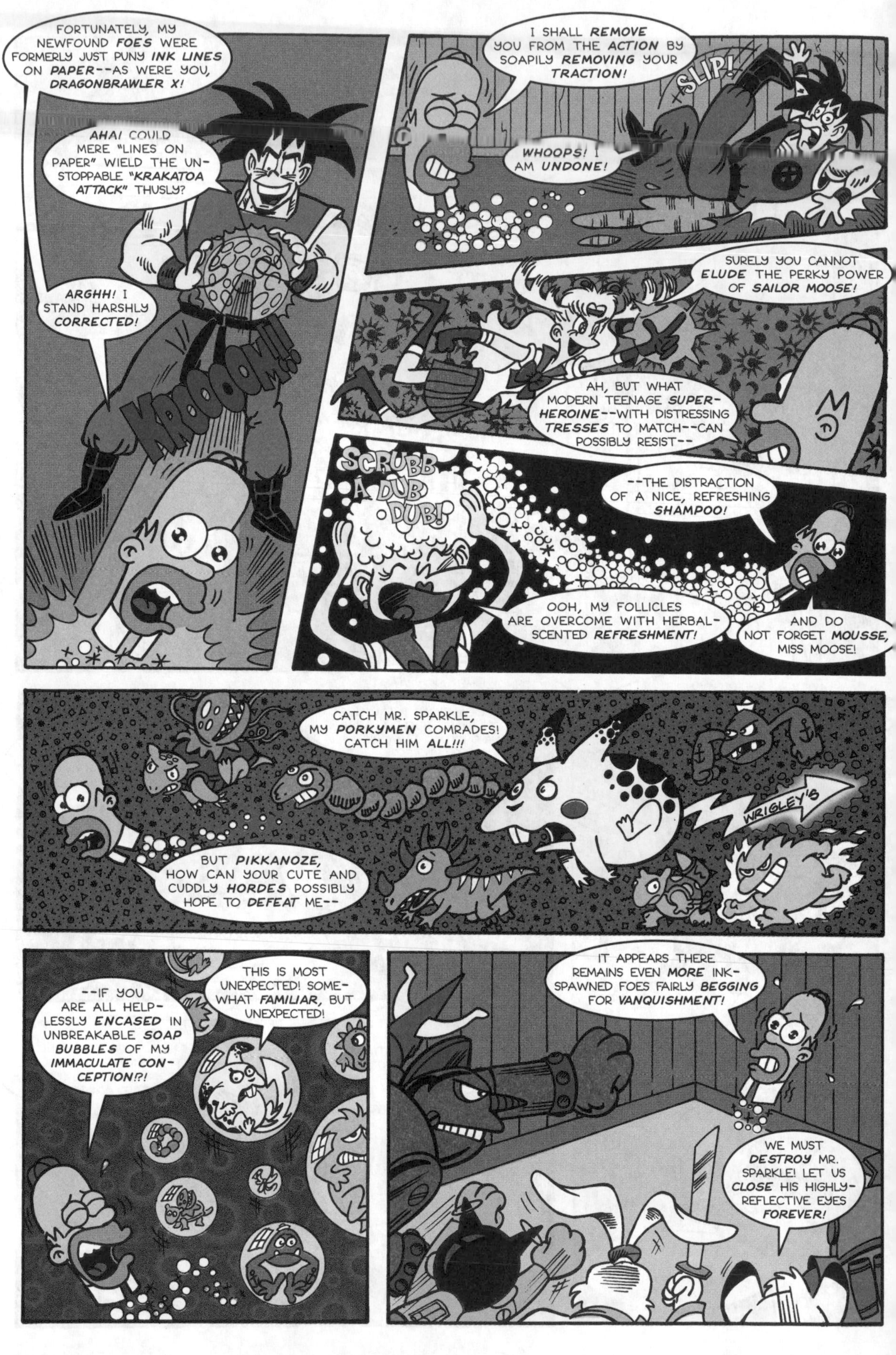
FORTUNATELY, MY NEWFOUND FOES WERE FORMERLY JUST PUNY INK LINES ON PAPER--AS WERE YOU, DRAGONBRAWLER X!
AHA! COULD MERE "LINES ON PAPER" WIELD THE UNSTOPPABLE "KRAKATOA ATTACK" THUSLY?
KROOOOM!!!
ARGHH! I STAND HARSHLY CORRECTED!
I SHALL REMOVE YOU FROM THE ACTION BY SOAPILY REMOVING YOUR TRACTION!
SLIP!
WHOOPS! I AM UNDONE!
SURELY YOU CANNOT ELUDE THE PERKY POWER OF SAILOR MOOSE!
AH, BUT WHAT MODERN TEENAGE SUPER-HEROINE--WITH DISTRESSING TRESSES TO MATCH--CAN POSSIBLY RESIST--
SCRUBB A DUB DUB!
--THE DISTRACTION OF A NICE, REFRESHING SHAMPOO!
OOH, MY FOLLICLES ARE OVERCOME WITH HERBAL-SCENTED REFRESHMENT!
AND DO NOT FORGET MOUSSE, MISS MOOSE!
CATCH MR. SPARKLE, MY PORKYMEN COMRADES! CATCH HIM ALL!!!
WRIGLEY'S
BUT PIKKANOZE, HOW CAN YOUR CUTE AND CUDDLY HORDES POSSIBLY HOPE TO DEFEAT ME--
--IF YOU ARE ALL HELPLESSLY ENCASED IN UNBREAKABLE SOAP BUBBLES OF MY IMMACULATE CONCEPTION!?!
THIS IS MOST UNEXPECTED! SOMEWHAT FAMILIAR, BUT UNEXPECTED!
IT APPEARS THERE REMAINS EVEN MORE INK-SPAWNED FOES FAIRLY BEGGING FOR VANQUISHMENT!
WE MUST DESTROY MR. SPARKLE! LET US CLOSE HIS HIGHLY-REFLECTIVE EYES FOREVER!

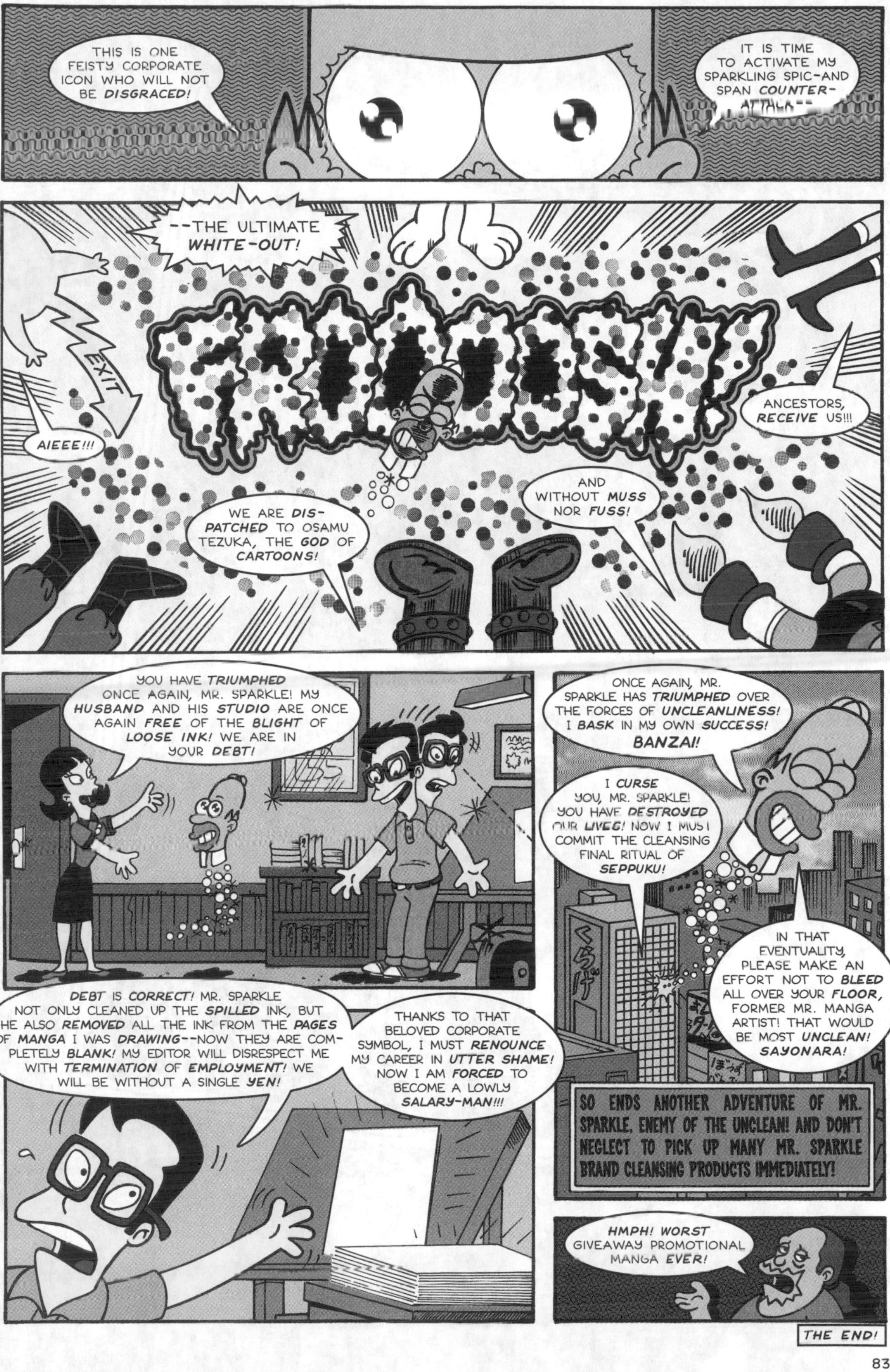

THIS IS ONE FEISTY CORPORATE ICON WHO WILL NOT BE DISGRACED!
IT IS TIME TO ACTIVATE MY SPARKLING SPIC-AND SPAN COUNTER-
--THE ULTIMATE WHITE-OUT!
EXIT
AIEEE!!!
ANCESTORS, RECEIVE US!!!
WE ARE DISPATCHED TO OSAMU TEZUKA, THE GOD OF CARTOONS!
AND WITHOUT MUSS NOR FUSS!
YOU HAVE TRIUMPHED ONCE AGAIN, MR. SPARKLE! MY HUSBAND AND HIS STUDIO ARE ONCE AGAIN FREE OF THE BLIGHT OF LOOSE INK! WE ARE IN YOUR DEBT!
ONCE AGAIN, MR. SPARKLE HAS TRIUMPHED OVER THE FORCES OF UNCLEANLINESS! I BASK IN MY OWN SUCCESS! BANZAI!
I CURSE YOU, MR. SPARKLE! YOU HAVE DESTROYED OUR LIVES! NOW I MUST COMMIT THE CLEANSING FINAL RITUAL OF SEPPUKU!
IN THAT EVENTUALITY, PLEASE MAKE AN EFFORT NOT TO BLEED ALL OVER YOUR FLOOR, FORMER MR. MANGA ARTIST! THAT WOULD BE MOST UNCLEAN! SAYONARA!
DEBT IS CORRECT! MR. SPARKLE NOT ONLY CLEANED UP THE SPILLED INK, BUT HE ALSO REMOVED ALL THE INK FROM THE PAGES OF MANGA I WAS DRAWING--NOW THEY ARE COMPLETELY BLANK! MY EDITOR WILL DISRESPECT ME WITH TERMINATION OF EMPLOYMENT! WE WILL BE WITHOUT A SINGLE YEN!
THANKS TO THAT BELOVED CORPORATE SYMBOL, I MUST RENOUNCE MY CAREER IN UTTER SHAME! NOW I AM FORCED TO BECOME A LOWLY SALARY-MAN!!!
SO ENDS ANOTHER ADVENTURE OF MR. SPARKLE, ENEMY OF THE UNCLEAN! AND DON'T NEGLECT TO PICK UP MANY MR. SPARKLE BRAND CLEANSING PRODUCTS IMMEDIATELY!
HMPH! WORST GIVEAWAY PROMOTIONAL MANGA EVER!
THE END!

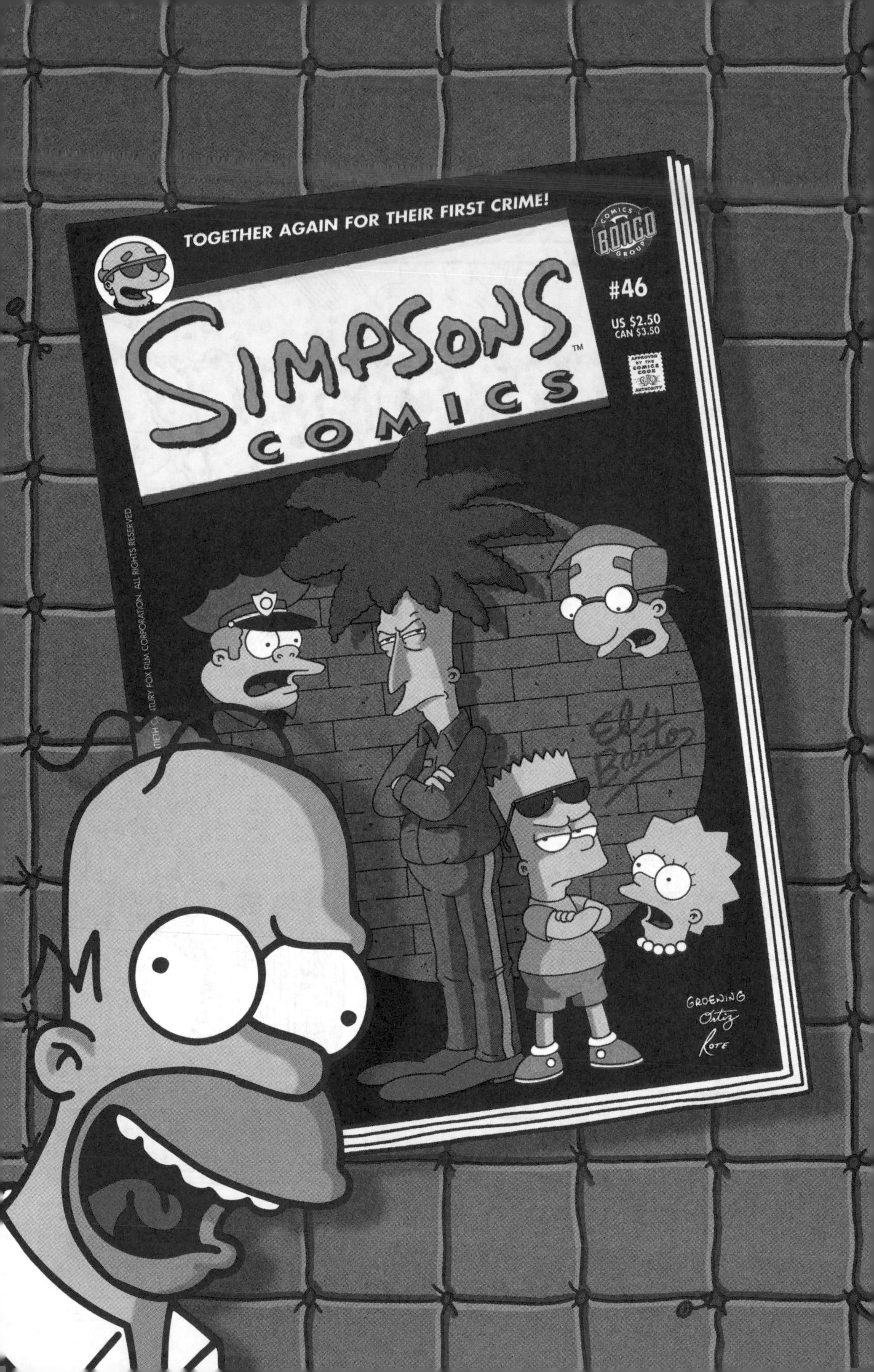

TOGETHER AGAIN FOR THEIR FIRST CRIME!
BONGO COMICS GROUP
SIMPSONS COMICS
#46
US $2.50
CAN $3.50
El Barto
GROENING
Ortiz
Rote

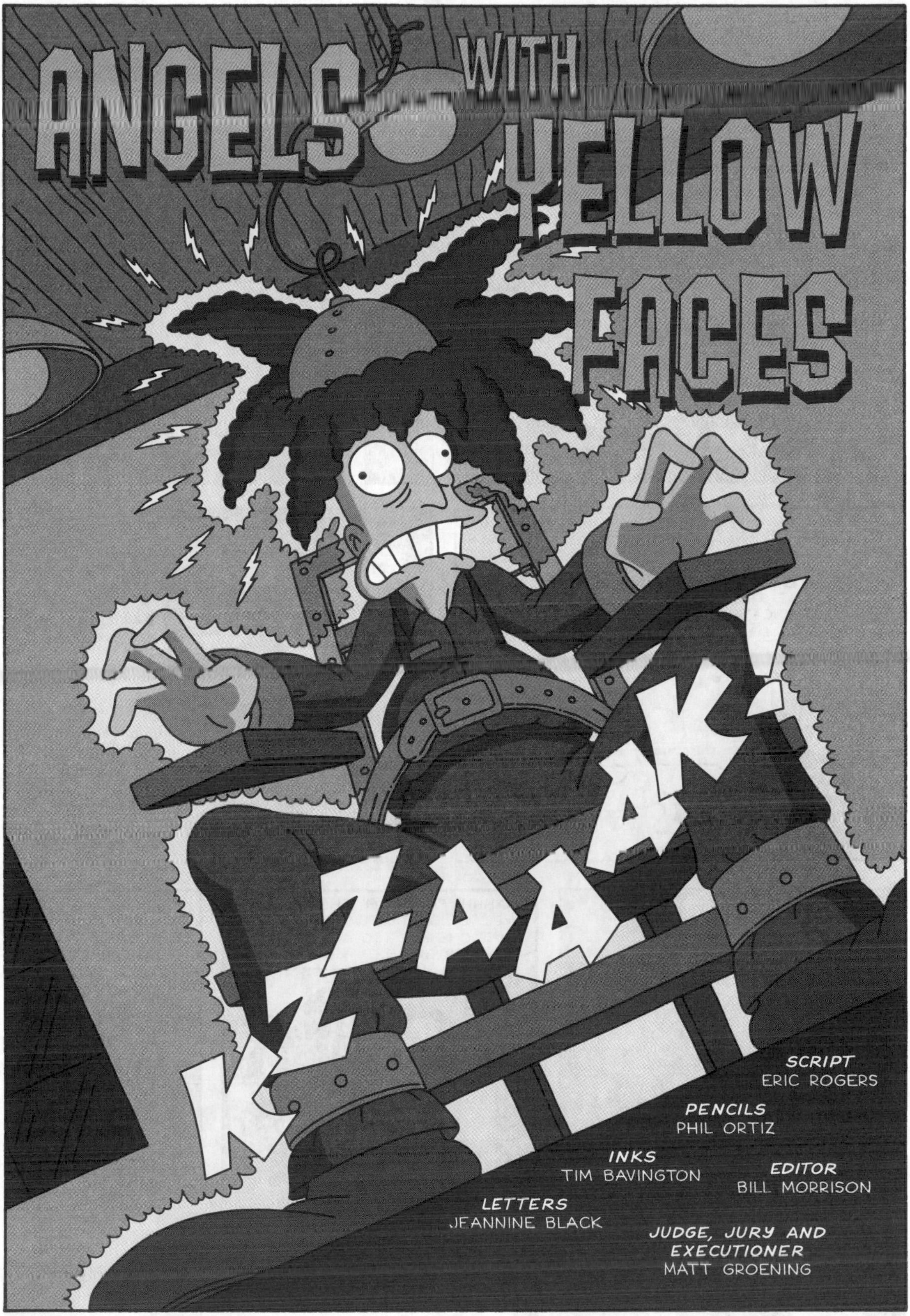
ANGELS WITH YELLOW FACES
KZZAAAK!
SCRIPT
ERIC ROGERS
PENCILS
PHIL ORTIZ
INKS
TIM BAVINGTON
EDITOR
BILL MORRISON
LETTERS
JEANNINE BLACK
JUDGE, JURY AND EXECUTIONER
MATT GROENING

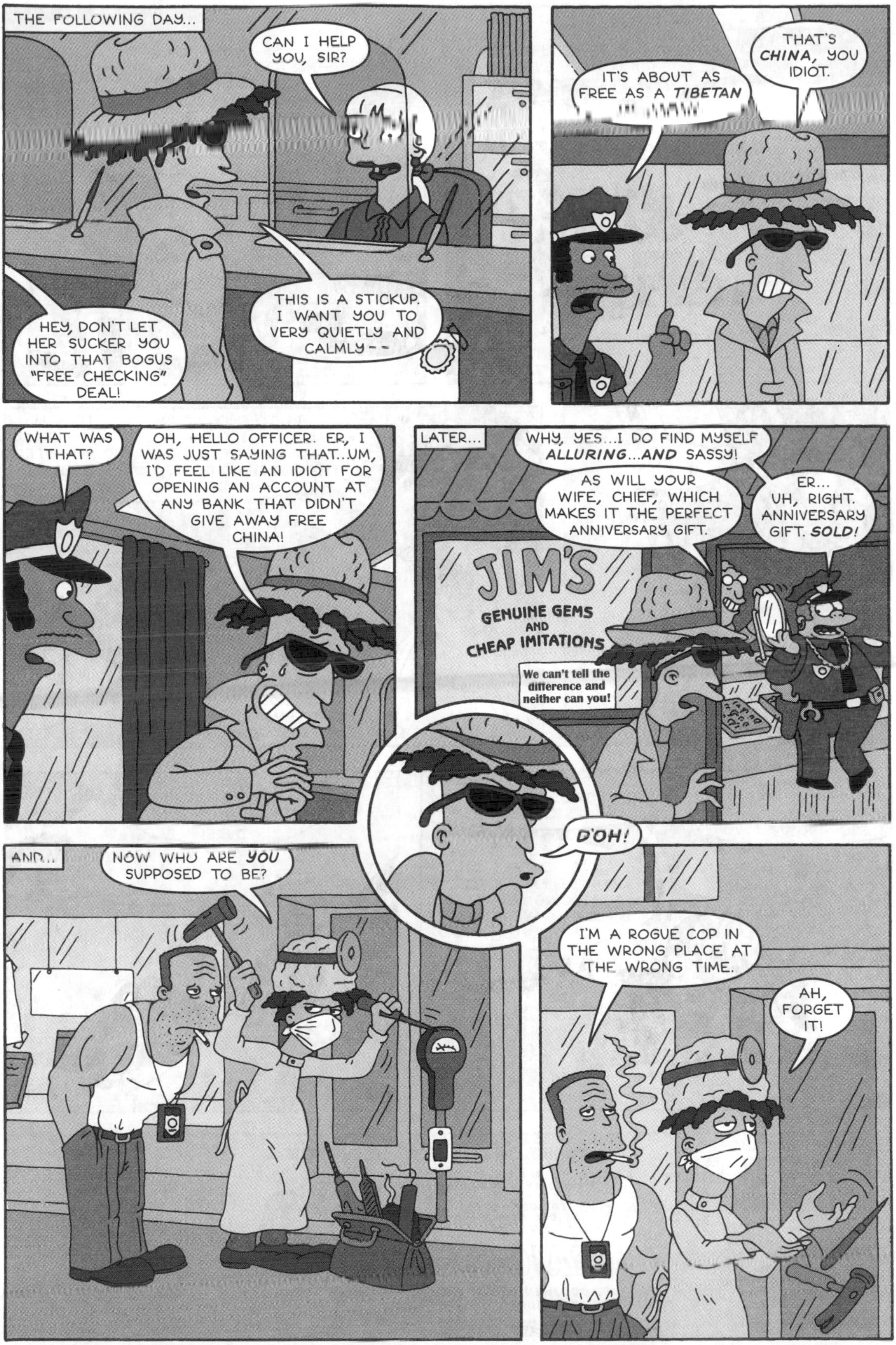
THE FOLLOWING DAY...
CAN I HELP YOU, SIR?
THIS IS A STICKUP. I WANT YOU TO VERY QUIETLY AND CALMLY--
HEY, DON'T LET HER SUCKER YOU INTO THAT BOGUS "FREE CHECKING" DEAL!
IT'S ABOUT AS FREE AS A TIBETAN
THAT'S CHINA, YOU IDIOT.
WHAT WAS THAT?
OH, HELLO OFFICER. ER, I WAS JUST SAYING THAT...UM, I'D FEEL LIKE AN IDIOT FOR OPENING AN ACCOUNT AT ANY BANK THAT DIDN'T GIVE AWAY FREE CHINA!
LATER...
WHY, YES...I DO FIND MYSELF ALLURING...AND SASSY!
AS WILL YOUR WIFE, CHIEF, WHICH MAKES IT THE PERFECT ANNIVERSARY GIFT.
ER... UH, RIGHT. ANNIVERSARY GIFT. SOLD!
JIM'S
GENUINE GEMS AND CHEAP IMITATIONS
We can't tell the difference and neither can you!
D'OH!
AND...
NOW WHO ARE YOU SUPPOSED TO BE?
I'M A ROGUE COP IN THE WRONG PLACE AT THE WRONG TIME.
AH, FORGET IT!

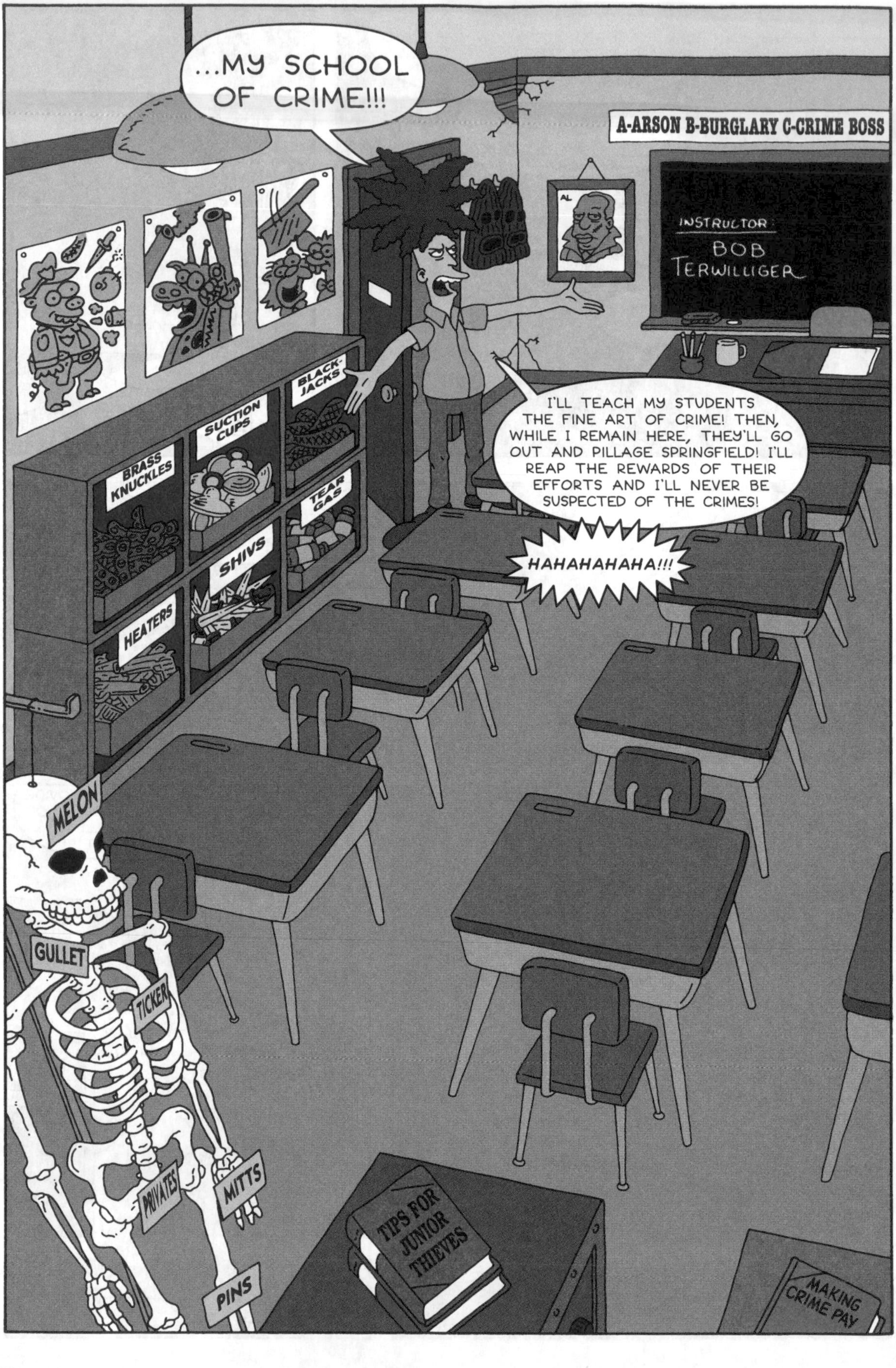
...MY SCHOOL OF CRIME!!!
A-ARSON B-BURGLARY C-CRIME BOSS
AL
INSTRUCTOR:
BOB TERWILLIGER
BLACK-JACKS
SUCTION CUPS
BRASS KNUCKLES
TEAR GAS
SHIVS
HEATERS
I'LL TEACH MY STUDENTS THE FINE ART OF CRIME! THEN, WHILE I REMAIN HERE, THEY'LL GO OUT AND PILLAGE SPRINGFIELD! I'LL REAP THE REWARDS OF THEIR EFFORTS AND I'LL NEVER BE SUSPECTED OF THE CRIMES!
HAHAHAHAHA!!!
MELON
GULLET
TICKER
PRIVATES
MITTS
PINS
TIPS FOR JUNIOR THIEVES
MAKING CRIME PAY

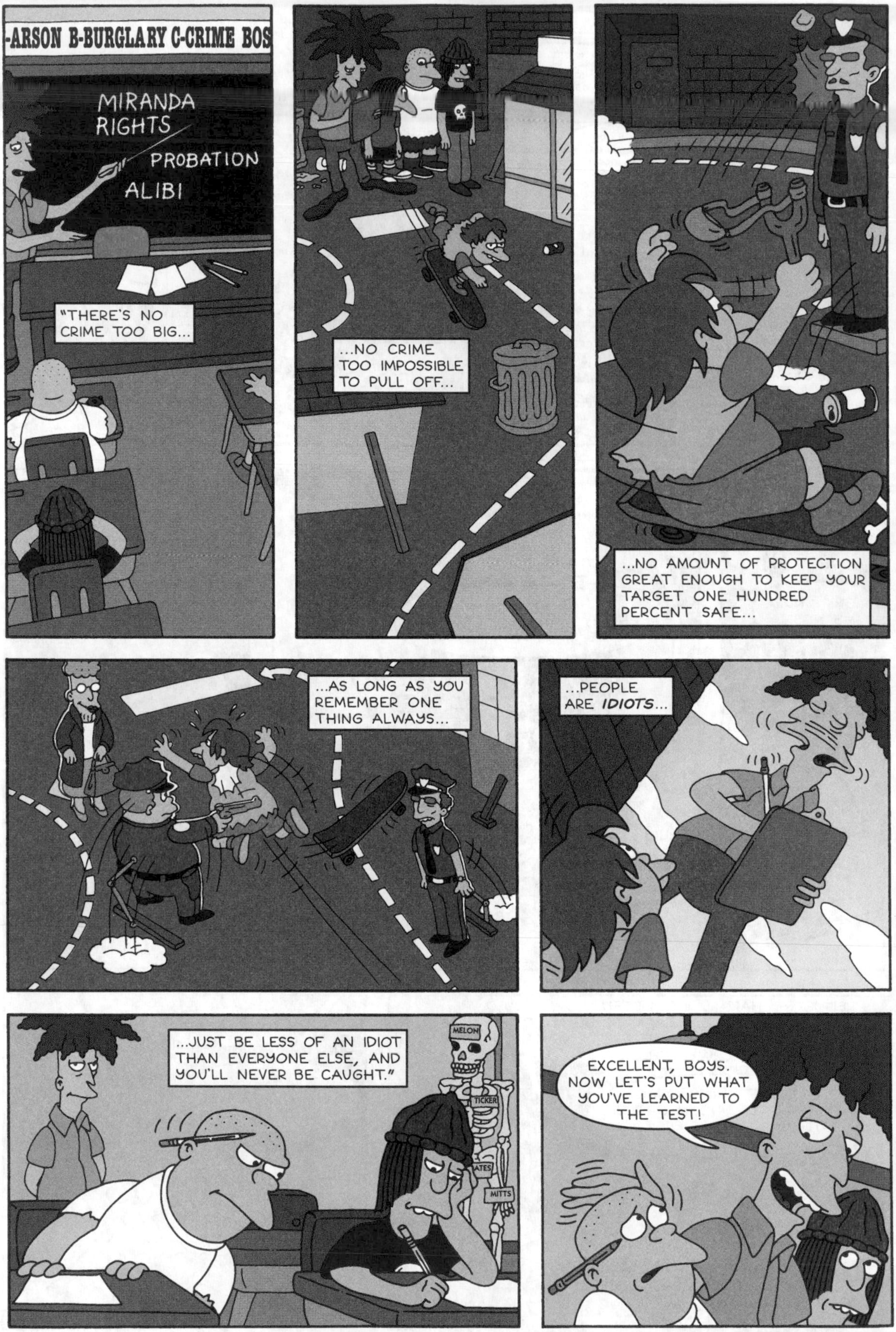
-ARSON B-BURGLARY C-CRIME BOS
MIRANDA RIGHTS
PROBATION
ALIBI
"THERE'S NO CRIME TOO BIG...
...NO CRIME TOO IMPOSSIBLE TO PULL OFF...
...NO AMOUNT OF PROTECTION GREAT ENOUGH TO KEEP YOUR TARGET ONE HUNDRED PERCENT SAFE...
...AS LONG AS YOU REMEMBER ONE THING ALWAYS...
...PEOPLE ARE *IDIOTS*...
...JUST BE LESS OF AN IDIOT THAN EVERYONE ELSE, AND YOU'LL NEVER BE CAUGHT."
MELON
TICKER
MITTS
EXCELLENT, BOYS. NOW LET'S PUT WHAT YOU'VE LEARNED TO THE TEST!

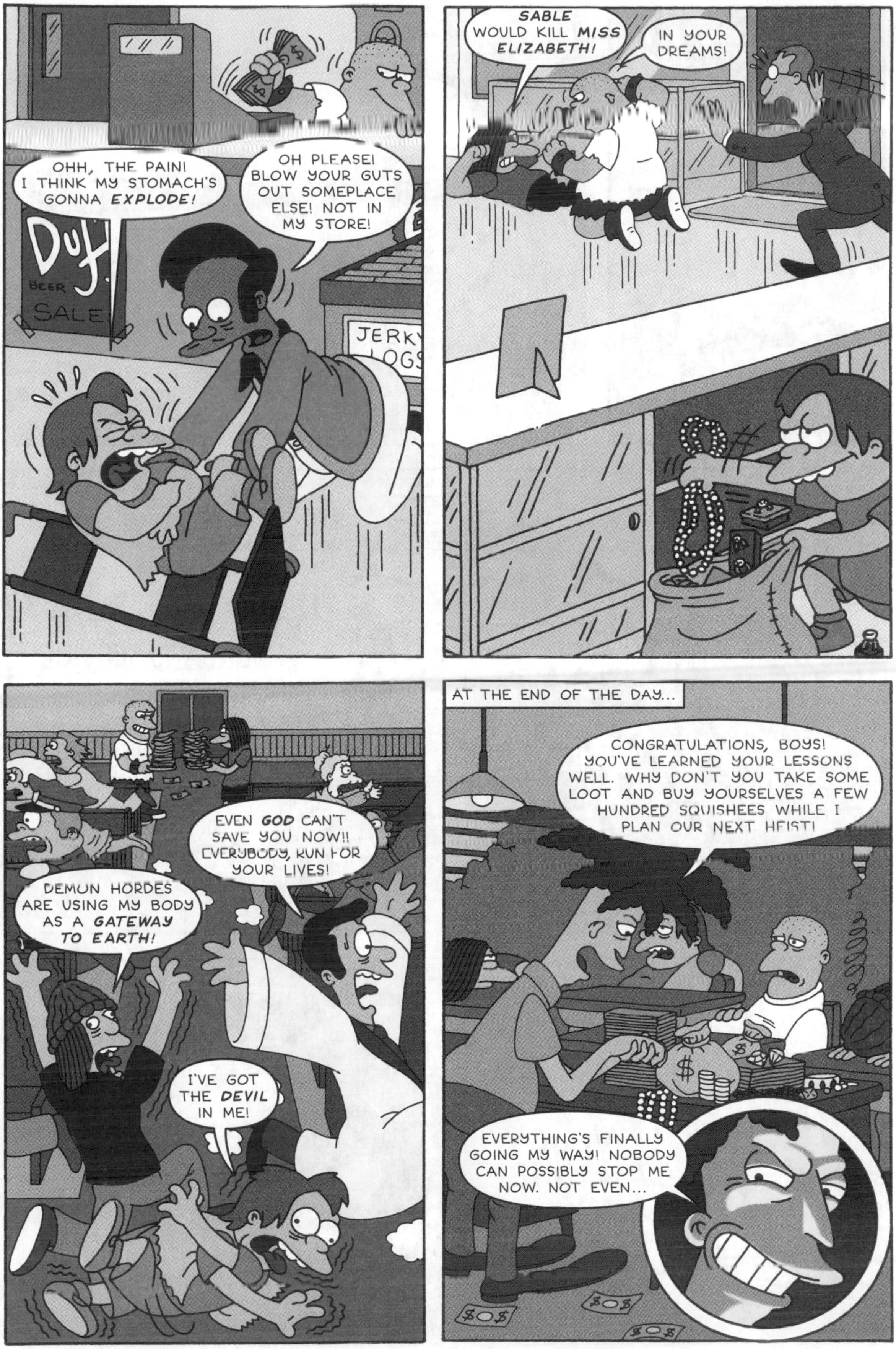
OHH, THE PAIN! I THINK MY STOMACH'S GONNA EXPLODE!
OH PLEASE! BLOW YOUR GUTS OUT SOMEPLACE ELSE! NOT IN MY STORE!
DUFF BEER SALE
JERKY LOGS
SABLE WOULD KILL MISS ELIZABETH!
IN YOUR DREAMS!
EVEN GOD CAN'T SAVE YOU NOW!! EVERYBODY, RUN FOR YOUR LIVES!
DEMON HORDES ARE USING MY BODY AS A GATEWAY TO EARTH!
I'VE GOT THE DEVIL IN ME!
AT THE END OF THE DAY...
CONGRATULATIONS, BOYS! YOU'VE LEARNED YOUR LESSONS WELL. WHY DON'T YOU TAKE SOME LOOT AND BUY YOURSELVES A FEW HUNDRED SQUISHEES WHILE I PLAN OUR NEXT HEIST!
EVERYTHING'S FINALLY GOING MY WAY! NOBODY CAN POSSIBLY STOP ME NOW. NOT EVEN...

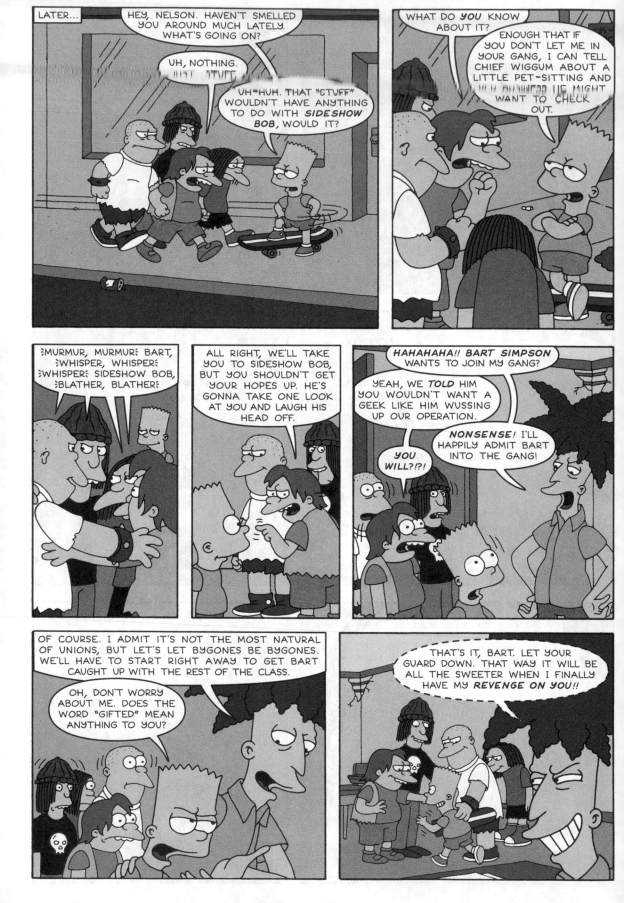

99

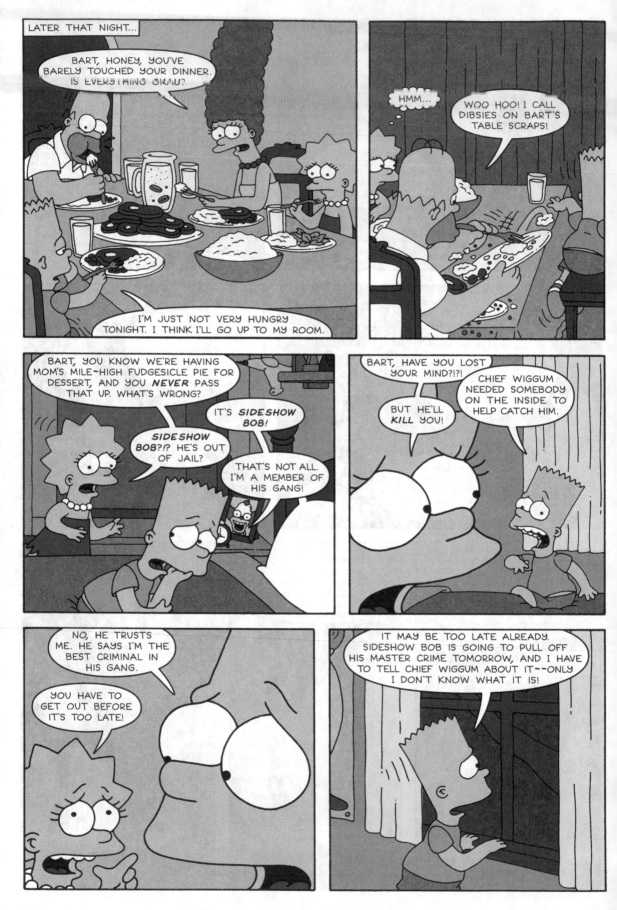

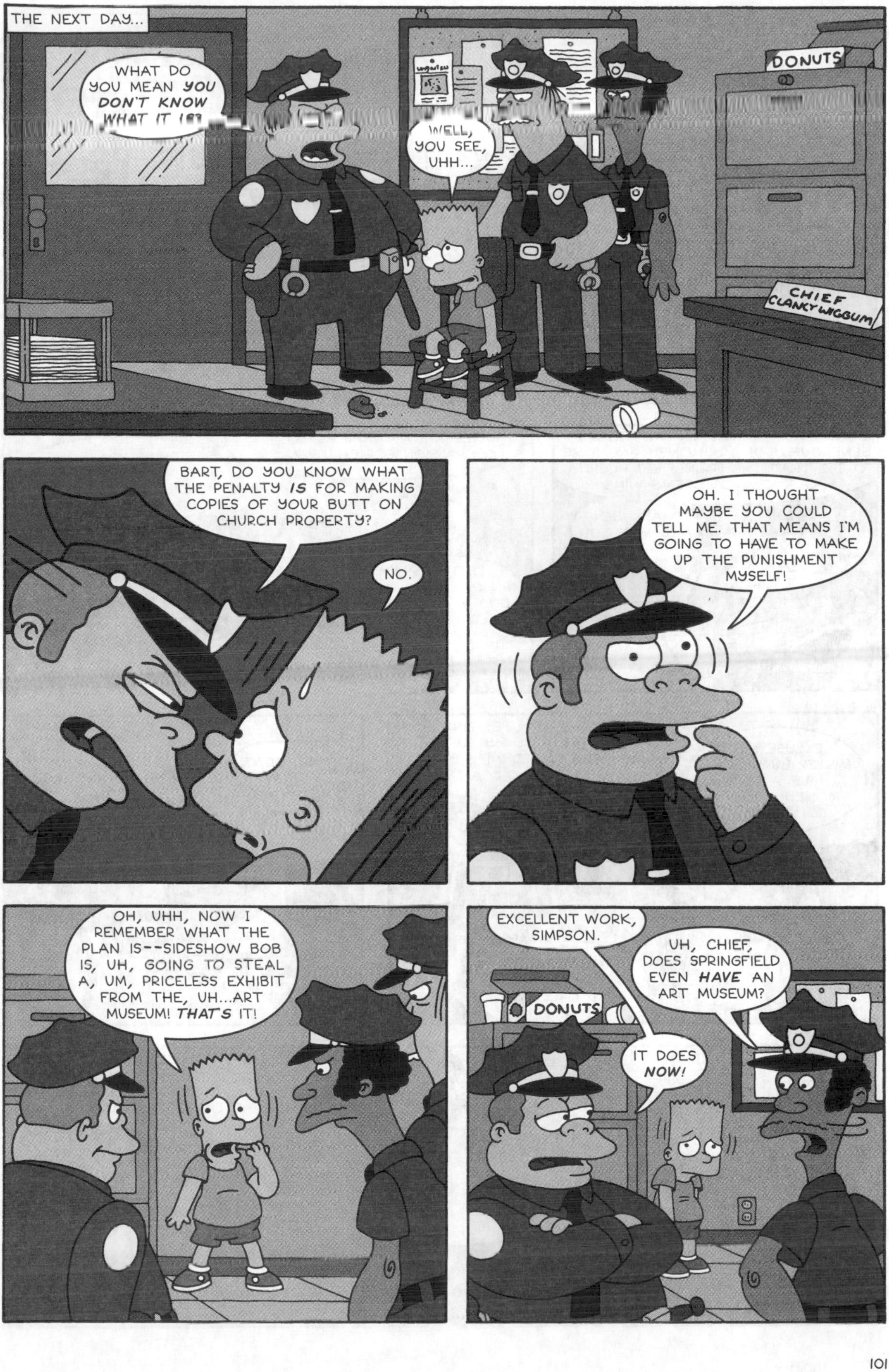

THE NEXT DAY...
WHAT DO YOU MEAN *YOU DON'T KNOW* WHAT IT IS?
WELL, YOU SEE, UHH...
DONUTS
CHIEF CLANKY WIGGUM
BART, DO YOU KNOW WHAT THE PENALTY *IS* FOR MAKING COPIES OF YOUR BUTT ON CHURCH PROPERTY?
NO.
OH. I THOUGHT MAYBE YOU COULD TELL ME. THAT MEANS I'M GOING TO HAVE TO MAKE UP THE PUNISHMENT MYSELF!
OH, UHH, NOW I REMEMBER WHAT THE PLAN IS--SIDESHOW BOB IS, UH, GOING TO STEAL A, UM, PRICELESS EXHIBIT FROM THE, UH...ART MUSEUM! *THAT'S* IT!
EXCELLENT WORK, SIMPSON.
UH, CHIEF, DOES SPRINGFIELD EVEN *HAVE* AN ART MUSEUM?
DONUTS
IT DOES *NOW!*

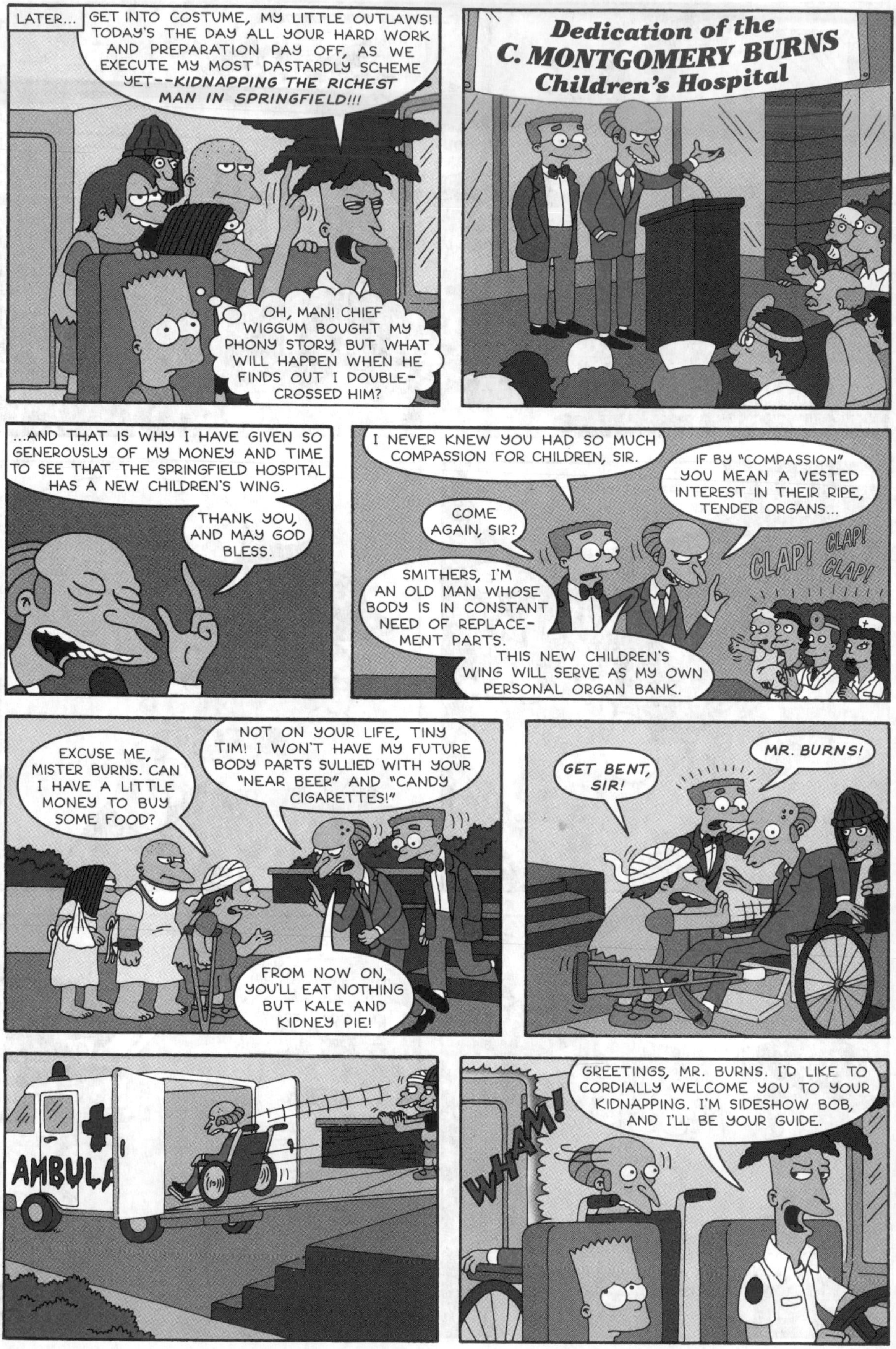
LATER...
GET INTO COSTUME, MY LITTLE OUTLAWS! TODAY'S THE DAY ALL YOUR HARD WORK AND PREPARATION PAY OFF, AS WE EXECUTE MY MOST DASTARDLY SCHEME YET--KIDNAPPING THE RICHEST MAN IN SPRINGFIELD!!!
OH, MAN! CHIEF WIGGUM BOUGHT MY PHONY STORY, BUT WHAT WILL HAPPEN WHEN HE FINDS OUT I DOUBLE-CROSSED HIM?
Dedication of the C. MONTGOMERY BURNS Children's Hospital
...AND THAT IS WHY I HAVE GIVEN SO GENEROUSLY OF MY MONEY AND TIME TO SEE THAT THE SPRINGFIELD HOSPITAL HAS A NEW CHILDREN'S WING.
THANK YOU, AND MAY GOD BLESS.
I NEVER KNEW YOU HAD SO MUCH COMPASSION FOR CHILDREN, SIR.
IF BY "COMPASSION" YOU MEAN A VESTED INTEREST IN THEIR RIPE, TENDER ORGANS...
COME AGAIN, SIR?
CLAP! CLAP! CLAP!
SMITHERS, I'M AN OLD MAN WHOSE BODY IS IN CONSTANT NEED OF REPLACEMENT PARTS.
THIS NEW CHILDREN'S WING WILL SERVE AS MY OWN PERSONAL ORGAN BANK.
EXCUSE ME, MISTER BURNS. CAN I HAVE A LITTLE MONEY TO BUY SOME FOOD?
NOT ON YOUR LIFE, TINY TIM! I WON'T HAVE MY FUTURE BODY PARTS SULLIED WITH YOUR "NEAR BEER" AND "CANDY CIGARETTES!"
FROM NOW ON, YOU'LL EAT NOTHING BUT KALE AND KIDNEY PIE!
GET BENT, SIR!
MR. BURNS!
AMBULA
WHAM!
GREETINGS, MR. BURNS. I'D LIKE TO CORDIALLY WELCOME YOU TO YOUR KIDNAPPING. I'M SIDESHOW BOB, AND I'LL BE YOUR GUIDE.

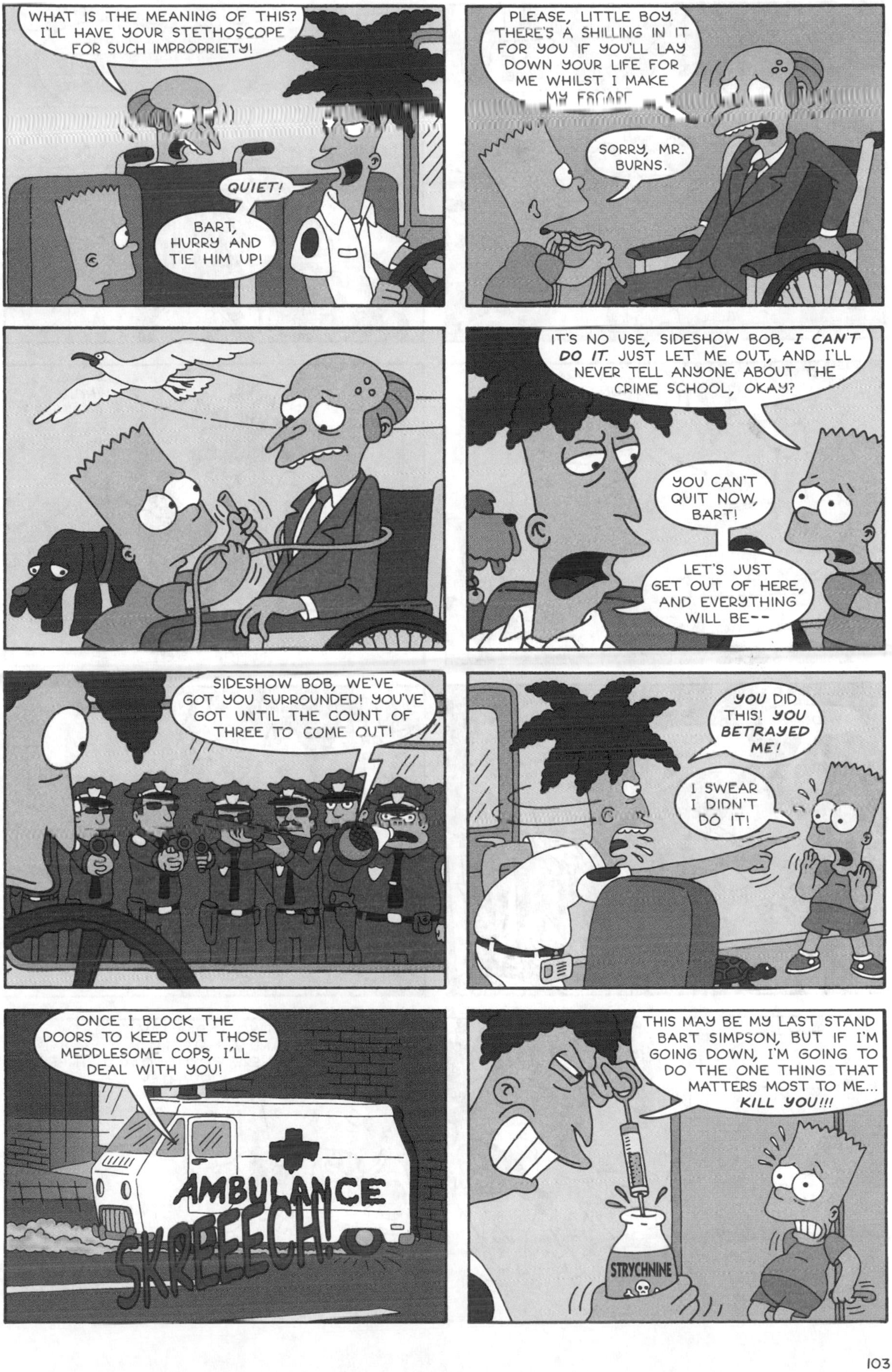
WHAT IS THE MEANING OF THIS? I'LL HAVE YOUR STETHOSCOPE FOR SUCH IMPROPRIETY!
QUIET!
BART, HURRY AND TIE HIM UP!
PLEASE, LITTLE BOY. THERE'S A SHILLING IN IT FOR YOU IF YOU'LL LAY DOWN YOUR LIFE FOR ME WHILST I MAKE MY ESCAPE
SORRY, MR. BURNS.
IT'S NO USE, SIDESHOW BOB, *I CAN'T DO IT*. JUST LET ME OUT, AND I'LL NEVER TELL ANYONE ABOUT THE CRIME SCHOOL, OKAY?
YOU CAN'T QUIT NOW, BART!
LET'S JUST GET OUT OF HERE, AND EVERYTHING WILL BE--
SIDESHOW BOB, WE'VE GOT YOU SURROUNDED! YOU'VE GOT UNTIL THE COUNT OF THREE TO COME OUT!
YOU DID THIS! *YOU BETRAYED ME!*
I SWEAR I DIDN'T DO IT!
ONCE I BLOCK THE DOORS TO KEEP OUT THOSE MEDDLESOME COPS, I'LL DEAL WITH YOU!
AMBULANCE
SKREEECH!
THIS MAY BE MY LAST STAND BART SIMPSON, BUT IF I'M GOING DOWN, I'M GOING TO DO THE ONE THING THAT MATTERS MOST TO ME... *KILL YOU!!!*
STRYCHNINE

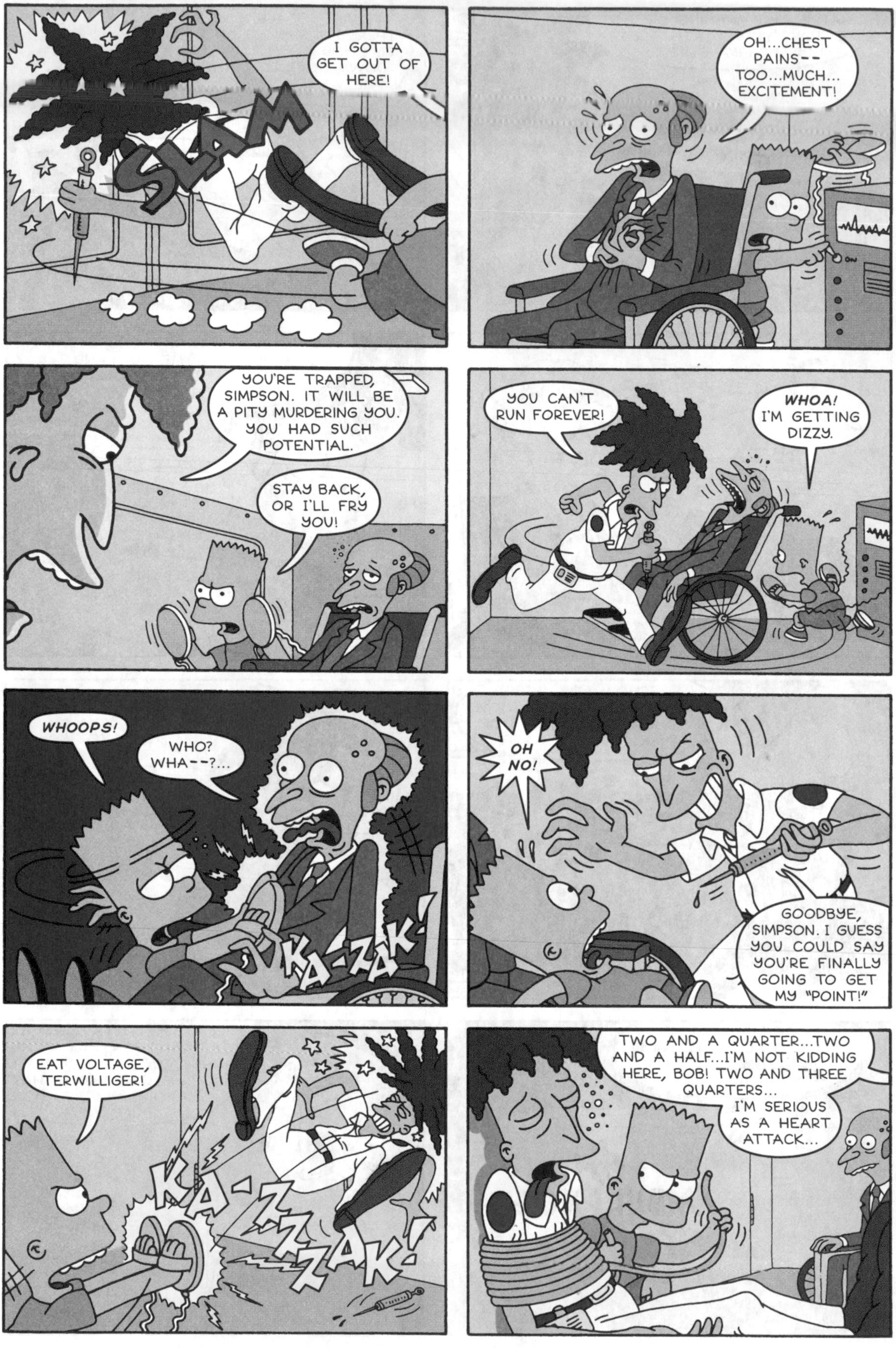

I GOTTA GET OUT OF HERE!
SLAM
OH...CHEST PAINS-- TOO...MUCH... EXCITEMENT!
YOU'RE TRAPPED, SIMPSON. IT WILL BE A PITY MURDERING YOU. YOU HAD SUCH POTENTIAL.
STAY BACK, OR I'LL FRY YOU!
YOU CAN'T RUN FOREVER!
WHOA! I'M GETTING DIZZY.
WHOOPS!
WHO? WHA--?...
KA-ZAK!
OH NO!
GOODBYE, SIMPSON. I GUESS YOU COULD SAY YOU'RE FINALLY GOING TO GET MY "POINT!"
EAT VOLTAGE, TERWILLIGER!
KA-ZZZZAK!
TWO AND A QUARTER...TWO AND A HALF...I'M NOT KIDDING HERE, BOB! TWO AND THREE QUARTERS...
I'M SERIOUS AS A HEART ATTACK...

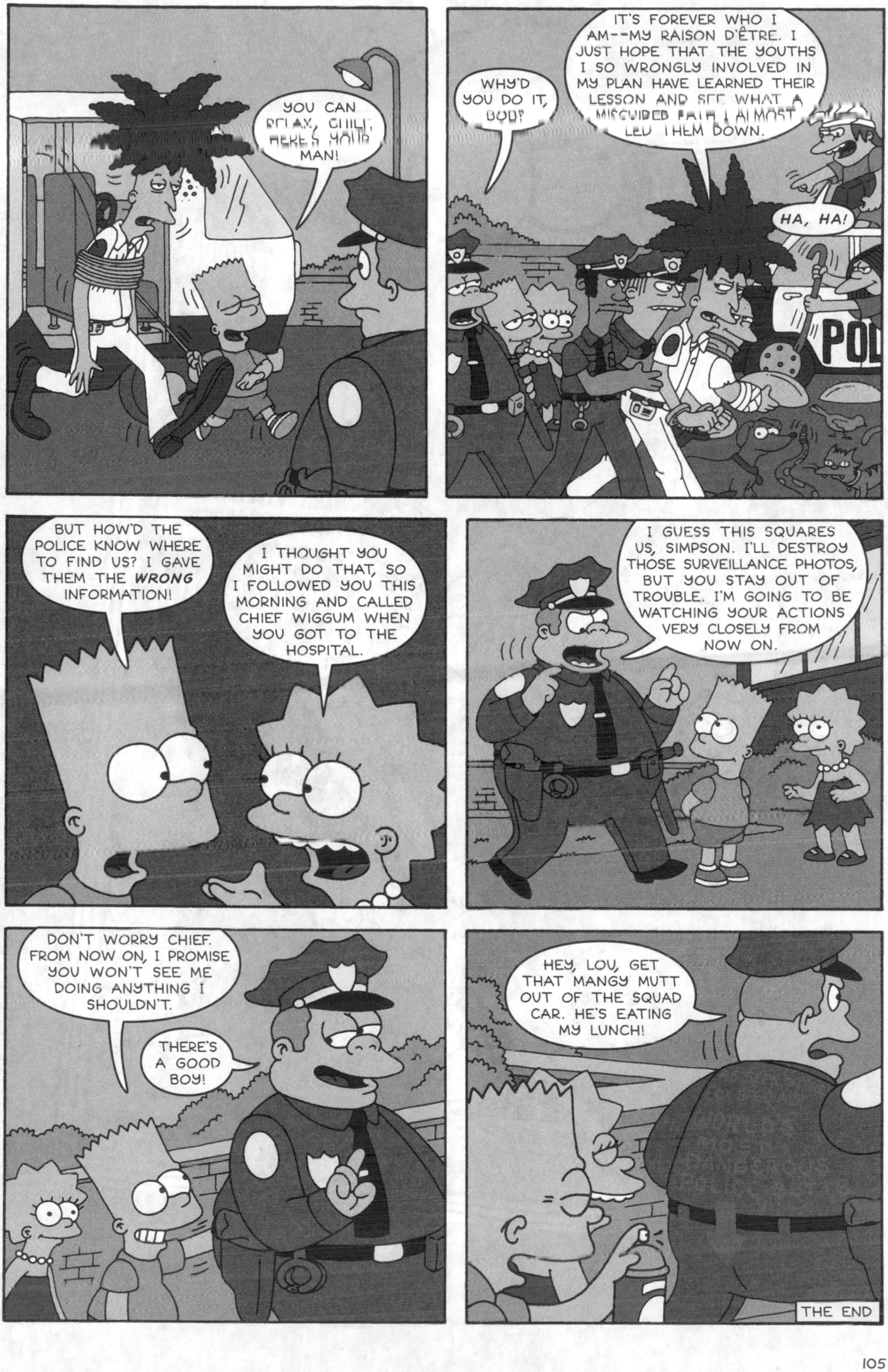
YOU CAN RELAX, CHIEF. HERE'S YOUR MAN!
WHY'D YOU DO IT, BOB?
IT'S FOREVER WHO I AM--MY RAISON D'ÊTRE. I JUST HOPE THAT THE YOUTHS I SO WRONGLY INVOLVED IN MY PLAN HAVE LEARNED THEIR LESSON AND SEE WHAT A MISGUIDED PATH I ALMOST LED THEM DOWN.
HA, HA!
POL
BUT HOW'D THE POLICE KNOW WHERE TO FIND US? I GAVE THEM THE **WRONG** INFORMATION!
I THOUGHT YOU MIGHT DO THAT, SO I FOLLOWED YOU THIS MORNING AND CALLED CHIEF WIGGUM WHEN YOU GOT TO THE HOSPITAL.
I GUESS THIS SQUARES US, SIMPSON. I'LL DESTROY THOSE SURVEILLANCE PHOTOS, BUT YOU STAY OUT OF TROUBLE. I'M GOING TO BE WATCHING YOUR ACTIONS VERY CLOSELY FROM NOW ON.
DON'T WORRY CHIEF. FROM NOW ON, I PROMISE YOU WON'T SEE ME DOING ANYTHING I SHOULDN'T.
THERE'S A GOOD BOY!
HEY, LOU, GET THAT MANGY MUTT OUT OF THE SQUAD CAR. HE'S EATING MY LUNCH!
THE END

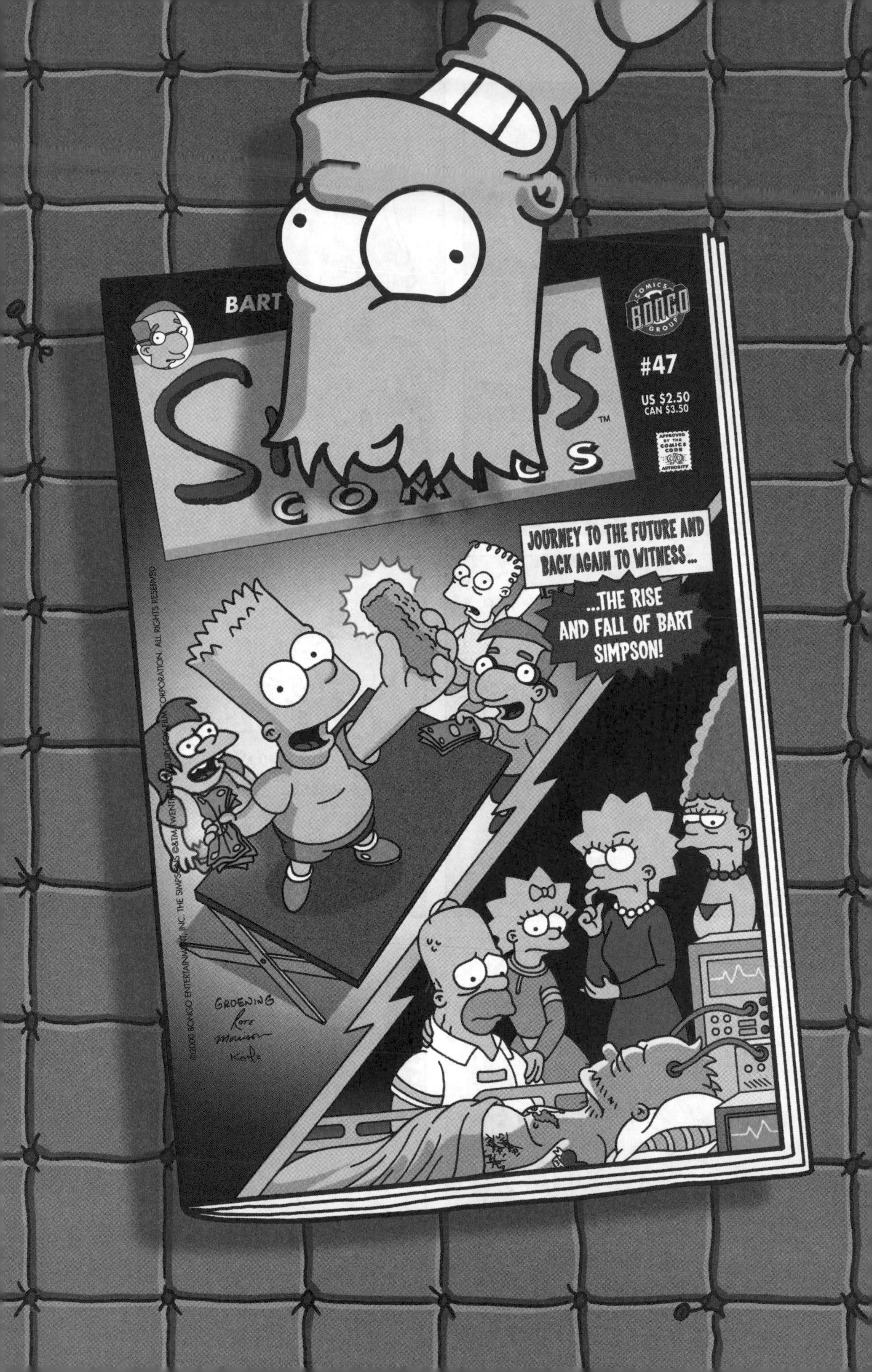

BART
#47
US $2.50
CAN $3.50
JOURNEY TO THE FUTURE AND BACK AGAIN TO WITNESS...
...THE RISE AND FALL OF BART SIMPSON!
GROENING

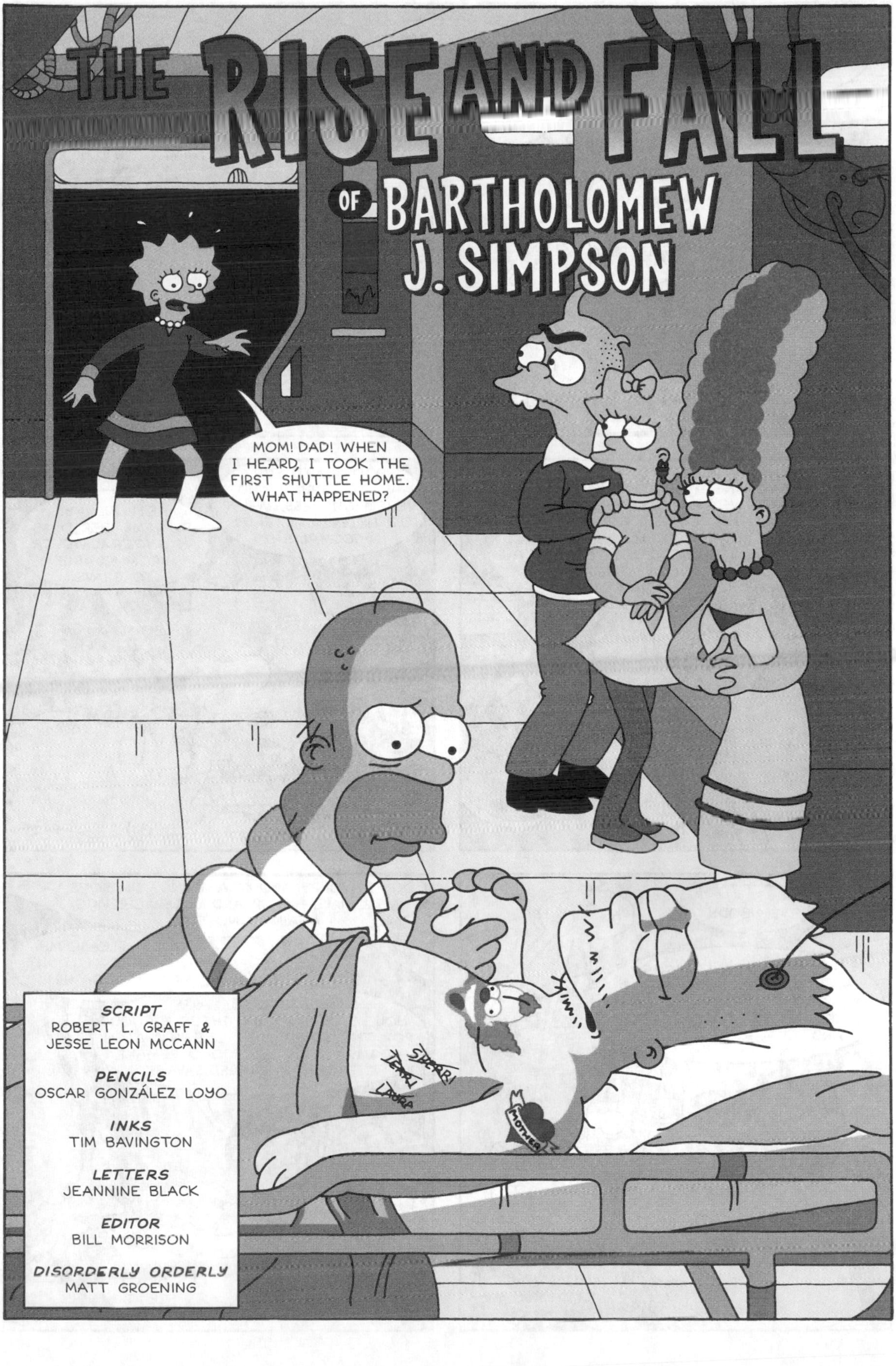
THE RISE AND FALL OF BARTHOLOMEW J. SIMPSON
MOM! DAD! WHEN I HEARD, I TOOK THE FIRST SHUTTLE HOME. WHAT HAPPENED?
SCRIPT
ROBERT L. GRAFF & JESSE LEON MCCANN
PENCILS
OSCAR GONZÁLEZ LOYO
INKS
TIM BAVINGTON
LETTERS
JEANNINE BLACK
EDITOR
BILL MORRISON
DISORDERLY ORDERLY
MATT GROENING
SHERRI
TERRI
LAURA
MOTHER

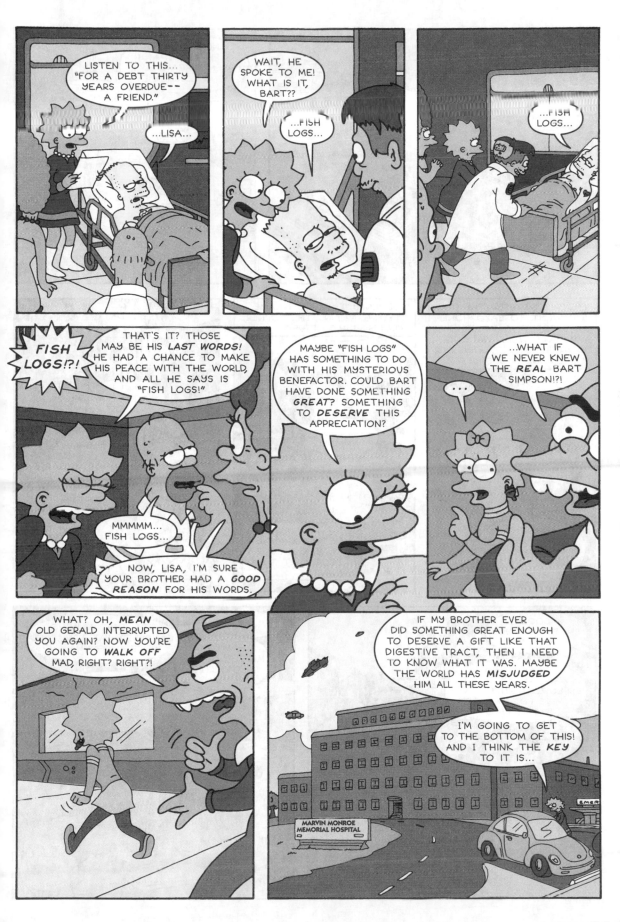

109

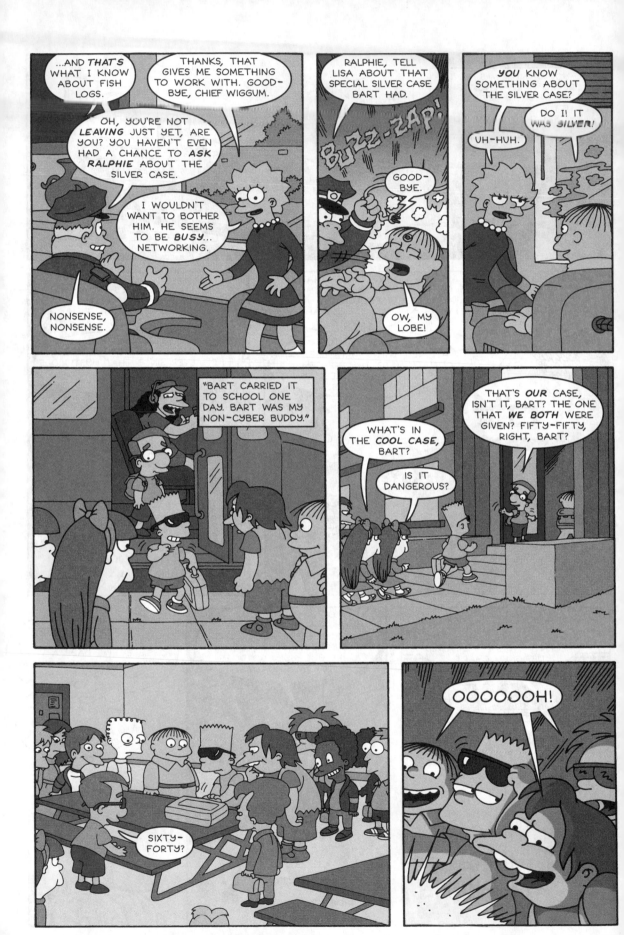

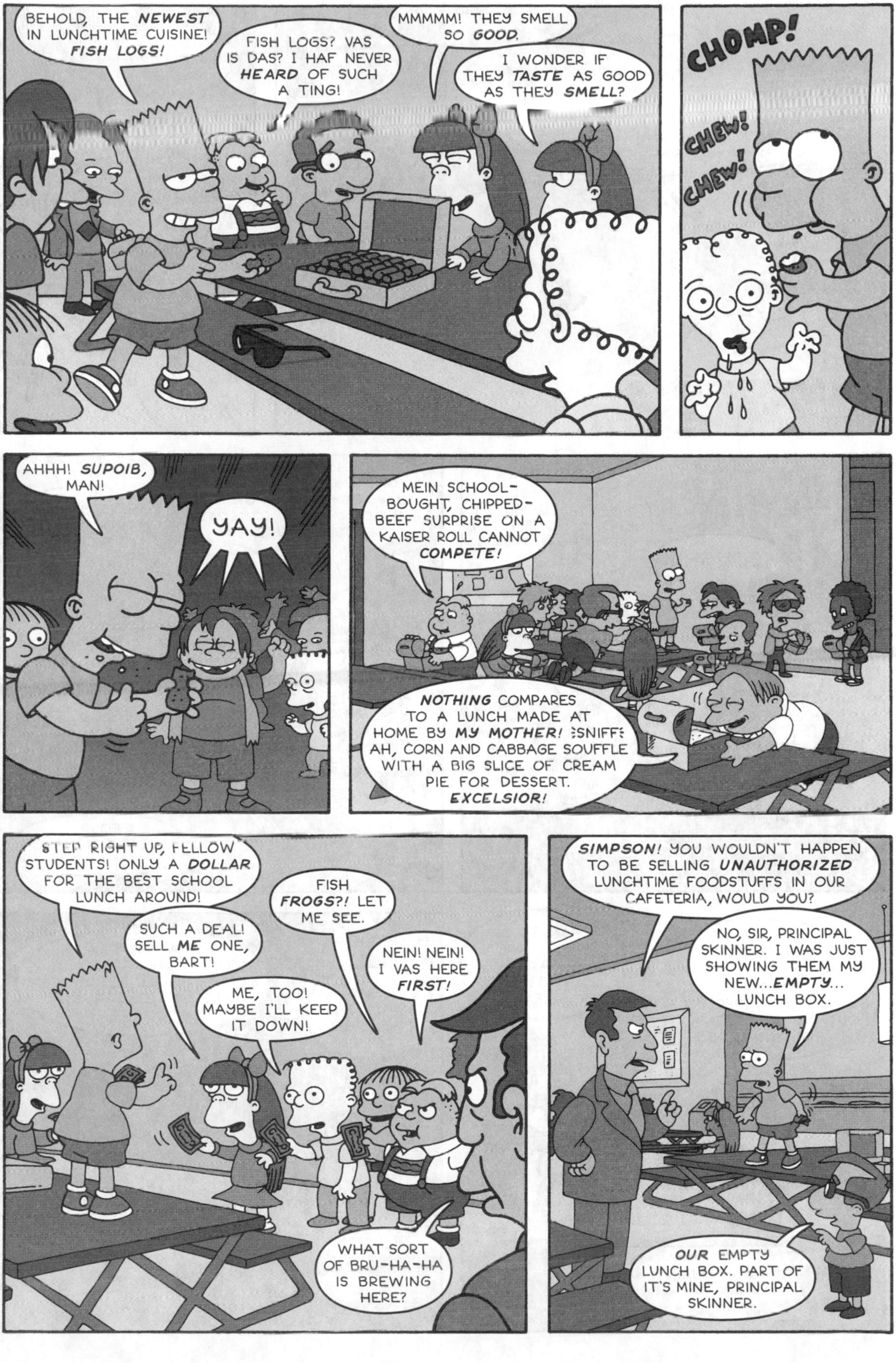

BEHOLD, THE NEWEST IN LUNCHTIME CUISINE! FISH LOGS!
FISH LOGS? VAS IS DAS? I HAF NEVER HEARD OF SUCH A TING!
MMMMM! THEY SMELL SO GOOD.
I WONDER IF THEY TASTE AS GOOD AS THEY SMELL?
CHOMP!
CHEW!
CHEW!
AHHH! SUPOIB, MAN!
YAY!
MEIN SCHOOL-BOUGHT, CHIPPED-BEEF SURPRISE ON A KAISER ROLL CANNOT COMPETE!
NOTHING COMPARES TO A LUNCH MADE AT HOME BY MY MOTHER! :SNIFF: AH, CORN AND CABBAGE SOUFFLE WITH A BIG SLICE OF CREAM PIE FOR DESSERT. EXCELSIOR!
STEP RIGHT UP, FELLOW STUDENTS! ONLY A DOLLAR FOR THE BEST SCHOOL LUNCH AROUND!
SUCH A DEAL! SELL ME ONE, BART!
FISH FROGS?! LET ME SEE.
NEIN! NEIN! I VAS HERE FIRST!
ME, TOO! MAYBE I'LL KEEP IT DOWN!
WHAT SORT OF BRU-HA-HA IS BREWING HERE?
SIMPSON! YOU WOULDN'T HAPPEN TO BE SELLING UNAUTHORIZED LUNCHTIME FOODSTUFFS IN OUR CAFETERIA, WOULD YOU?
NO, SIR, PRINCIPAL SKINNER. I WAS JUST SHOWING THEM MY NEW...EMPTY... LUNCH BOX.
OUR EMPTY LUNCH BOX. PART OF IT'S MINE, PRINCIPAL SKINNER.

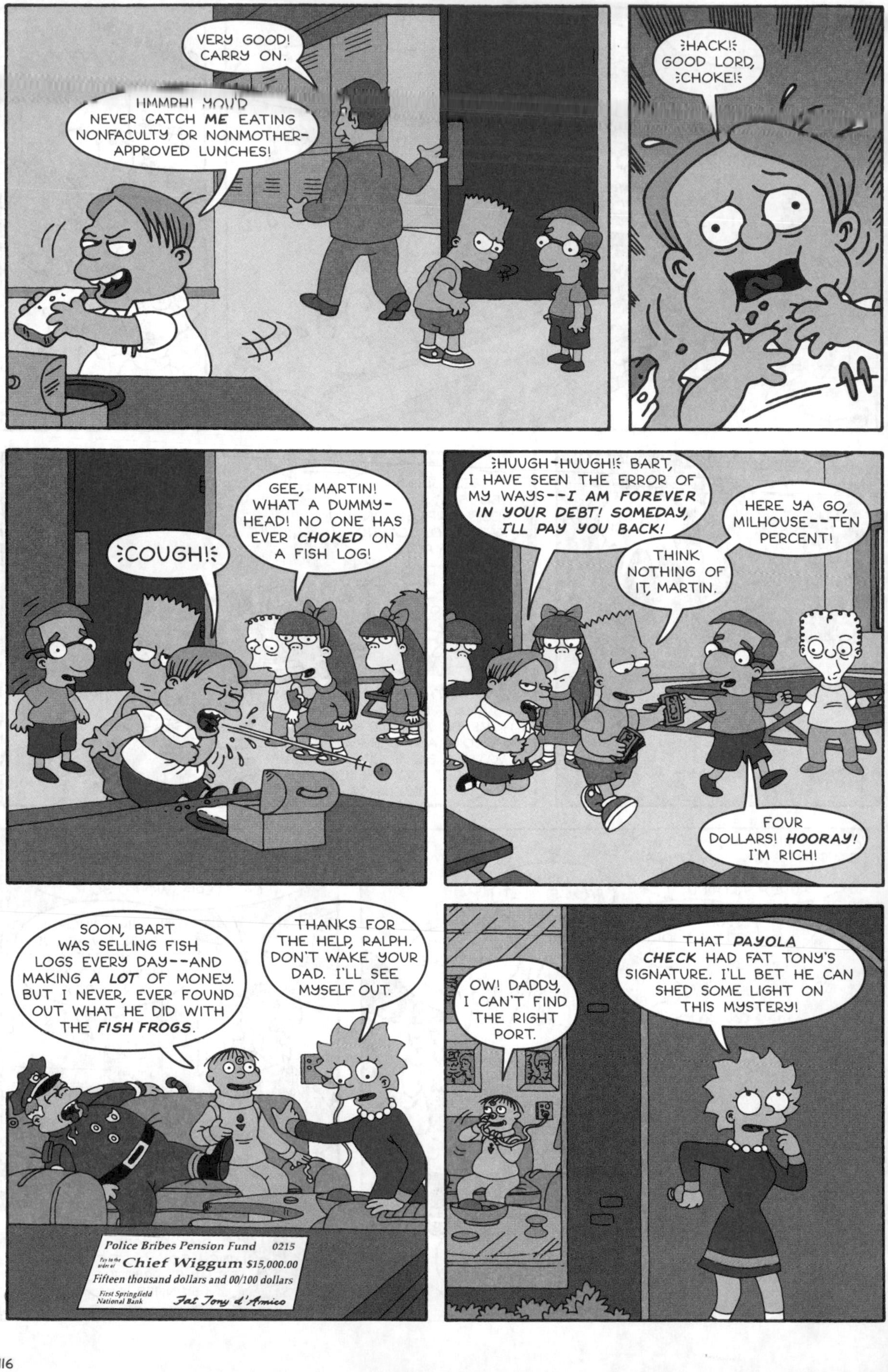

VERY GOOD! CARRY ON.
HMMPH! YOU'D NEVER CATCH **ME** EATING NONFACULTY OR NONMOTHER-APPROVED LUNCHES!
HACK! GOOD LORD, CHOKE!
COUGH!
GEE, MARTIN! WHAT A DUMMY-HEAD! NO ONE HAS EVER **CHOKED** ON A FISH LOG!
HUUGH-HUUGH! BART, I HAVE SEEN THE ERROR OF MY WAYS--***I AM FOREVER IN YOUR DEBT! SOMEDAY, I'LL PAY YOU BACK!***
THINK NOTHING OF IT, MARTIN.
HERE YA GO, MILHOUSE--TEN PERCENT!
FOUR DOLLARS! ***HOORAY!*** I'M RICH!
SOON, BART WAS SELLING FISH LOGS EVERY DAY--AND MAKING ***A LOT*** OF MONEY. BUT I NEVER, EVER FOUND OUT WHAT HE DID WITH THE ***FISH FROGS***.
THANKS FOR THE HELP, RALPH. DON'T WAKE YOUR DAD. I'LL SEE MYSELF OUT.
Police Bribes Pension Fund 0215
Pay to the order of Chief Wiggum $15,000.00
Fifteen thousand dollars and 00/100 dollars
First Springfield National Bank
Fat Tony d'Amico
OW! DADDY, I CAN'T FIND THE RIGHT PORT.
THAT ***PAYOLA CHECK*** HAD FAT TONY'S SIGNATURE. I'LL BET HE CAN SHED SOME LIGHT ON THIS MYSTERY!

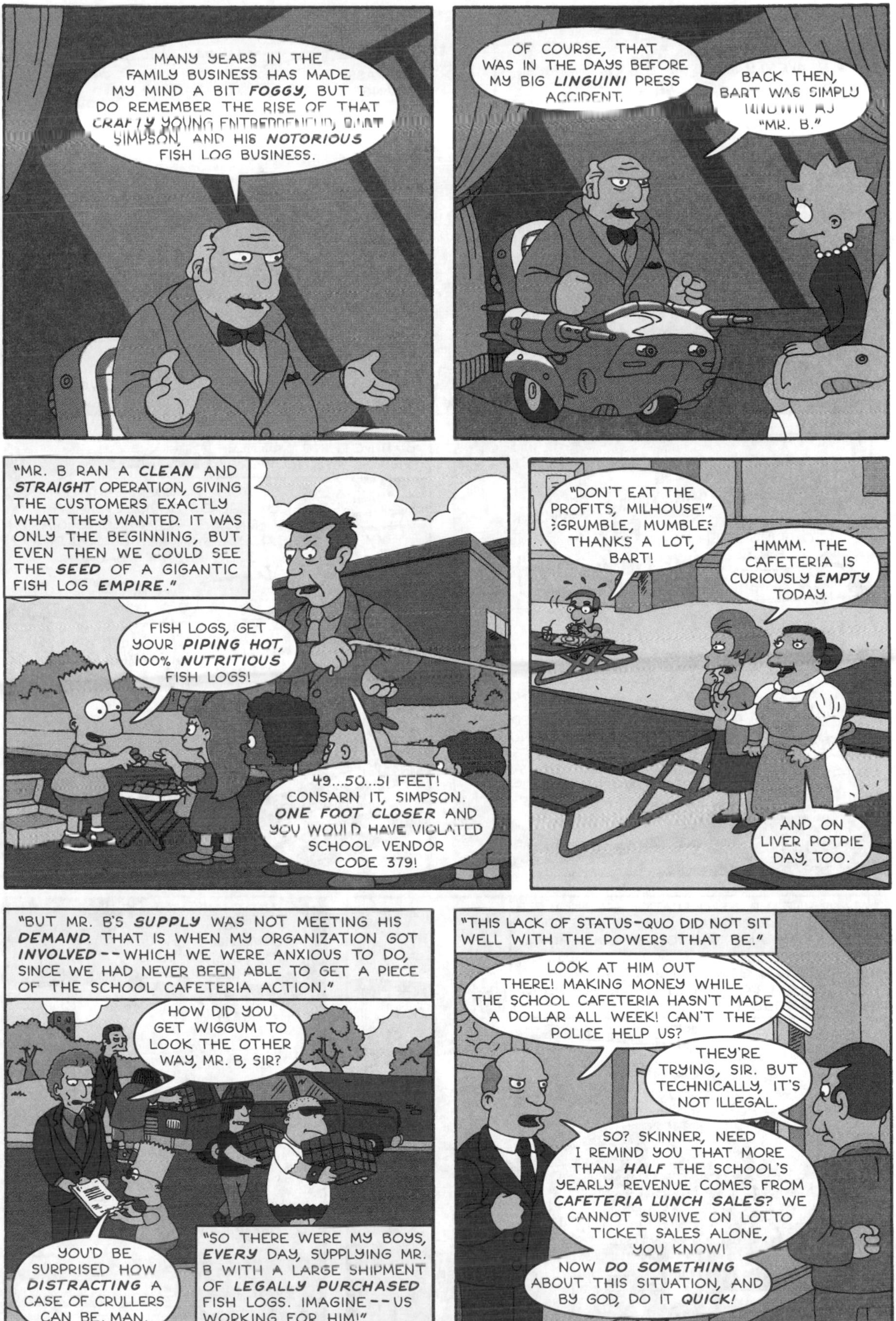
MANY YEARS IN THE FAMILY BUSINESS HAS MADE MY MIND A BIT *FOGGY*, BUT I DO REMEMBER THE RISE OF THAT *CRAFTY* YOUNG ENTREPRENEUR, BART SIMPSON, AND HIS *NOTORIOUS* FISH LOG BUSINESS.
OF COURSE, THAT WAS IN THE DAYS BEFORE MY BIG *LINGUINI* PRESS ACCIDENT.
BACK THEN, BART WAS SIMPLY KNOWN AS "MR. B."
"MR. B RAN A *CLEAN* AND *STRAIGHT* OPERATION, GIVING THE CUSTOMERS EXACTLY WHAT THEY WANTED. IT WAS ONLY THE BEGINNING, BUT EVEN THEN WE COULD SEE THE *SEED* OF A GIGANTIC FISH LOG *EMPIRE*."
FISH LOGS, GET YOUR *PIPING HOT*, 100% *NUTRITIOUS* FISH LOGS!
49...50...51 FEET! CONSARN IT, SIMPSON. *ONE FOOT CLOSER* AND YOU WOULD HAVE VIOLATED SCHOOL VENDOR CODE 379!
"DON'T EAT THE PROFITS, MILHOUSE!" ¿GRUMBLE, MUMBLE¿ THANKS A LOT, BART!
HMMM. THE CAFETERIA IS CURIOUSLY *EMPTY* TODAY.
AND ON LIVER POTPIE DAY, TOO.
"BUT MR. B'S *SUPPLY* WAS NOT MEETING HIS *DEMAND*. THAT IS WHEN MY ORGANIZATION GOT *INVOLVED*--WHICH WE WERE ANXIOUS TO DO, SINCE WE HAD NEVER BEEN ABLE TO GET A PIECE OF THE SCHOOL CAFETERIA ACTION."
HOW DID YOU GET WIGGUM TO LOOK THE OTHER WAY, MR. B, SIR?
YOU'D BE SURPRISED HOW *DISTRACTING* A CASE OF CRULLERS CAN BE, MAN.
"SO THERE WERE MY BOYS, *EVERY* DAY, SUPPLYING MR. B WITH A LARGE SHIPMENT OF *LEGALLY PURCHASED* FISH LOGS. IMAGINE--US WORKING FOR HIM!"
"THIS LACK OF STATUS-QUO DID NOT SIT WELL WITH THE POWERS THAT BE."
LOOK AT HIM OUT THERE! MAKING MONEY WHILE THE SCHOOL CAFETERIA HASN'T MADE A DOLLAR ALL WEEK! CAN'T THE POLICE HELP US?
THEY'RE TRYING, SIR. BUT TECHNICALLY, IT'S NOT ILLEGAL.
SO? SKINNER, NEED I REMIND YOU THAT MORE THAN *HALF* THE SCHOOL'S YEARLY REVENUE COMES FROM *CAFETERIA LUNCH SALES*? WE CANNOT SURVIVE ON LOTTO TICKET SALES ALONE, YOU KNOW!
NOW *DO SOMETHING* ABOUT THIS SITUATION, AND BY GOD, DO IT *QUICK*!

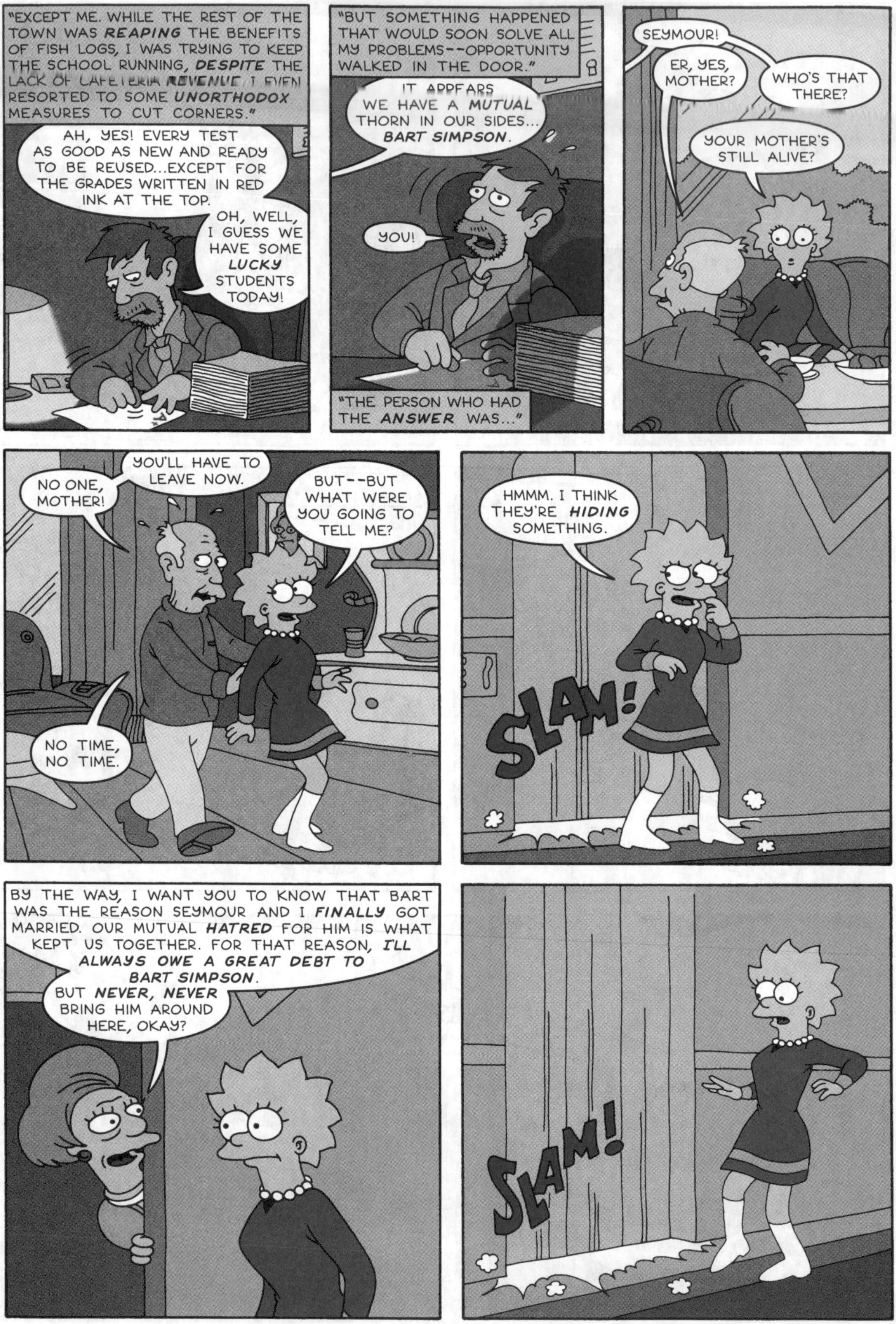
"EXCEPT ME. WHILE THE REST OF THE TOWN WAS *REAPING* THE BENEFITS OF FISH LOGS, I WAS TRYING TO KEEP THE SCHOOL RUNNING, *DESPITE* THE LACK OF CAFETERIA REVENUE. I EVEN RESORTED TO SOME *UNORTHODOX* MEASURES TO CUT CORNERS."
AH, YES! EVERY TEST AS GOOD AS NEW AND READY TO BE REUSED...EXCEPT FOR THE GRADES WRITTEN IN RED INK AT THE TOP.
OH, WELL, I GUESS WE HAVE SOME *LUCKY* STUDENTS TODAY!
"BUT SOMETHING HAPPENED THAT WOULD SOON SOLVE ALL MY PROBLEMS--OPPORTUNITY WALKED IN THE DOOR."
IT APPEARS WE HAVE A *MUTUAL* THORN IN OUR SIDES... *BART SIMPSON*.
YOU!
"THE PERSON WHO HAD THE *ANSWER* WAS..."
SEYMOUR!
ER, YES, MOTHER?
WHO'S THAT THERE?
YOUR MOTHER'S STILL ALIVE?
NO ONE, MOTHER!
YOU'LL HAVE TO LEAVE NOW.
BUT--BUT WHAT WERE YOU GOING TO TELL ME?
NO TIME, NO TIME.
HMMM. I THINK THEY'RE *HIDING* SOMETHING.
SLAM!
BY THE WAY, I WANT YOU TO KNOW THAT BART WAS THE REASON SEYMOUR AND I *FINALLY* GOT MARRIED. OUR MUTUAL *HATRED* FOR HIM IS WHAT KEPT US TOGETHER. FOR THAT REASON, *I'LL ALWAYS OWE A GREAT DEBT TO BART SIMPSON*.
BUT *NEVER, NEVER* BRING HIM AROUND HERE, OKAY?
SLAM!

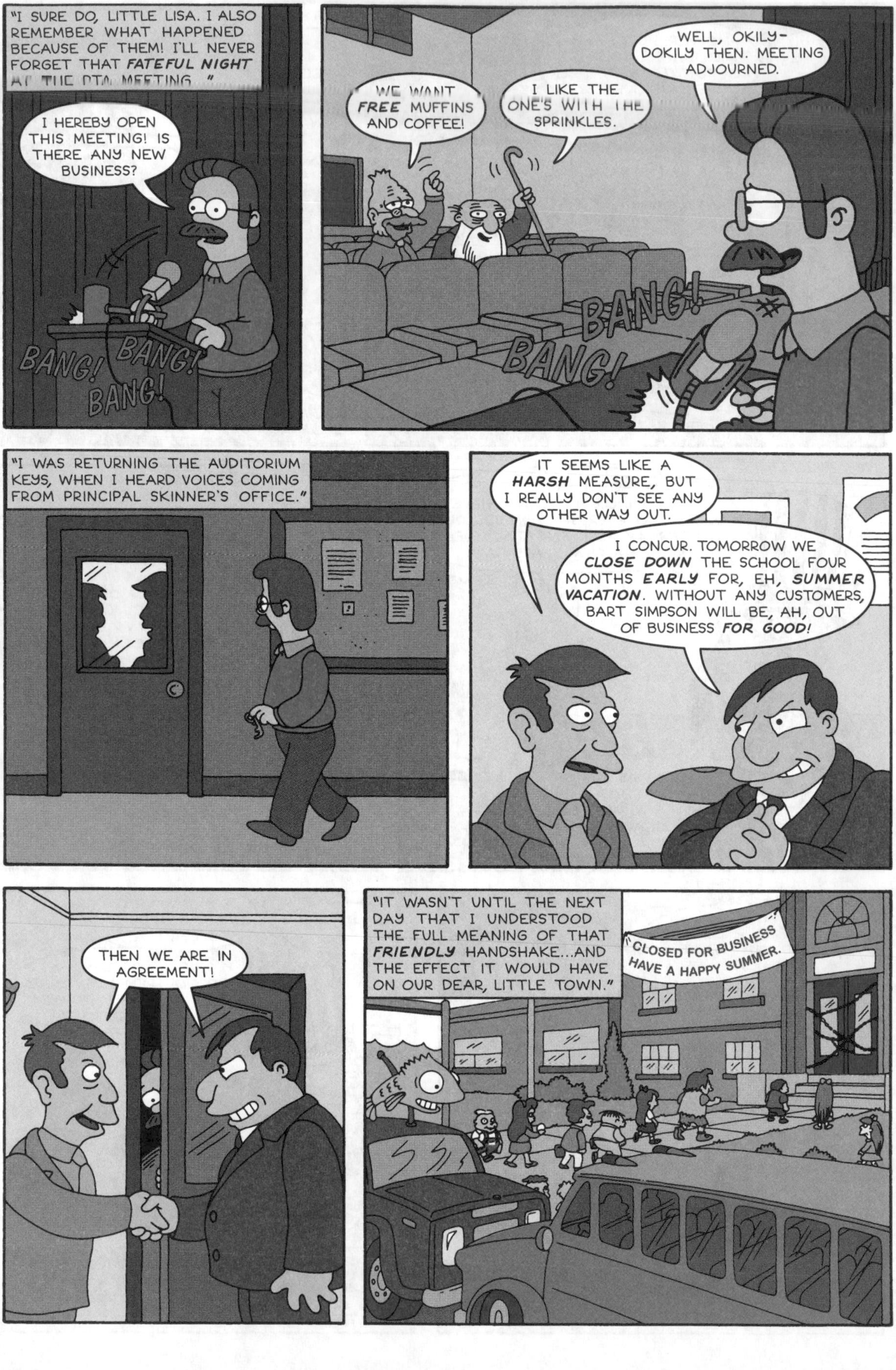
"I SURE DO, LITTLE LISA. I ALSO REMEMBER WHAT HAPPENED BECAUSE OF THEM! I'LL NEVER FORGET THAT FATEFUL NIGHT AT THE PTA MEETING."
I HEREBY OPEN THIS MEETING! IS THERE ANY NEW BUSINESS?
BANG! BANG! BANG!
WE WANT FREE MUFFINS AND COFFEE!
I LIKE THE ONE'S WITH THE SPRINKLES.
WELL, OKILY-DOKILY THEN. MEETING ADJOURNED.
BANG! BANG!
"I WAS RETURNING THE AUDITORIUM KEYS, WHEN I HEARD VOICES COMING FROM PRINCIPAL SKINNER'S OFFICE."
IT SEEMS LIKE A HARSH MEASURE, BUT I REALLY DON'T SEE ANY OTHER WAY OUT.
I CONCUR. TOMORROW WE CLOSE DOWN THE SCHOOL FOUR MONTHS EARLY FOR, EH, SUMMER VACATION. WITHOUT ANY CUSTOMERS, BART SIMPSON WILL BE, AH, OUT OF BUSINESS FOR GOOD!
THEN WE ARE IN AGREEMENT!
"IT WASN'T UNTIL THE NEXT DAY THAT I UNDERSTOOD THE FULL MEANING OF THAT FRIENDLY HANDSHAKE...AND THE EFFECT IT WOULD HAVE ON OUR DEAR, LITTLE TOWN."
CLOSED FOR BUSINESS
HAVE A HAPPY SUMMER.

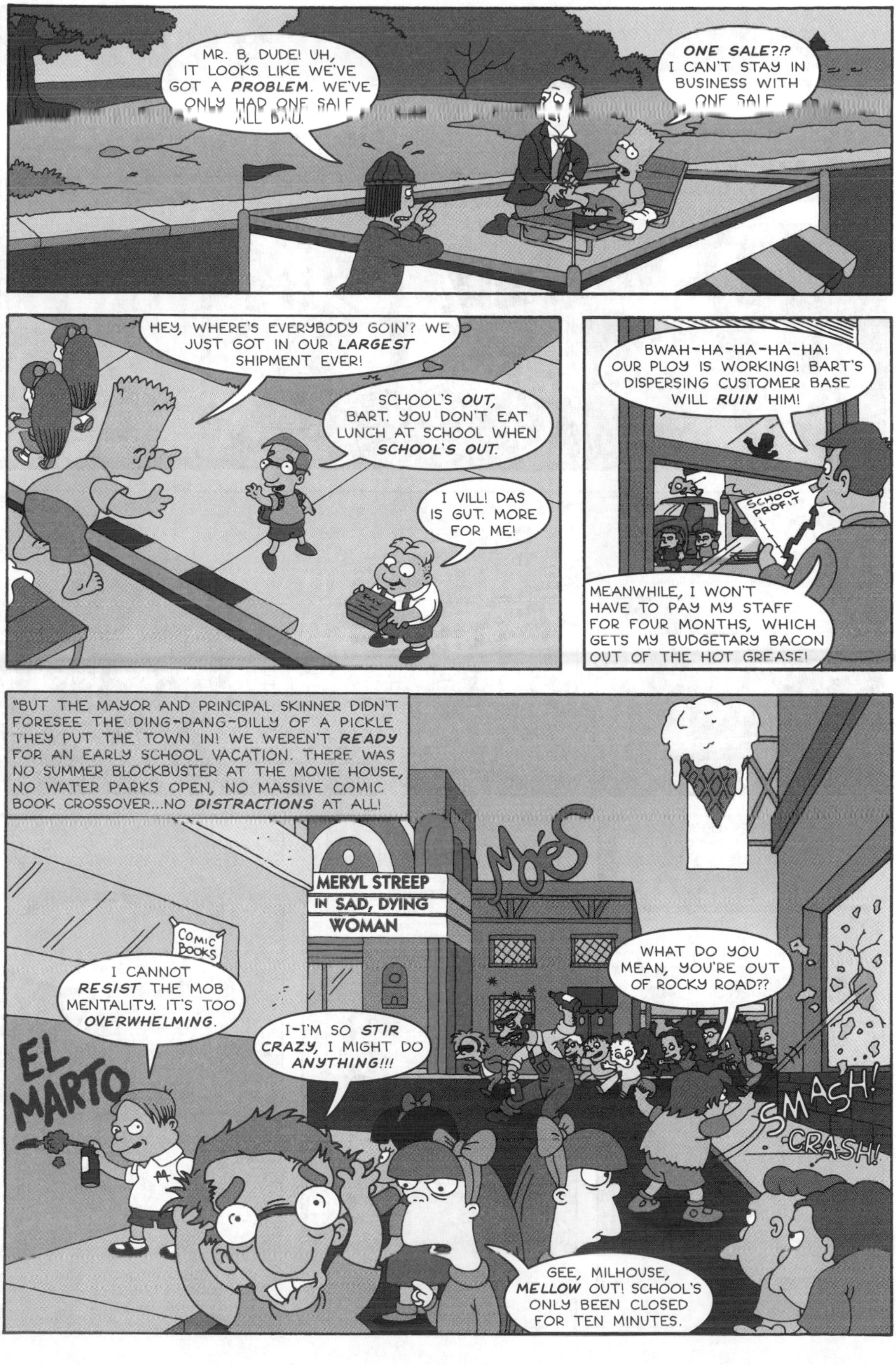

MR. B, DUDE! UH, IT LOOKS LIKE WE'VE GOT A **PROBLEM**. WE'VE ONLY HAD ONE SALE ALL DAY.
ONE SALE?!? I CAN'T STAY IN BUSINESS WITH ONE SALE
HEY, WHERE'S EVERYBODY GOIN'? WE JUST GOT IN OUR ***LARGEST*** SHIPMENT EVER!
SCHOOL'S ***OUT,*** BART. YOU DON'T EAT LUNCH AT SCHOOL WHEN ***SCHOOL'S OUT.***
I VILL! DAS IS GUT. MORE FOR ME!
BWAH-HA-HA-HA-HA! OUR PLOY IS WORKING! BART'S DISPERSING CUSTOMER BASE WILL ***RUIN*** HIM!
SCHOOL PROFIT
MEANWHILE, I WON'T HAVE TO PAY MY STAFF FOR FOUR MONTHS, WHICH GETS MY BUDGETARY BACON OUT OF THE HOT GREASE!
"BUT THE MAYOR AND PRINCIPAL SKINNER DIDN'T FORESEE THE DING-DANG-DILLY OF A PICKLE THEY PUT THE TOWN IN! WE WEREN'T ***READY*** FOR AN EARLY SCHOOL VACATION. THERE WAS NO SUMMER BLOCKBUSTER AT THE MOVIE HOUSE, NO WATER PARKS OPEN, NO MASSIVE COMIC BOOK CROSSOVER...NO ***DISTRACTIONS*** AT ALL!
MERYL STREEP IN SAD, DYING WOMAN
MOE'S
COMIC BOOKS
I CANNOT ***RESIST*** THE MOB MENTALITY. IT'S TOO ***OVERWHELMING***.
EL MARTO
I-I'M SO ***STIR CRAZY,*** I MIGHT DO ***ANYTHING!!!***
WHAT DO YOU MEAN, YOU'RE OUT OF ROCKY ROAD??
SMASH!
-CRASH!
GEE, MILHOUSE, ***MELLOW*** OUT! SCHOOL'S ONLY BEEN CLOSED FOR TEN MINUTES.

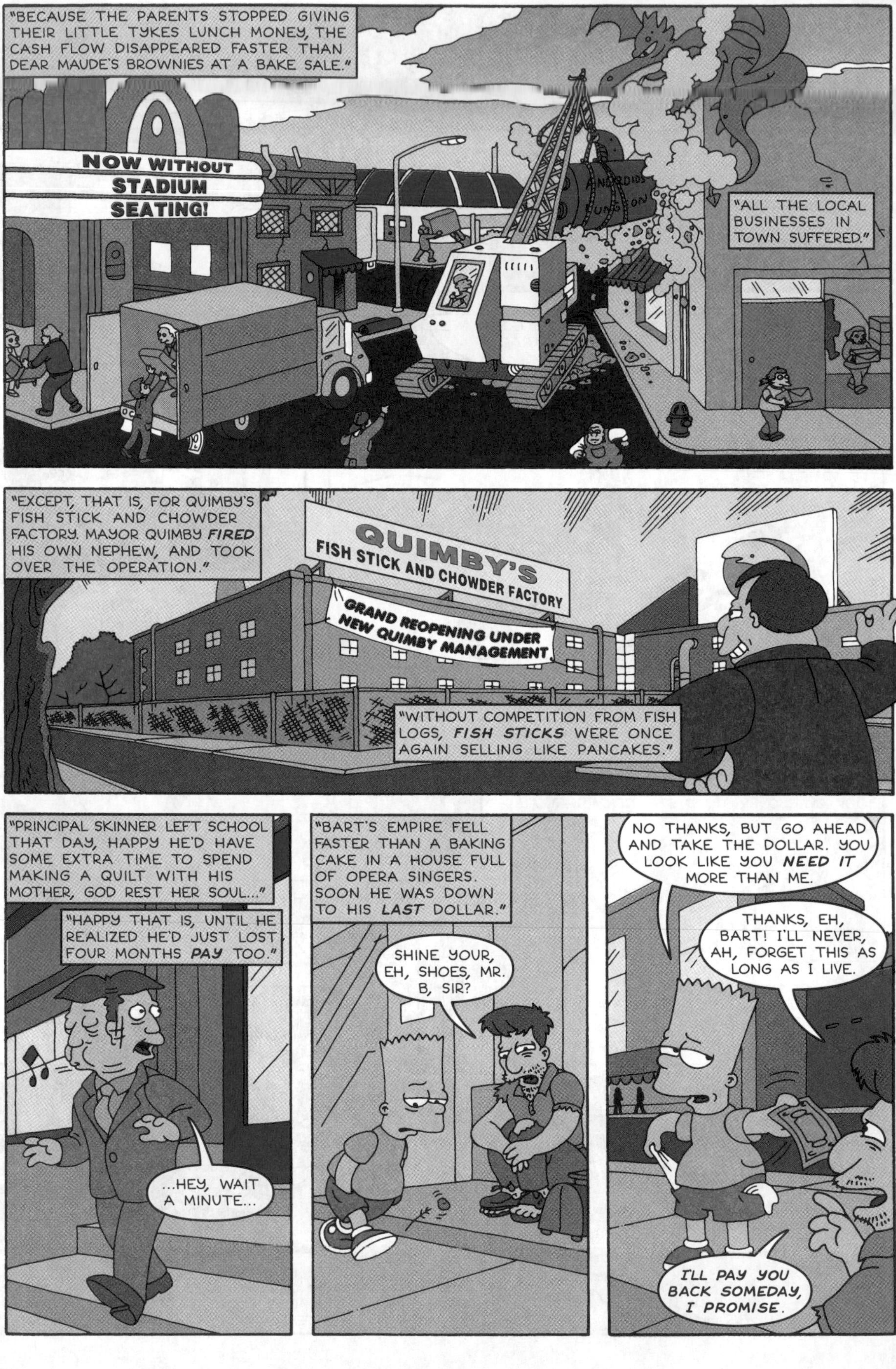
"BECAUSE THE PARENTS STOPPED GIVING THEIR LITTLE TYKES LUNCH MONEY, THE CASH FLOW DISAPPEARED FASTER THAN DEAR MAUDE'S BROWNIES AT A BAKE SALE."
NOW WITHOUT STADIUM SEATING!
"ALL THE LOCAL BUSINESSES IN TOWN SUFFERED."
"EXCEPT, THAT IS, FOR QUIMBY'S FISH STICK AND CHOWDER FACTORY. MAYOR QUIMBY FIRED HIS OWN NEPHEW, AND TOOK OVER THE OPERATION."
QUIMBY'S FISH STICK AND CHOWDER FACTORY
GRAND REOPENING UNDER NEW QUIMBY MANAGEMENT
"WITHOUT COMPETITION FROM FISH LOGS, FISH STICKS WERE ONCE AGAIN SELLING LIKE PANCAKES."
"PRINCIPAL SKINNER LEFT SCHOOL THAT DAY, HAPPY HE'D HAVE SOME EXTRA TIME TO SPEND MAKING A QUILT WITH HIS MOTHER, GOD REST HER SOUL..."
"HAPPY THAT IS, UNTIL HE REALIZED HE'D JUST LOST FOUR MONTHS PAY TOO."
...HEY, WAIT A MINUTE...
"BART'S EMPIRE FELL FASTER THAN A BAKING CAKE IN A HOUSE FULL OF OPERA SINGERS. SOON HE WAS DOWN TO HIS LAST DOLLAR."
SHINE YOUR, EH, SHOES, MR. B, SIR?
NO THANKS, BUT GO AHEAD AND TAKE THE DOLLAR. YOU LOOK LIKE YOU NEED IT MORE THAN ME.
THANKS, EH, BART! I'LL NEVER, AH, FORGET THIS AS LONG AS I LIVE.
I'LL PAY YOU BACK SOMEDAY, I PROMISE.

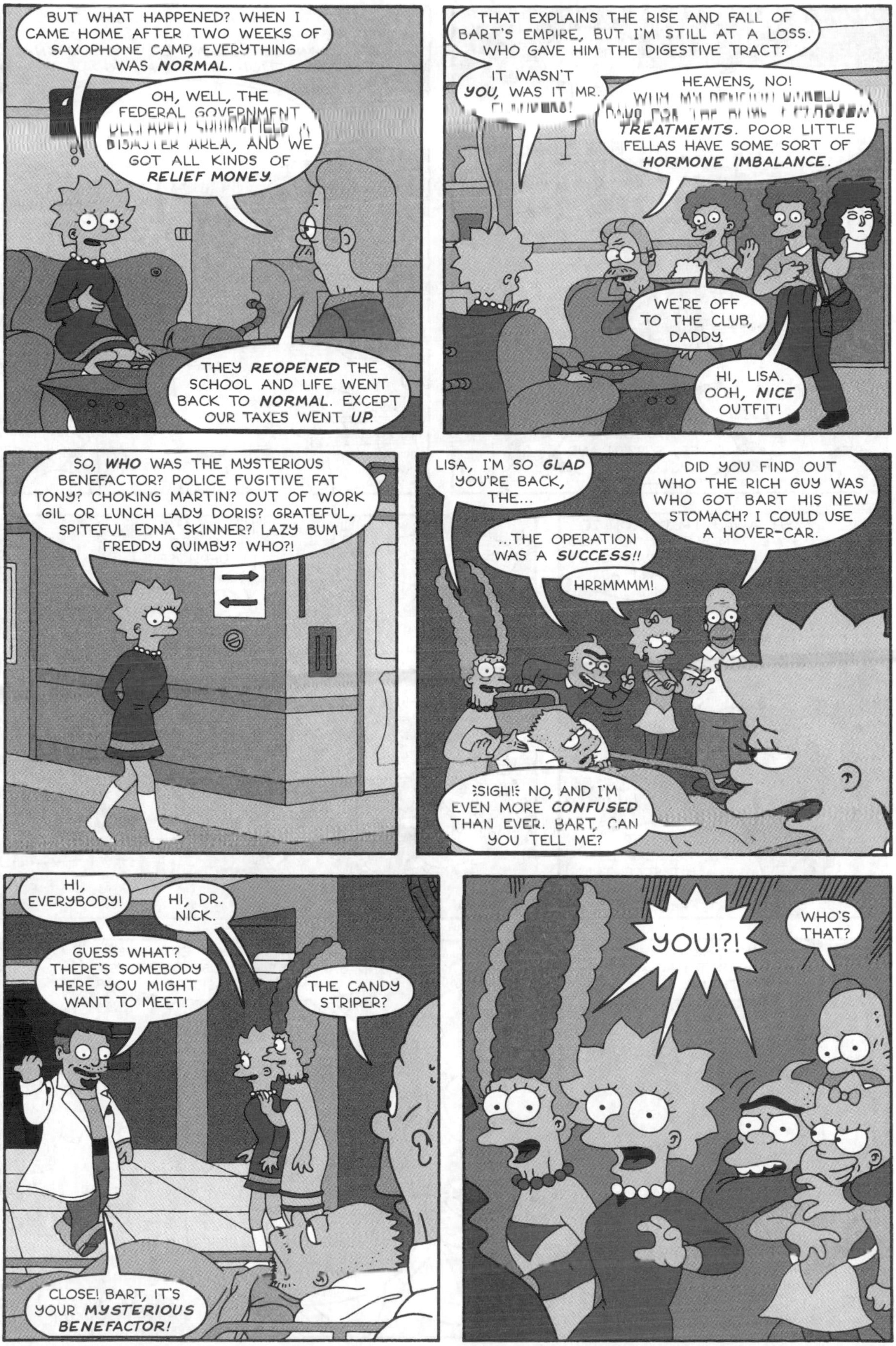

BUT WHAT HAPPENED? WHEN I CAME HOME AFTER TWO WEEKS OF SAXOPHONE CAMP, EVERYTHING WAS **NORMAL**.
OH, WELL, THE FEDERAL GOVERNMENT DISASTER AREA, AND WE GOT ALL KINDS OF **RELIEF MONEY**.
THEY **REOPENED** THE SCHOOL AND LIFE WENT BACK TO **NORMAL**. EXCEPT OUR TAXES WENT **UP**.
THAT EXPLAINS THE RISE AND FALL OF BART'S EMPIRE, BUT I'M STILL AT A LOSS. WHO GAVE HIM THE DIGESTIVE TRACT?
IT WASN'T **YOU**, WAS IT MR.
HEAVENS, NO!
TREATMENTS. POOR LITTLE FELLAS HAVE SOME SORT OF **HORMONE IMBALANCE**.
WE'RE OFF TO THE CLUB, DADDY.
HI, LISA. OOH, **NICE** OUTFIT!
SO, **WHO** WAS THE MYSTERIOUS BENEFACTOR? POLICE FUGITIVE FAT TONY? CHOKING MARTIN? OUT OF WORK GIL OR LUNCH LADY DORIS? GRATEFUL, SPITEFUL EDNA SKINNER? LAZY BUM FREDDY QUIMBY? WHO?!
LISA, I'M SO **GLAD** YOU'RE BACK, THE...
...THE OPERATION WAS A **SUCCESS!!**
HRRMMMM!
DID YOU FIND OUT WHO THE RICH GUY WAS WHO GOT BART HIS NEW STOMACH? I COULD USE A HOVER-CAR.
:SIGH!: NO, AND I'M EVEN MORE **CONFUSED** THAN EVER. BART, CAN YOU TELL ME?
HI, EVERYBODY!
HI, DR. NICK.
GUESS WHAT? THERE'S SOMEBODY HERE YOU MIGHT WANT TO MEET!
THE CANDY STRIPER?
CLOSE! BART, IT'S YOUR **MYSTERIOUS BENEFACTOR!**
YOU!?!
WHO'S THAT?

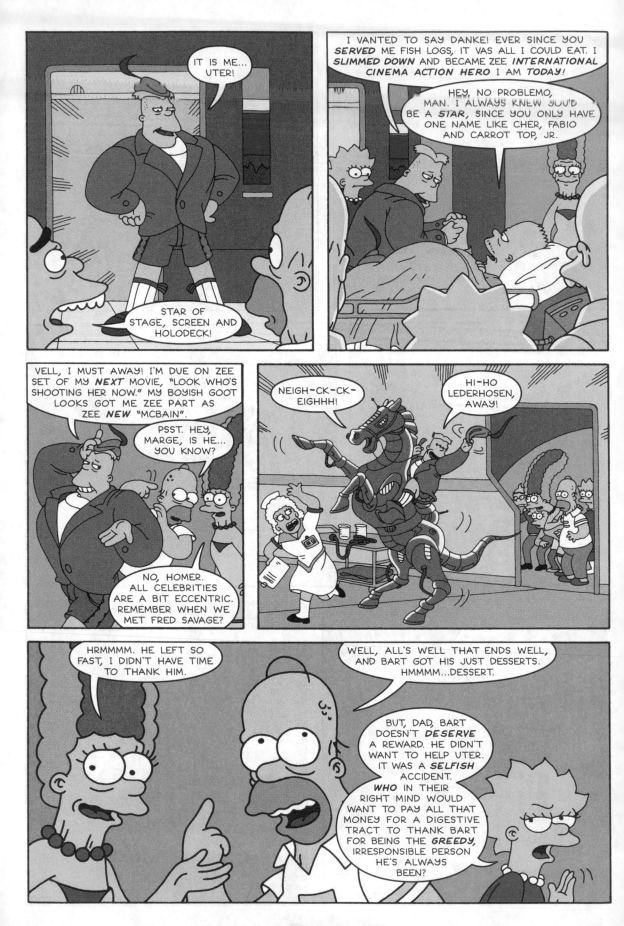

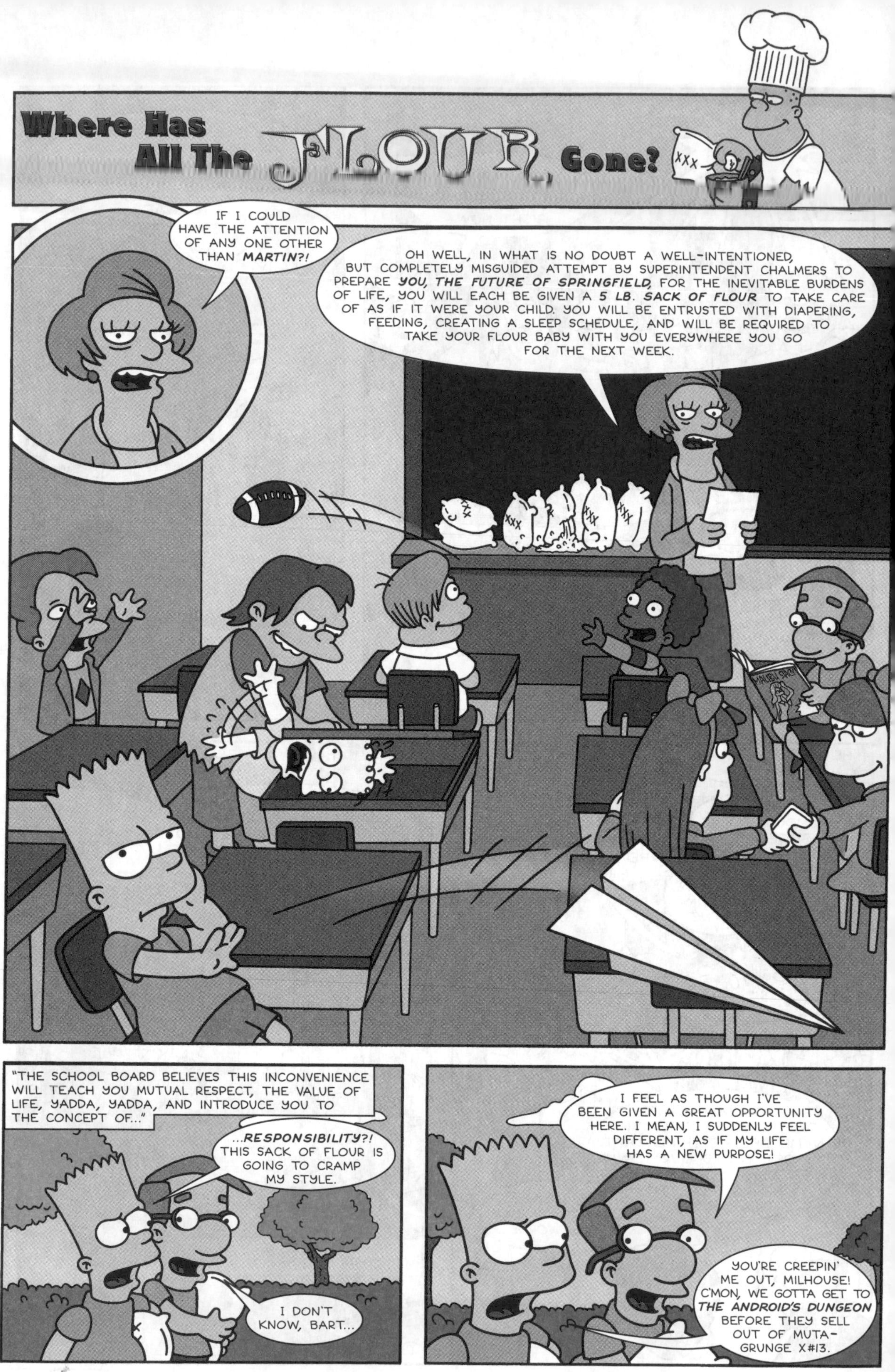
Where Has All The FLOUR Gone?
XXX
IF I COULD HAVE THE ATTENTION OF ANY ONE OTHER THAN MARTIN?!
OH WELL, IN WHAT IS NO DOUBT A WELL-INTENTIONED, BUT COMPLETELY MISGUIDED ATTEMPT BY SUPERINTENDENT CHALMERS TO PREPARE YOU, THE FUTURE OF SPRINGFIELD, FOR THE INEVITABLE BURDENS OF LIFE, YOU WILL EACH BE GIVEN A 5 LB. SACK OF FLOUR TO TAKE CARE OF AS IF IT WERE YOUR CHILD. YOU WILL BE ENTRUSTED WITH DIAPERING, FEEDING, CREATING A SLEEP SCHEDULE, AND WILL BE REQUIRED TO TAKE YOUR FLOUR BABY WITH YOU EVERYWHERE YOU GO FOR THE NEXT WEEK.
"THE SCHOOL BOARD BELIEVES THIS INCONVENIENCE WILL TEACH YOU MUTUAL RESPECT, THE VALUE OF LIFE, YADDA, YADDA, AND INTRODUCE YOU TO THE CONCEPT OF..."
...RESPONSIBILITY?! THIS SACK OF FLOUR IS GOING TO CRAMP MY STYLE.
I DON'T KNOW, BART...
I FEEL AS THOUGH I'VE BEEN GIVEN A GREAT OPPORTUNITY HERE. I MEAN, I SUDDENLY FEEL DIFFERENT, AS IF MY LIFE HAS A NEW PURPOSE!
YOU'RE CREEPIN' ME OUT, MILHOUSE! C'MON, WE GOTTA GET TO THE ANDROID'S DUNGEON BEFORE THEY SELL OUT OF MUTA-GRUNGE X#13.

129

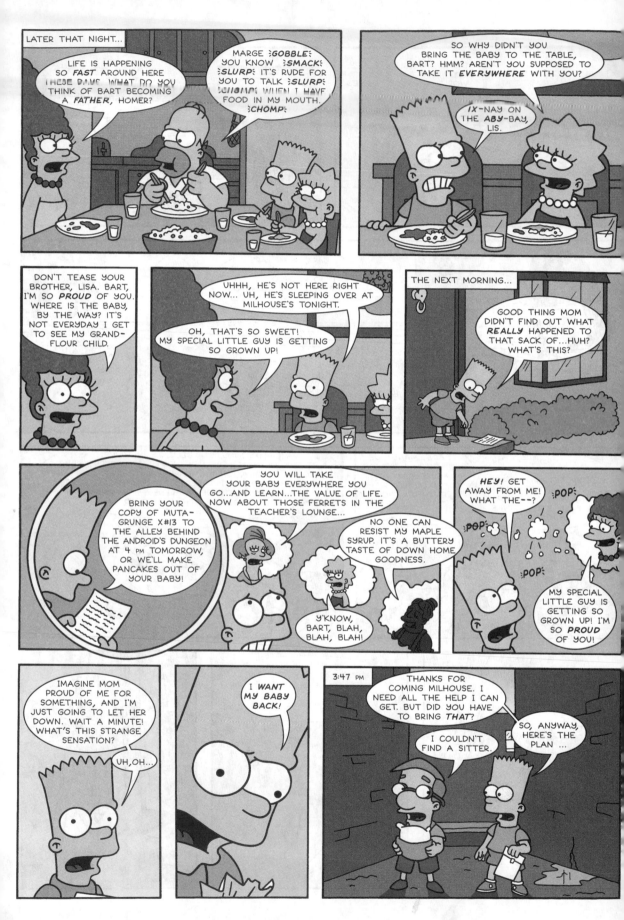

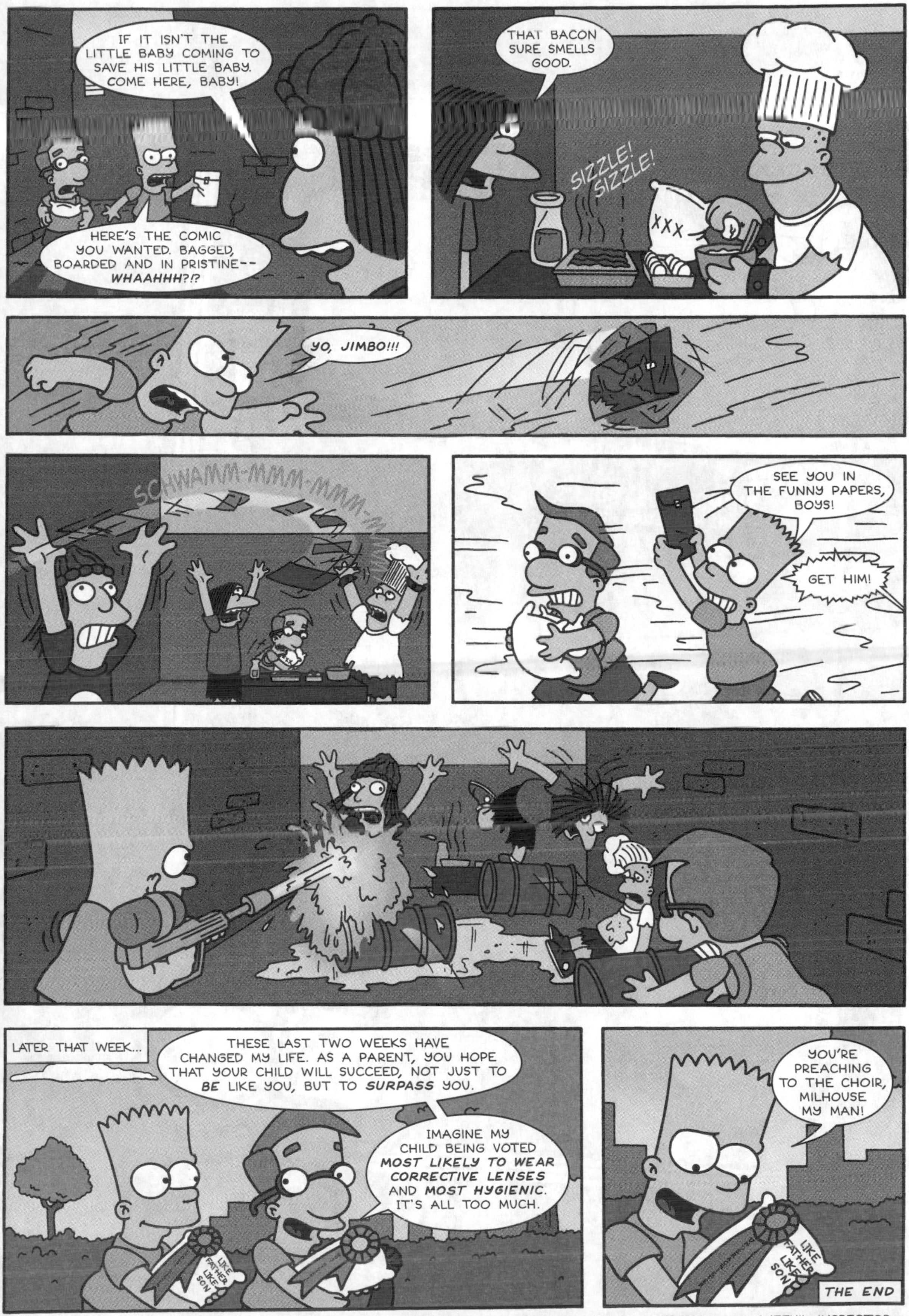
IF IT ISN'T THE LITTLE BABY COMING TO SAVE HIS LITTLE BABY. COME HERE, BABY!
HERE'S THE COMIC YOU WANTED. BAGGED, BOARDED AND IN PRISTINE-- WHAAHHH?!?
THAT BACON SURE SMELLS GOOD.
SIZZLE! SIZZLE!
XXX
YO, JIMBO!!!
SCHWAMM-MMM-MMM-M
SEE YOU IN THE FUNNY PAPERS, BOYS!
GET HIM!
LATER THAT WEEK...
THESE LAST TWO WEEKS HAVE CHANGED MY LIFE. AS A PARENT, YOU HOPE THAT YOUR CHILD WILL SUCCEED, NOT JUST TO BE LIKE YOU, BUT TO SURPASS YOU.
IMAGINE MY CHILD BEING VOTED MOST LIKELY TO WEAR CORRECTIVE LENSES AND MOST HYGIENIC. IT'S ALL TOO MUCH.
LIKE FATHER LIKE SON
YOU'RE PREACHING TO THE CHOIR, MILHOUSE MY MAN!
LIKE FATHER LIKE SON
THE END

STORY TERRY DELEGEANE | PENCILS ERICK TRAN | INKS STEVE STEERE, JR. | LETTERS KAREN BATES | COLORS NATHAN KANE | EDITOR BILL MORRISON | WEEVIL INSPECTOR MATT GROENING

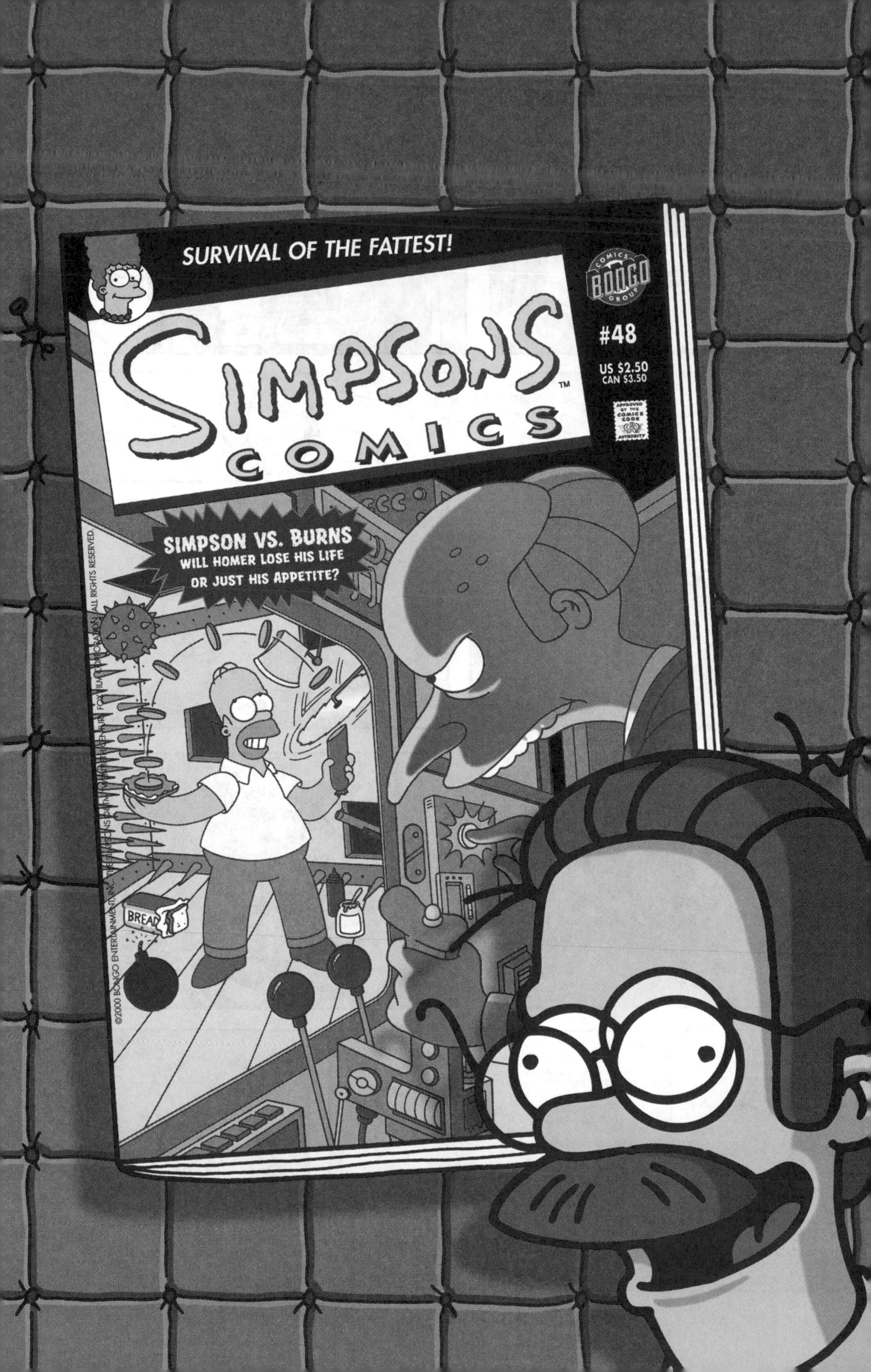
SURVIVAL OF THE FATTEST!
COMICS BONGO GROUP
SIMPSONS™ COMICS
#48
US $2.50
CAN $3.50
APPROVED BY THE COMICS CODE AUTHORITY
SIMPSON VS. BURNS
WILL HOMER LOSE HIS LIFE OR JUST HIS APPETITE?
©2000 BONGO ENTERTAINMENT, INC.
ALL RIGHTS RESERVED.
BREAD

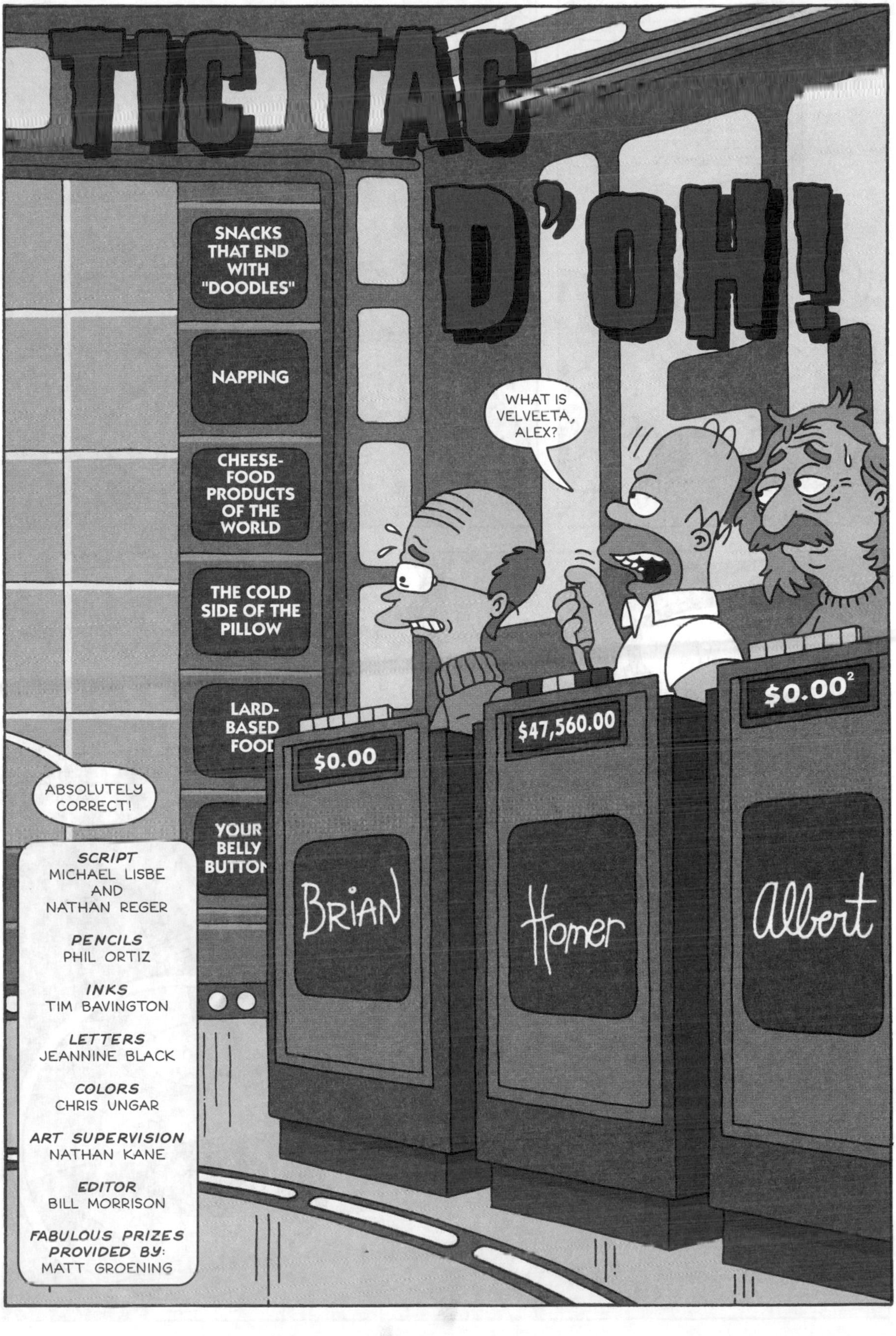

TIC TAC D'OH!
SNACKS THAT END WITH "DOODLES"
NAPPING
CHEESE-FOOD PRODUCTS OF THE WORLD
THE COLD SIDE OF THE PILLOW
LARD-BASED FOOD
YOUR BELLY BUTTON
ABSOLUTELY CORRECT!
WHAT IS VELVEETA, ALEX?
$0.00
$47,560.00
$0.00²
Brian
Homer
Albert
SCRIPT MICHAEL LISBE AND NATHAN REGER
PENCILS PHIL ORTIZ
INKS TIM BAVINGTON
LETTERS JEANNINE BLACK
COLORS CHRIS UNGAR
ART SUPERVISION NATHAN KANE
EDITOR BILL MORRISON
FABULOUS PRIZES PROVIDED BY: MATT GROENING

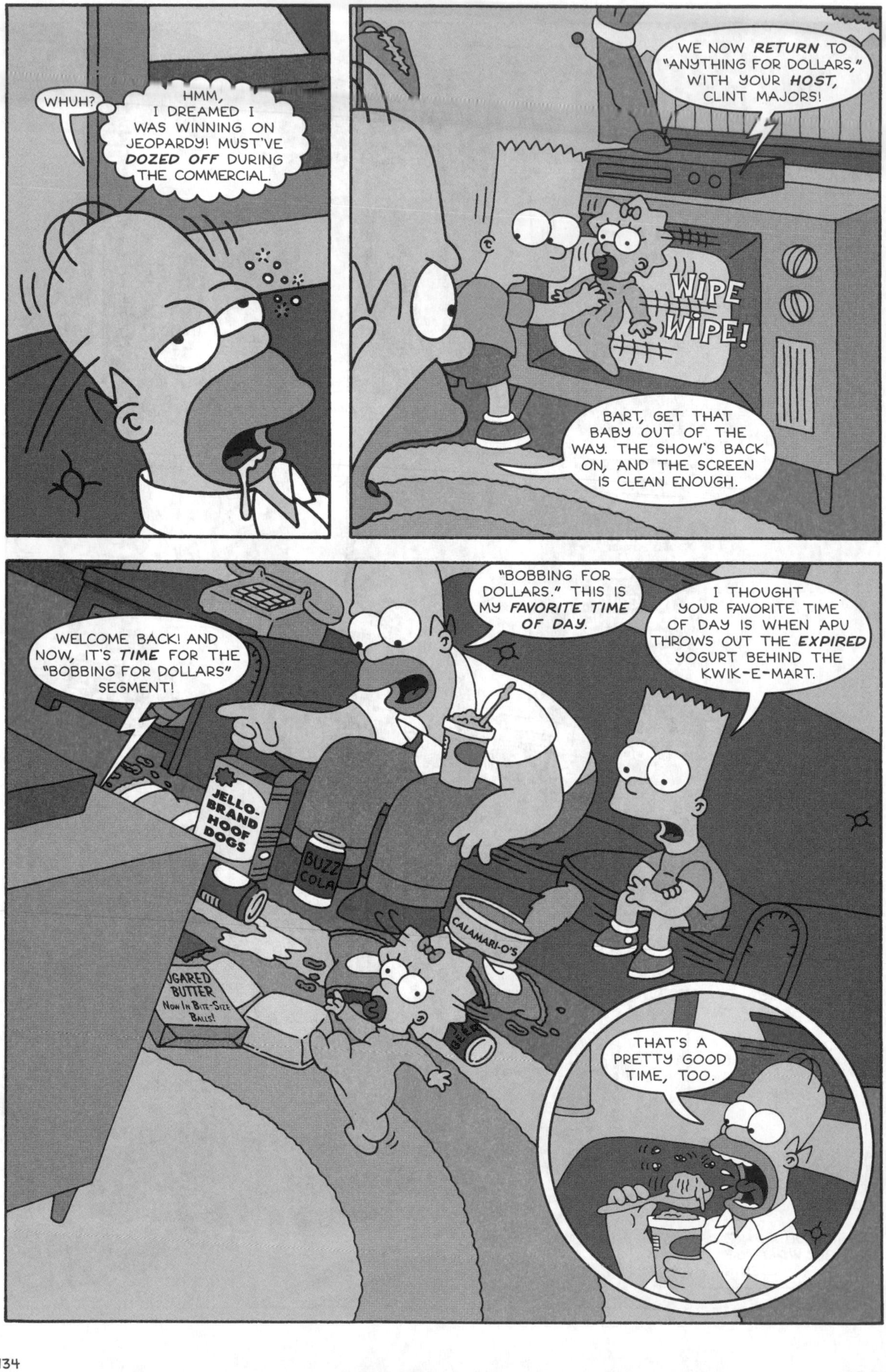
WHUH?
HMM, I DREAMED I WAS WINNING ON JEOPARDY! MUST'VE DOZED OFF DURING THE COMMERCIAL.
WE NOW RETURN TO "ANYTHING FOR DOLLARS," WITH YOUR HOST, CLINT MAJORS!
WIPE WIPE!
BART, GET THAT BABY OUT OF THE WAY. THE SHOW'S BACK ON, AND THE SCREEN IS CLEAN ENOUGH.
WELCOME BACK! AND NOW, IT'S TIME FOR THE "BOBBING FOR DOLLARS" SEGMENT!
"BOBBING FOR DOLLARS." THIS IS MY FAVORITE TIME OF DAY.
I THOUGHT YOUR FAVORITE TIME OF DAY IS WHEN APU THROWS OUT THE EXPIRED YOGURT BEHIND THE KWIK-E-MART.
JELLO-BRAND HOOF DOGS
BUZZ COLA
CALAMARI-O'S
SUGARED BUTTER Now In Bite-Size Balls!
THAT'S A PRETTY GOOD TIME, TOO.

Our second-place contestant will receive a copy of the book *Cooking With Pepper: Salt's Nasty Friend*. Contestants are responsible for their own medical bills. If you'd like to be a contestant on *Anything For Dollars*, send a letter with your original birth certificate, two crisp ten-dollar bills, and a conch shell to Krusty-Lu Studios, P.O. Box 911, Springfield, USA.

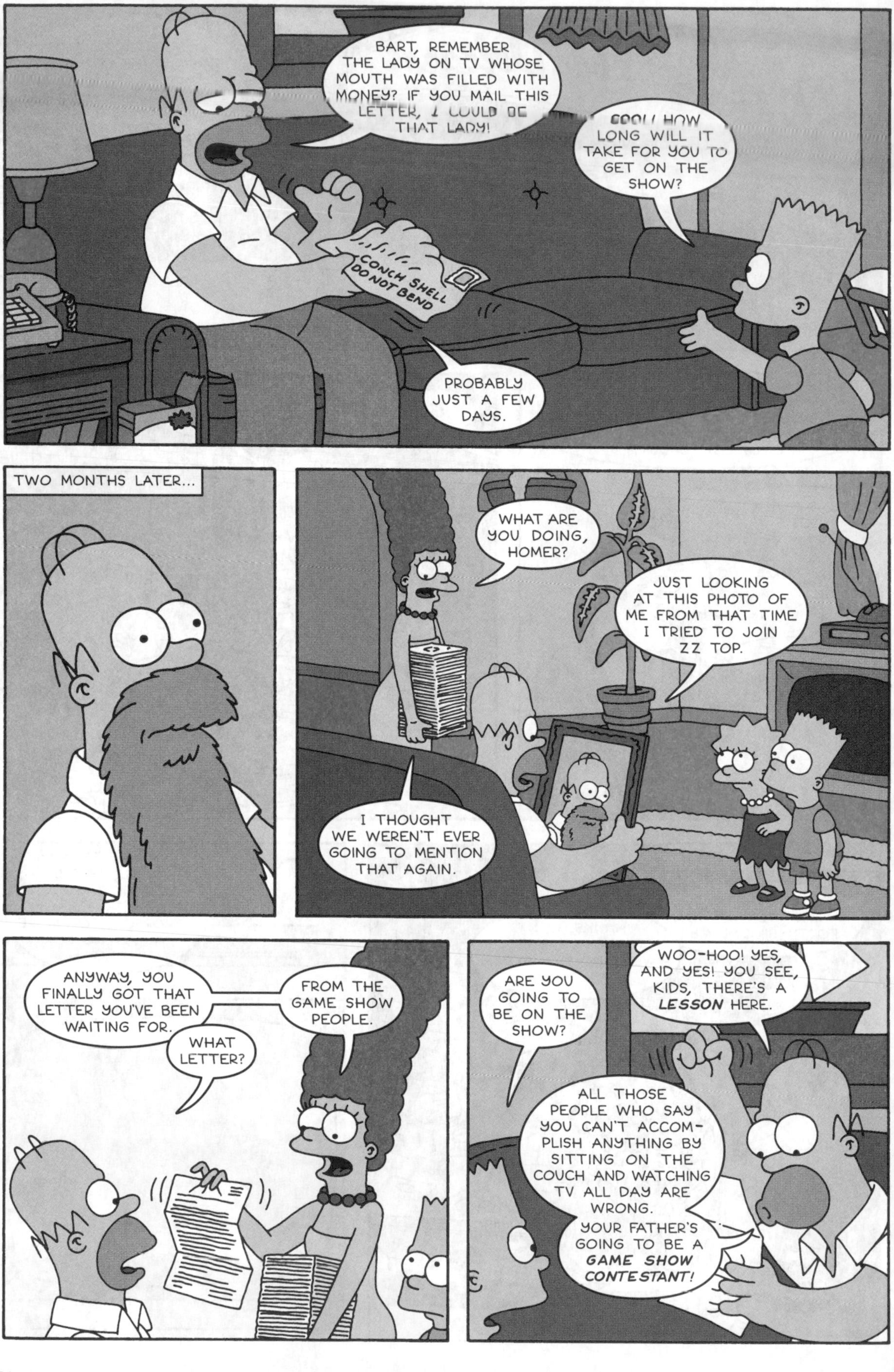
BART, REMEMBER THE LADY ON TV WHOSE MOUTH WAS FILLED WITH MONEY? IF YOU MAIL THIS LETTER, I COULD BE THAT LADY!
CONCH SHELL DO NOT BEND
COOL! HOW LONG WILL IT TAKE FOR YOU TO GET ON THE SHOW?
PROBABLY JUST A FEW DAYS.
TWO MONTHS LATER...
WHAT ARE YOU DOING, HOMER?
JUST LOOKING AT THIS PHOTO OF ME FROM THAT TIME I TRIED TO JOIN ZZ TOP.
I THOUGHT WE WEREN'T EVER GOING TO MENTION THAT AGAIN.
ANYWAY, YOU FINALLY GOT THAT LETTER YOU'VE BEEN WAITING FOR.
FROM THE GAME SHOW PEOPLE.
WHAT LETTER?
ARE YOU GOING TO BE ON THE SHOW?
WOO-HOO! YES, AND YES! YOU SEE, KIDS, THERE'S A ***LESSON*** HERE.
ALL THOSE PEOPLE WHO SAY YOU CAN'T ACCOMPLISH ANYTHING BY SITTING ON THE COUCH AND WATCHING TV ALL DAY ARE WRONG.
YOUR FATHER'S GOING TO BE A ***GAME SHOW CONTESTANT!***

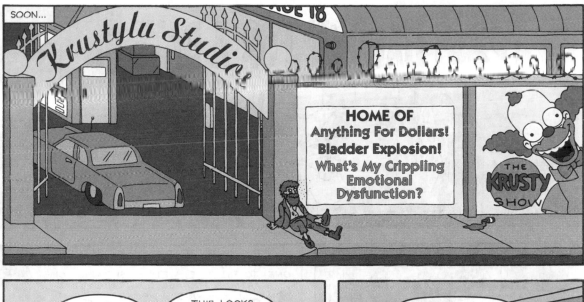

SOON...

Krustylu Studio

HOME OF
Anything For Dollars!
Bladder Explosion!
What's My Crippling
Emotional
Dysfunction?

THE KRUSTY SHOW

DO YOU KNOW WHERE YOU'RE GOING?

THIS LOOKS LIKE A STUDIO DOOR. IT'S PROBABLY IN HERE.

ARE YOU ONE OF THE CONTESTANTS?

YES.

WE'VE BEEN *WAITING* FOR YOU. SIGN THESE FORMS AND FOLLOW ME. YOUR FAMILY CAN GO SIT IN THE AUDIENCE.

GOOD LUCK, HOMER.

STUDIO C

THAT WAS MY WIFE AND KIDS. THEY'RE REALLY *ROOTING* FOR ME TO WIN.

WIFE AND KIDS?!! THEY MUST HAVE A REALLY *OPEN* MARRIAGE!

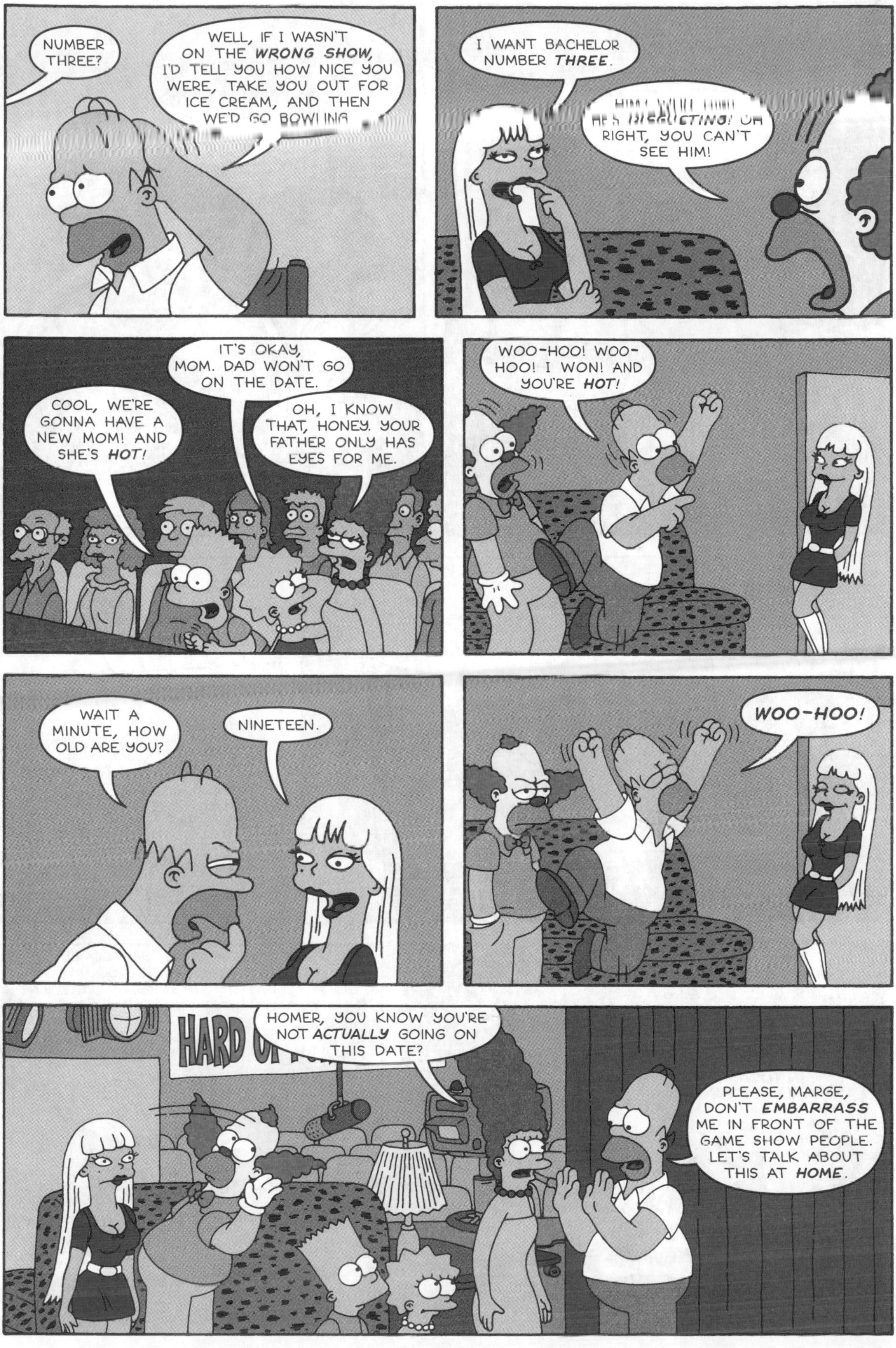
NUMBER THREE?
WELL, IF I WASN'T ON THE *WRONG SHOW,* I'D TELL YOU HOW NICE YOU WERE, TAKE YOU OUT FOR ICE CREAM, AND THEN WE'D GO BOWLING
I WANT BACHELOR NUMBER *THREE*.
RIGHT, YOU CAN'T SEE HIM!
IT'S OKAY, MOM. DAD WON'T GO ON THE DATE.
COOL, WE'RE GONNA HAVE A NEW MOM! AND SHE'S *HOT*!
OH, I KNOW THAT, HONEY. YOUR FATHER ONLY HAS EYES FOR ME.
WOO-HOO! WOO-HOO! I WON! AND YOU'RE *HOT*!
WAIT A MINUTE, HOW OLD ARE YOU?
NINETEEN.
WOO-HOO!
HARD
HOMER, YOU KNOW YOU'RE NOT *ACTUALLY* GOING ON THIS DATE?
PLEASE, MARGE, DON'T *EMBARRASS* ME IN FRONT OF THE GAME SHOW PEOPLE. LET'S TALK ABOUT THIS AT *HOME*.

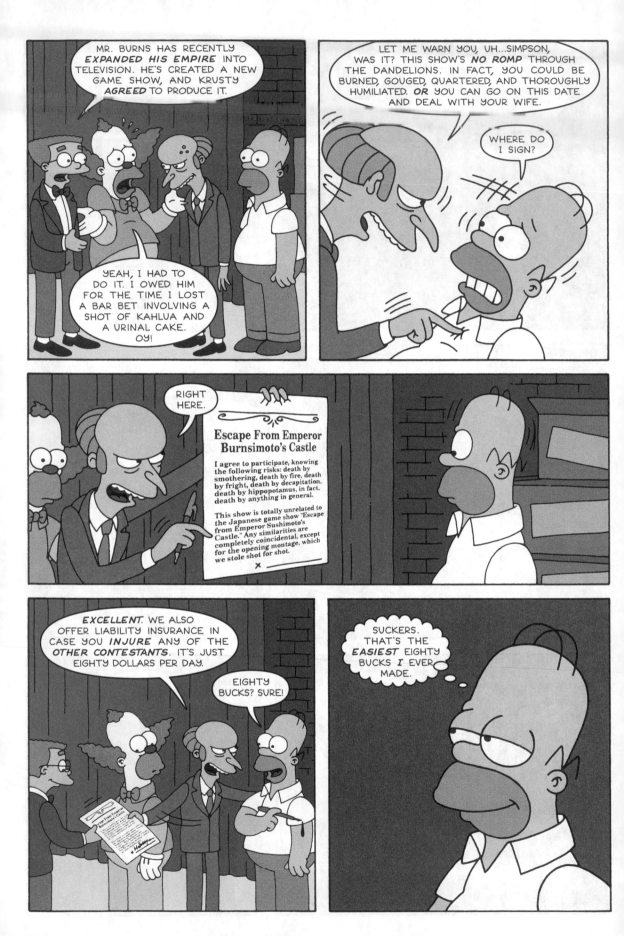

GAME DAY!

HOMER, IT'S FIVE IN THE MORNING.

THEY NEED ME THERE EARLY TO MEASURE ME FOR A COFFIN.

I DON'T KNOW, HOMIE. THIS SOUNDS *DANGEROUS*!

MARGE, MR. BURNS WOULD NEVER PUT ANYONE IN *REAL* DANGER.

THERE'S MY MONOCLE, SMITHERS. A LITTLE TO THE LEFT. NEXT TO THAT IRRA-DIATED ROD.

IT *BURNS*, SIR!

HOMER, I DON'T LIKE THIS. I WANT TO BE THERE IN CASE SOMETHING GOES WRONG.

MARGE, THE RULES SPECIFICALLY STATE THAT NO *NEXT OF KIN* ARE ALLOWED ON THE PREMISES-- SOMETHING ABOUT NO *WITNESSES*.

EVERYTHING IS GOING TO BE FINE, HONEY. WHAT COULD GO *WRONG*? I'VE SEEN EVERY EPISODE OF "TRUTH OR CONSEQUENCES," AND I CAN'T IMAGINE THAT THIS SHOW HAS ANYTHING WORSE THAN WHAT BOB BARKER DISHES OUT.

SOON...

CONTESTANTS. THAT'S ME!

BURNSIMOTO CASTLE

CONTESTANTS

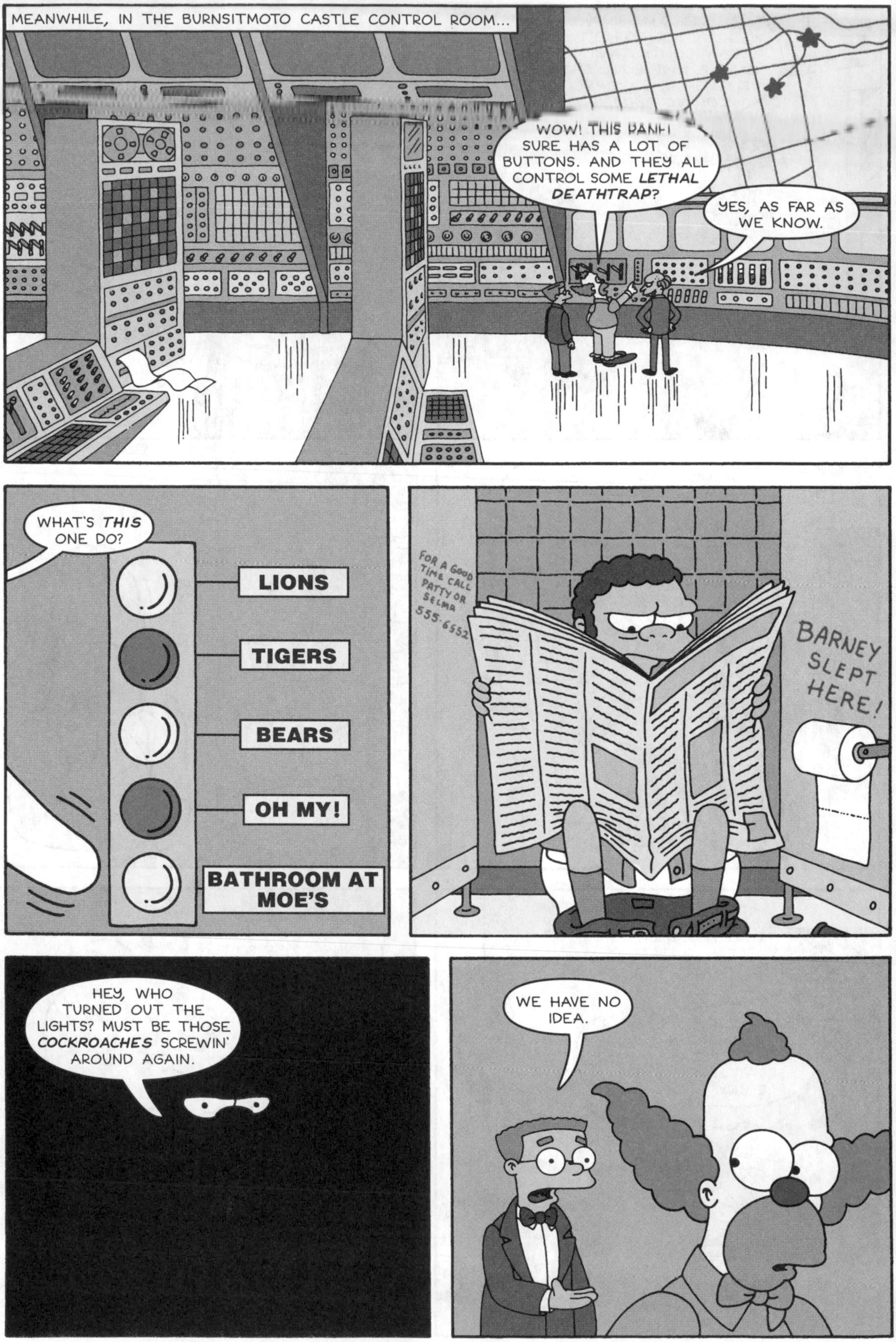

MEANWHILE, IN THE BURNSITMOTO CASTLE CONTROL ROOM...
WOW! THIS PANEL SURE HAS A LOT OF BUTTONS. AND THEY ALL CONTROL SOME *LETHAL DEATHTRAP?*
YES, AS FAR AS WE KNOW.
WHAT'S *THIS* ONE DO?
LIONS
TIGERS
BEARS
OH MY!
BATHROOM AT MOE'S
FOR A GOOD TIME CALL PATTY OR SELMA 555-6552
BARNEY SLEPT HERE!
HEY, WHO TURNED OUT THE LIGHTS? MUST BE THOSE *COCKROACHES* SCREWIN' AROUND AGAIN.
WE HAVE NO IDEA.

THIS IS [???] REPORTING LIVE OUTSIDE OF BURNSIMOTO CASTLE.

THIS GAME SHOW, *BANNED* IN EVERY STATE EXCEPT FOR OUR STATE AND, OF COURSE, UTAH, WILL SOON SEND THREE CONVICTS, TWO MENTAL PATIENTS, A HOMELESS GUY, A CIRCUS FREAK, AND ONE LAZY [???] CONTESTANTS

IN THIS REPORTER'S OPINION, JUST THE TOUCH OF *DARWINISM* OUR SOCIETY *NEEDS*.

OH MY!

MEANWHILE...

THIS IS GONNA BE A PIECE OF CAKE.

BOP!

KLIK!

HMM...

BOP!

KLIK!

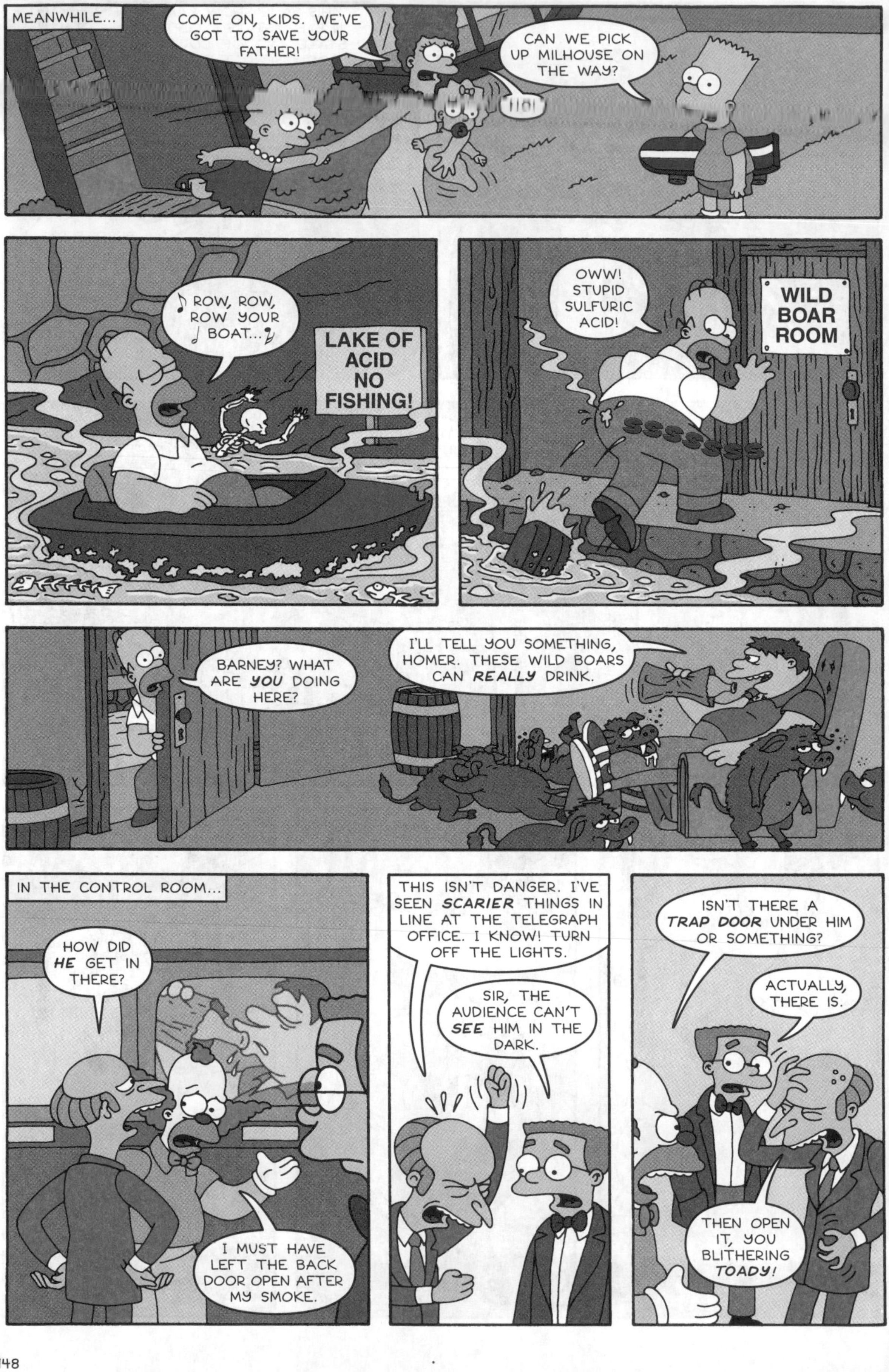

MEANWHILE...
COME ON, KIDS. WE'VE GOT TO SAVE YOUR FATHER!
CAN WE PICK UP MILHOUSE ON THE WAY?
ROW, ROW, ROW YOUR BOAT...
LAKE OF ACID NO FISHING!
OWW! STUPID SULFURIC ACID!
WILD BOAR ROOM
SSSSSSSS
BARNEY? WHAT ARE YOU DOING HERE?
I'LL TELL YOU SOMETHING, HOMER. THESE WILD BOARS CAN REALLY DRINK.
IN THE CONTROL ROOM...
HOW DID HE GET IN THERE?
I MUST HAVE LEFT THE BACK DOOR OPEN AFTER MY SMOKE.
THIS ISN'T DANGER. I'VE SEEN SCARIER THINGS IN LINE AT THE TELEGRAPH OFFICE. I KNOW! TURN OFF THE LIGHTS.
SIR, THE AUDIENCE CAN'T SEE HIM IN THE DARK.
ISN'T THERE A TRAP DOOR UNDER HIM OR SOMETHING?
ACTUALLY, THERE IS.
THEN OPEN IT, YOU BLITHERING TOADY!

D'OHHHHHHHHHH!

CLICK!

FWWWUMP!

HEE, HEE!

LICK!

LICK!

MEANWHILE...

BURNSIMOTO CASTLE 5 MILES

BACK IN THE CONTROL ROOM...

I *TOLD* YOU THAT WOULDN'T WORK!

UH, KRUSTY, IF YOU RECALL, MR. BURNS' *ORIGINAL* PLAN CALLED FOR THE CONTEST-ANTS TO BE DRESSED IN A RUBBER CHEW-TOY SUIT AND DIPPED IN STEAK SAUCE.

I'LL HAVE YOU KNOW, KRUSTY, MY AUNTIE WAS *EATEN ALIVE* BY A ROVING BAND OF *PUPPIES* DURING THE LEAN YEARS OF THE HOOVER ADMINISTRATION. DON'T TELL *ME* WHAT WORKS AND WHAT DOESN'T.

THIS IS RIDICULOUS! SMITHERS, LET ME TAKE A LOOK AT THOSE BUTTONS. WE NEED ONE THAT WILL REALLY COOK HIS GOOSE.

WELL, UNLESS YOU'VE GOT A *VODKA* BUTTON, I'LL BE BACK IN FIFTEEN MINUTES.

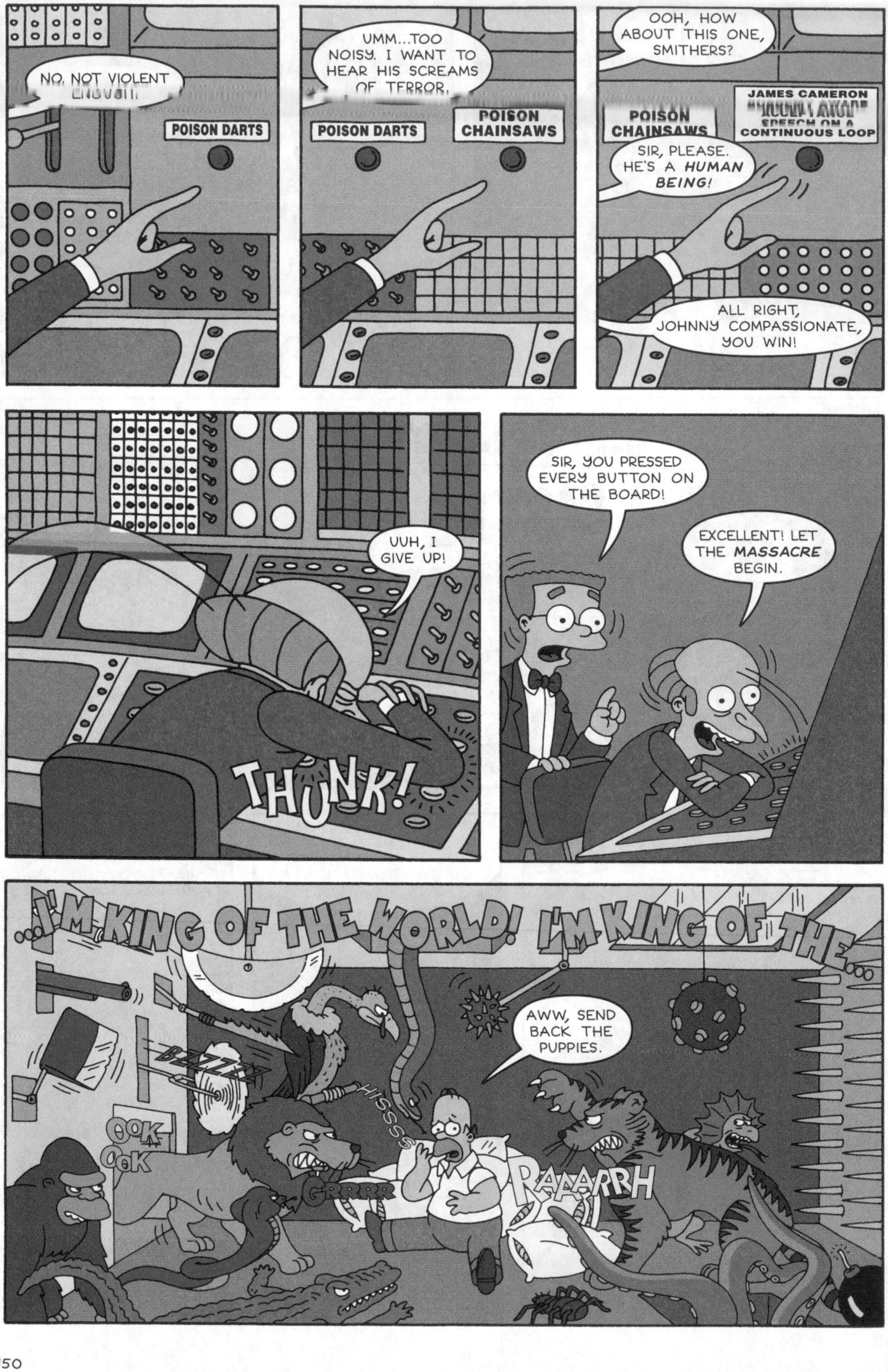

NO, NOT VIOLENT
POISON DARTS
UMM...TOO NOISY. I WANT TO HEAR HIS SCREAMS OF TERROR.
POISON DARTS
POISON CHAINSAWS
OOH, HOW ABOUT THIS ONE, SMITHERS?
POISON CHAINSAWS
JAMES CAMERON
SPEECH ON A CONTINUOUS LOOP
SIR, PLEASE. HE'S A *HUMAN BEING!*
ALL RIGHT, JOHNNY COMPASSIONATE, YOU WIN!
UUH, I GIVE UP!
THUNK!
SIR, YOU PRESSED EVERY BUTTON ON THE BOARD!
EXCELLENT! LET THE *MASSACRE* BEGIN.
...I'M KING OF THE WORLD! I'M KING OF THE...
BZZZT
HISSSS
AWW, SEND BACK THE PUPPIES.
OOK OOK
GRRRRR
RAAARRH

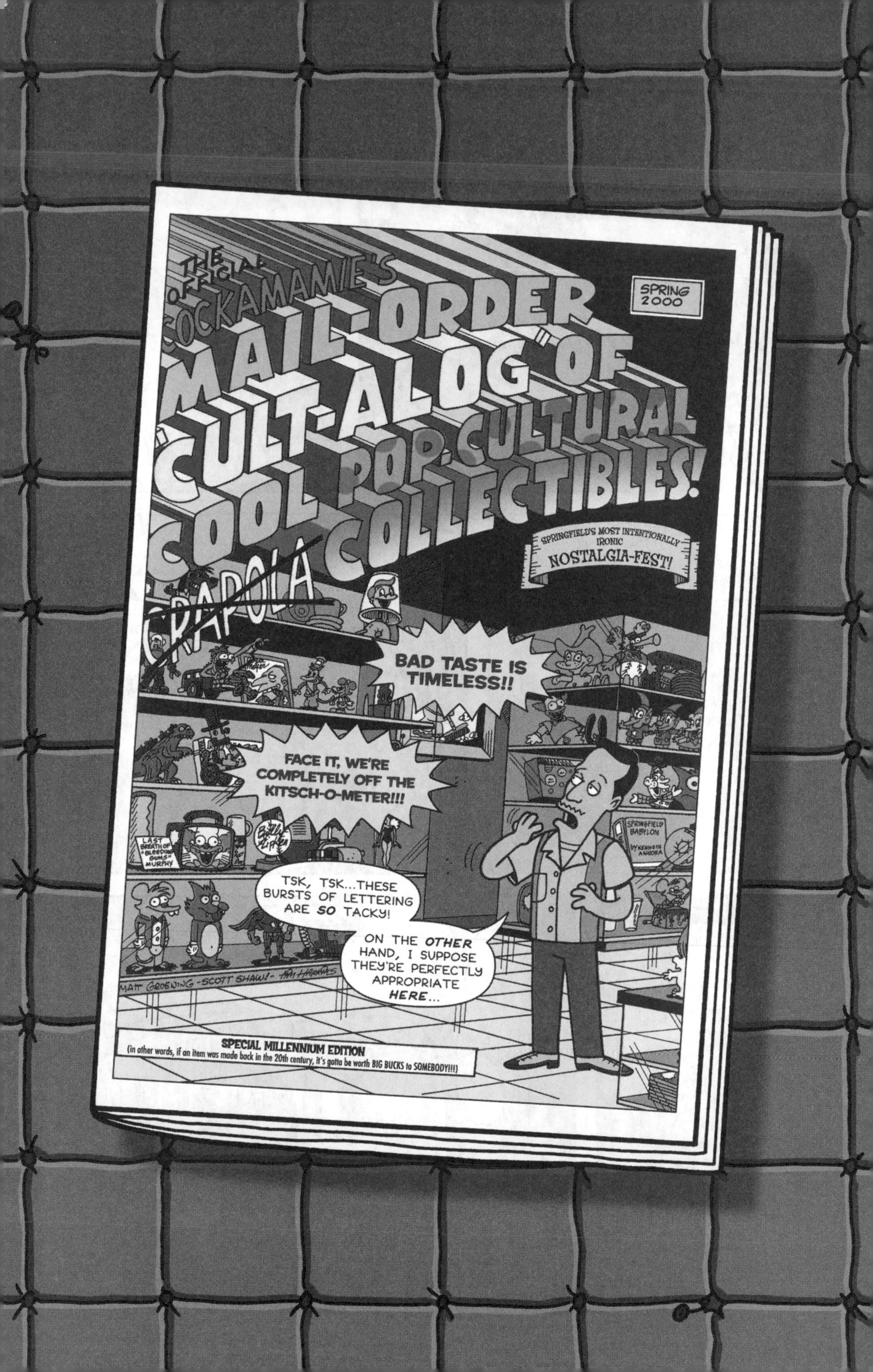
THE OFFICIAL
COCKAMAMIE'S
MAIL-ORDER
"CULT-ALOG" OF
COOL POP-CULTURAL
CRAPOLA
COLLECTIBLES!
SPRING 2000
SPRINGFIELD'S MOST INTENTIONALLY IRONIC NOSTALGIA-FEST!
BAD TASTE IS TIMELESS!!
FACE IT, WE'RE COMPLETELY OFF THE KITSCH-O-METER!!!
LAST BREATH OF "BLEEDING GUMS" MURPHY
SPRINGFIELD BABYLON by KENNETH ANGORA
TSK, TSK...THESE BURSTS OF LETTERING ARE SO TACKY!
ON THE OTHER HAND, I SUPPOSE THEY'RE PERFECTLY APPROPRIATE HERE...
MATT GROENING - SCOTT SHAW! -
SPECIAL MILLENNIUM EDITION
(in other words, if an item was made back in the 20th century, it's gotta be worth BIG BUCKS to SOMEBODY!!!)

HELLO, I'M *JOHN*, THE OWNER AND MANAGER OF *COCKAMAMIE'S* COLLECTIBLE SHOP!

COCKAMAMIE'S MAIL ORDER "CULT-ALOG" OF COOL POP-CULTURAL CRAPOLA...ER, COLLECTIBLES, OUR LATEST COLLECTOR'S CATALOG, CHOCK-FULL OF THINGS THAT ARE EITHER *TRAGICALLY LUDICROUS* OR *LUDICROUSLY TRAGIC!*

WRITTEN AND DRAWN BY SCOTT SHAW!	INKED BY TIM HARKINS	COLORED BY CHRIS UNGAR	LETTERED BY KAREN BATES	EDITED BY BILL MORRISON	NIGHT WATCHMAN MATT GROENING

DIE-CAST "SCHLOCK WHEELS" CAR

NEW FOR 1991! SCHLOCK WHEELS

1991 "The Homer" 1/64 scale

$19.95

LIMITED EDITION!

Just as the short-lived "Homer" automobile was responsible for the corporate failure of its manufacturer, Powell Motors, this 1/64th scale auto was responsible for the sudden collapse of ITS parent factory!

Mint condition on card.

"THE HAPPY LITTLE ELVES" INSECT HABITARIUM

$12.95

What could possibly make the Happy Little Elves even HAPPIER? Their very own INSECT ZOO! (The unfortunate elf-to-bug SIZE RATIO make for a delightfully SICK tableau!) We'll even throw in the insects at no extra charge! Fine condition.

UNCIRCULATED "POOCHIE THE ROCKIN' DOG" ITEMS

For the lot: $1.98 (or best offer)

(COMPLETE WITH TEST-MARKET DISPLAY!)

SPECIAL WAREHOUSE FIND!

HEY KIDS! DIG IT! WHOA!

As you may recall, Poochie died on the way back to his home planet, (so they say), but fortunately for us, he left these great prototype products in his wake (including OFFICIAL POOCHIE CORNCOB HOLDERS, OFFICIAL POOCHIE FLY-PAPER and THE OFFICIAL POOCHIE PROGRAMMABLE BOOMERANG-WITH-A-BRAIN), all of which went undistributed. Absolutely untouched. Mint condition in display.

DIRK "RADIOACTIVE MAN" RICHTER

TO MARK! WITH 1,000-ROENTGEN REGARDS, DIRK RICHTER

$74.95

Autographed "To MARK, with 1,000-roentgen regards, DIRK RICHTER." This rare item is an absolute MUST for any SERIOUS Radioactive Man collector especially if your name is "MARK"!)

Fine condition.

"LARD LAD" PLASTIC COIN BANK AND PETROLEUM GEL DISPENSER

Grease my palm with $24.95 and it's yours!

$ $ $

It's a plastic COIN BANK! (You can "feed" his doughnut!) It's a PETROLEUM GEL DISPENSER! (Just rub his hairdo for a blast of hygenic goo!) It's two totally dissimilar items in one! (Also available in GLAZED, RAINBOW-SPRINKLED and BEEF TALLOW models.)

Slick condition.

"MALIBU STACY'S" HAWAIIAN TIMESHARE CONDO

SWEATY PALMS BEACH CONDOS

VACANCY

$49.95

This hot-pink paradise, manufactured by the Petrochem Petrochemical Corporation, features a lanai, a hot tub, beach access, a working miniature piña colada blender, and a never-ending sales pitch seminar. (Malibu Stacy NOT included.) Fine condition.

"KRUSTY THE CLOWN" KEYHOLE CAMERA

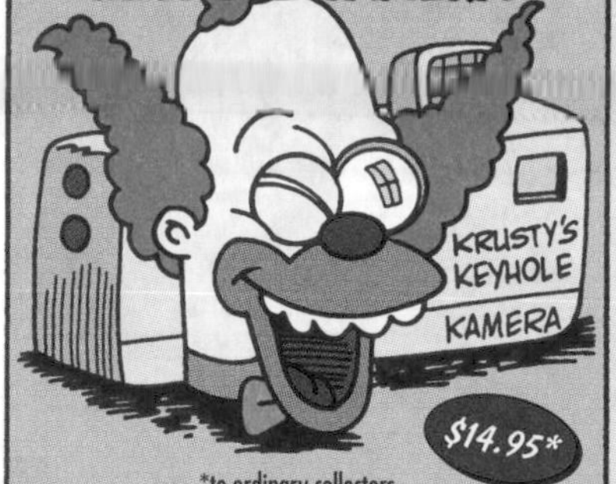

KRUSTY'S KEYHOLE KAMERA
$14.95*

*to ordinary collectors
($1495.00 to Mayor "Diamond Joe" Quimby)

Not many of these have survived over the years, since most of them were destroyed by irate parents and neighbors, especially whenever Mom and Dad were getting frisky! And it includes an undeveloped roll of film! Who knows WHOSE pictures are on that film, possibly even Mayor "Diamond Joe" Quimby, whose nephew Freddie is rumored to be it's original owner!

Very fine condition.

"McBAIN" EXPLODING FOREIGN EMBASSY PLAYSET

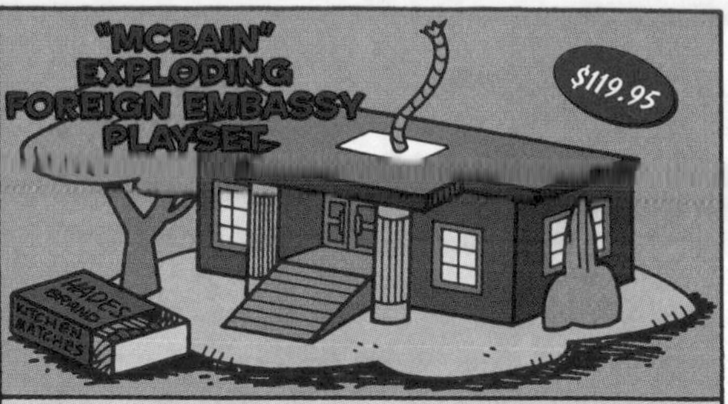

$119.95
HADES BRAND KITCHEN MATCHES

Complete in the box, this was concurrently issued to tie in with the feature film, "McBAIN III: A Big Honkin' Line in the Sand," starring Rainier Wolfcastle. Magnesium fuse and box of official "McBain" kitchen matches included! Mint condition (for the time being…)

"ITCHY AND SCRATCHY" LAWN DARTS

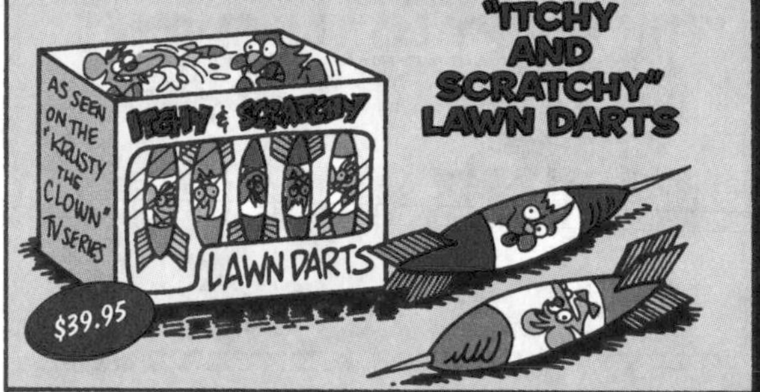

AS SEEN ON THE "KRUSTY THE CLOWN" TV SERIES
ITCHY & SCRATCHY
LAWN DARTS
$39.95

These are EXTREMELY RARE items (inexplicably pulled from the toy shelves by some pesky parents' group). Aside from some minor red stains, these are in very fine condition.

"ITCHY AND SCRATCHY" FIRST AID KIT

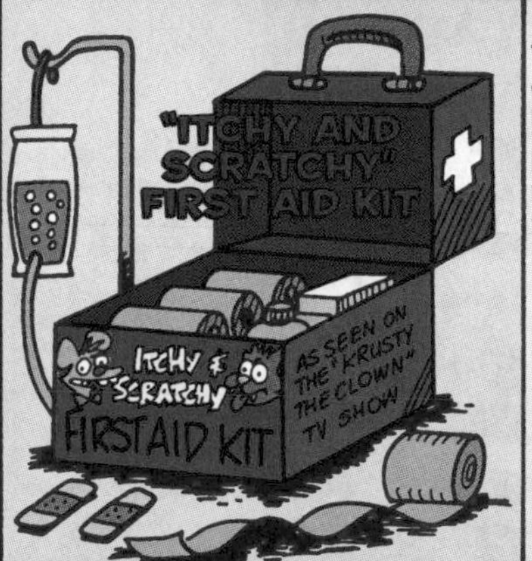

ITCHY & SCRATCHY
FIRST AID KIT
AS SEEN ON THE "KRUSTY THE CLOWN" TV SHOW

This medical kit comes with antiseptic, bandages, "pretend" painkillers and everything else needed to treat those pesky PUNCTURE WOUNDS!

Very good condition.

$69.95

"ITCHY AND SCRATCHY" HOME TAXIDERMY SET

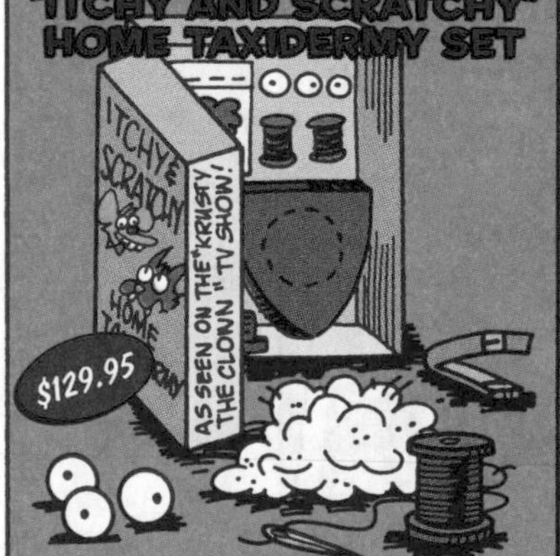

ITCHY & SCRATCHY
AS SEEN ON THE "KRUSTY THE CLOWN" TV SHOW!
$129.95

This unusual item was marketed in the happenstance that the use of the Itchy and Scratchy First Aid Kit wasn't nearly as effective as originally expected. Complete with plenty of kapok stuffing, spools of high-test sewing thread, and an industrial-strength staple gun.

Mint condition.

"TRUCKASAURUS" MODEL

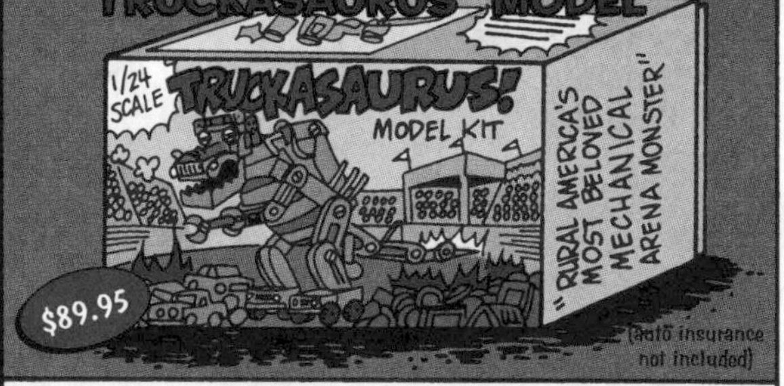

1/24 SCALE
TRUCKASAURUS!
MODEL KIT
"RURAL AMERICA'S MOST BELOVED MECHANICAL ARENA MONSTER"
$89.95
(auto insurance not included)

This 1/24th scale model of rural America's favorite scrapheap behemoth is still mint in its box! (Which is probably where you'd be better off keeping it, unless you don't mind seeing Truckasaurus EAT the rest of the vintage model cars in your collection!)

LURLEEN LUMPKIN COUNTRY-WESTERN DEMO RECORDINGS

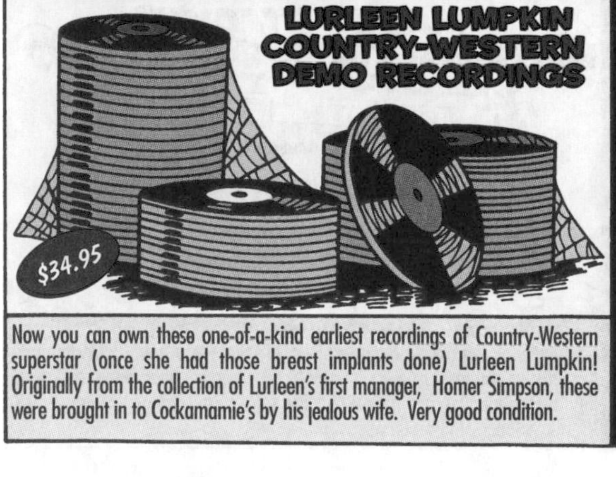

$34.95

Now you can own these one-of-a-kind earliest recordings of Country-Western superstar (once she had those breast implants done) Lurleen Lumpkin! Originally from the collection of Lurleen's first manager, Homer Simpson, these were brought in to Cockamamie's by his jealous wife. Very good condition.

DENIM JACKET

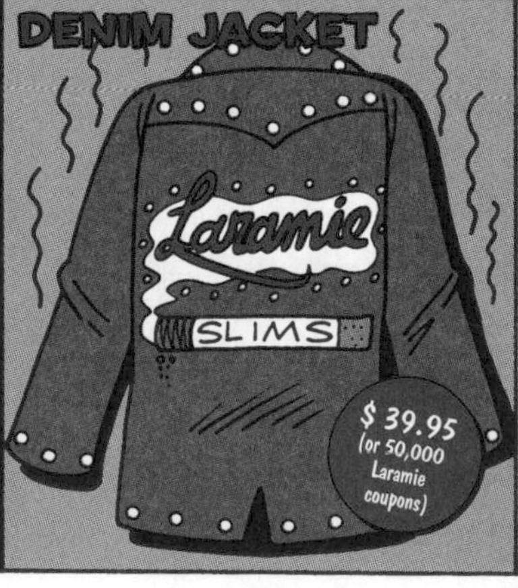

Laramie
SLIMS
$ 39.95 (or 50,000 Laramie coupons)

We picked up this item at an estate sale. It was worn only once by its original owner (before she checked into the hospital), a heavy smoker of Laramie Slims cigarettes! The jacket still stinks of cigarettes, otherwise it's in mint condition.

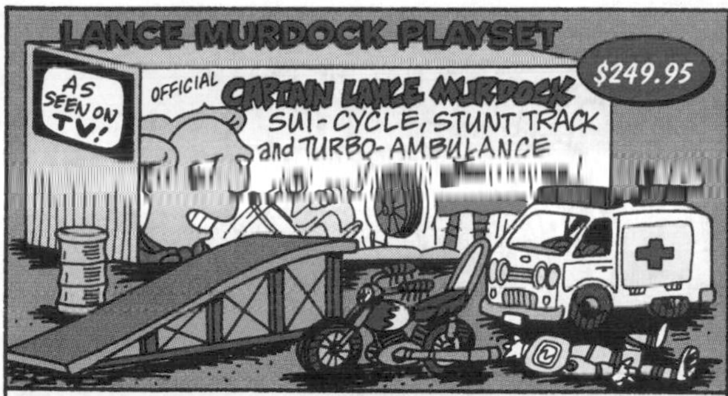
LANCE MURDOCK PLAYSET
$249.95
AS SEEN ON TV!
OFFICIAL
CAPTAIN LANCE MURDOCK
SUI-CYCLE, STUNT TRACK and TURBO-AMBULANCE

Who doesn't remember motorcycle daredevil Captain Lance Murdock? (Except, of course, Murdock himself, who's suffered amnesia ever since his last cycle-stunt went so horribly wrong...). This exciting set is in mint condition, except for the Lance Murdock action figure (which is in somewhat poor condition).

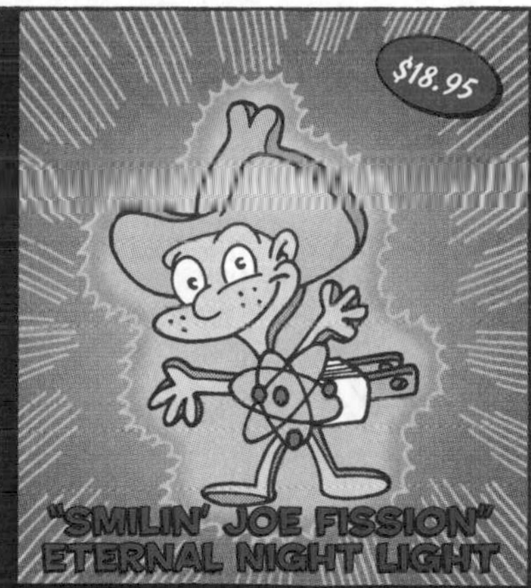
$18.95
"SMILIN' JOE FISSION" ETERNAL NIGHT LIGHT

Molded in the distinctive shape of everyone's favorite nuclear spokes-character, this little beauty will brighten up your collectibles cabinet – no electricity required! (Cockamamie's denies any responsibility for radiation burns or genetic mutations.)

Glowingly bright mint condition.

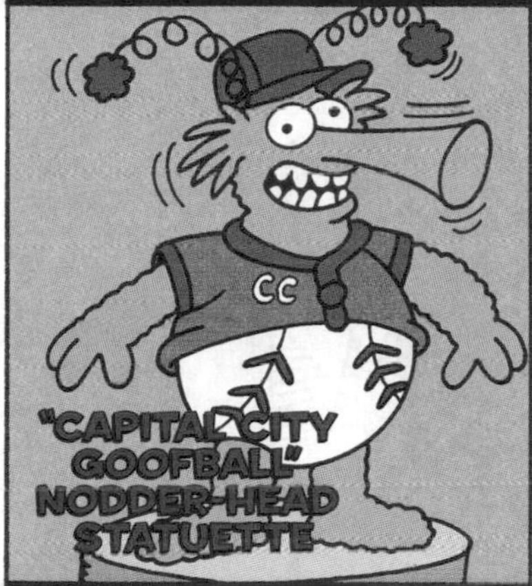
CC
"CAPITAL CITY GOOFBALL" NODDER-HEAD STATUETTE

Personally, the appeal of organized sports completely eludes me but this mint condition mascot's constantly wobbling cranium will provide hours of fun for any and all, baseball fans or not! Why, it's almost HYPNOTIC! You are getting s l e e p y ... s l e e p y ...you will send me--

$29.95

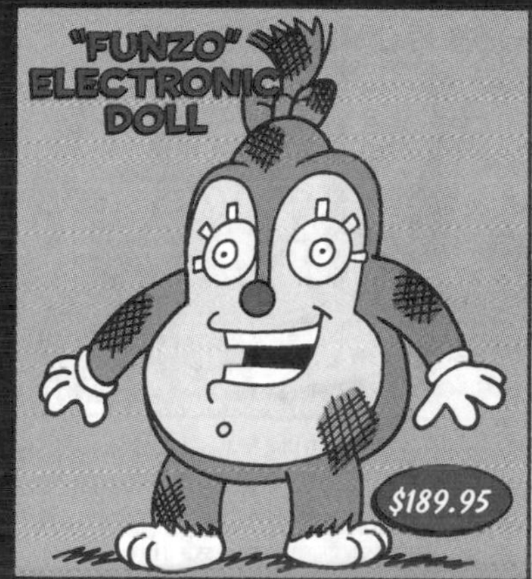
"FUNZO" ELECTRONIC DOLL
$189.95

"ALL-RIGHTY!" This is believed to be the last semi-intact interactive "FUNZO" doll to survive its frenzied, but mercifully short craze! Get him before he gets YOU! Slightly fire-damaged, so I can't grade it higher than "good" condition.

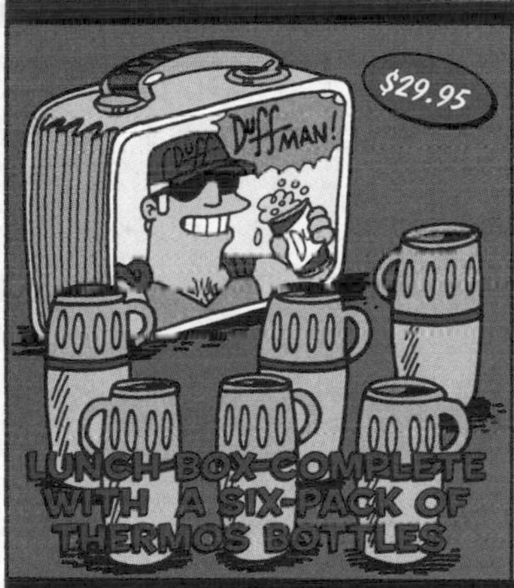
$29.95
DUFF
Duff MAN!
LUNCH-BOX COMPLETE WITH A SIX-PACK OF THERMOS BOTTLES

This brightly lithographed metal lunch box features Duff Man, the overly-familiar beer-swilling superhero used to publicize Duff Beer back in the '70's. (Attention, Barney Gumble – we know you're out there; this box fairly cries out for YOU!)

Very fine condition (at least, to bloodshot, bleary eyes.)

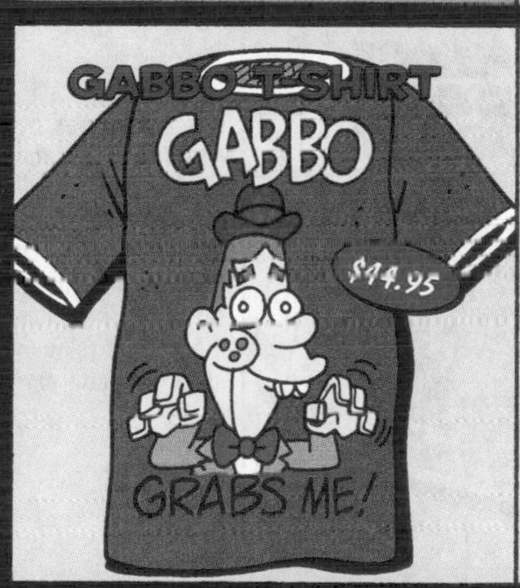
GABBO T-SHIRT
GABBO
$14.95
GRABS ME!

"Wooden" it be nice to own this colorful item? Here's a nostalgic reminder of Springfield's brief affair with has-been ventriloquist Arthur Crandall's lovable dummy, "GABBO."

Good condition, with slight splintering.

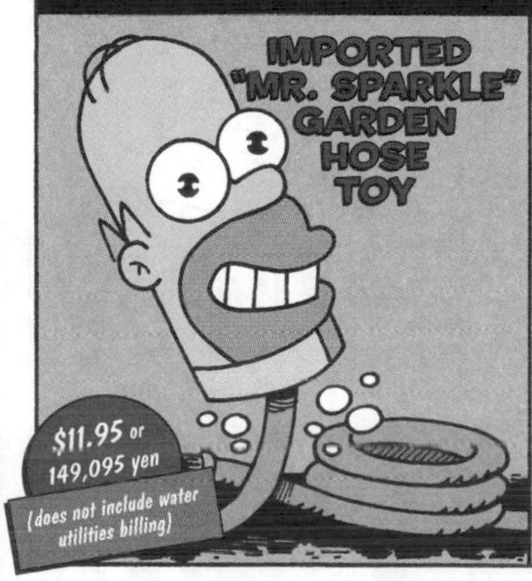
IMPORTED "MR. SPARKLE" GARDEN HOSE TOY
$11.95 or 149,095 yen
(does not include water utilities billing)

Look out, straight from Japan, here comes that disrespecter of uncleanliness, Mr. Sparkle (or at least a fairly faithful approximation of the honorable one!) Just hook him up, turn on the faucet and watch Mr. Sparkle "take a bite out of grime!"

Very, very, very, VERY clean condition, mint-plus, even! (Sheesh!)

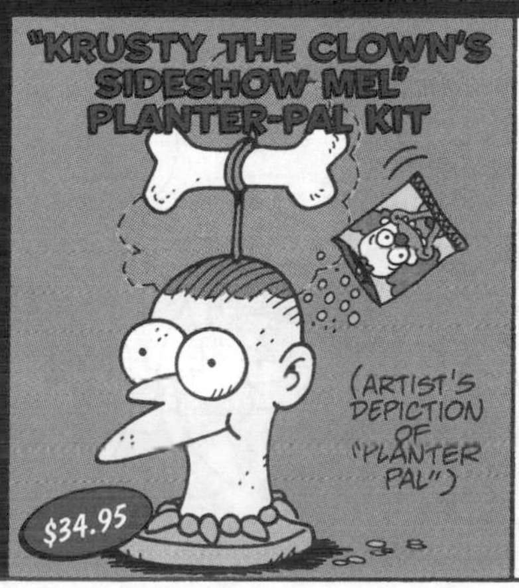
"KRUSTY THE CLOWN'S SIDESHOW MEL" PLANTER-PAL KIT
(ARTIST'S DEPICTION OF "PLANTER PAL")
$34.95

Remember that familiar slogan, "Hey, kids, create lots of far-out hairstyles for Sideshow Mel!"? These hydroponic planters haven't been seen since the mid-1980's, when it was discovered that the seeds included in the kits were of the Cannabis sativa variety. Mint condition, in box.

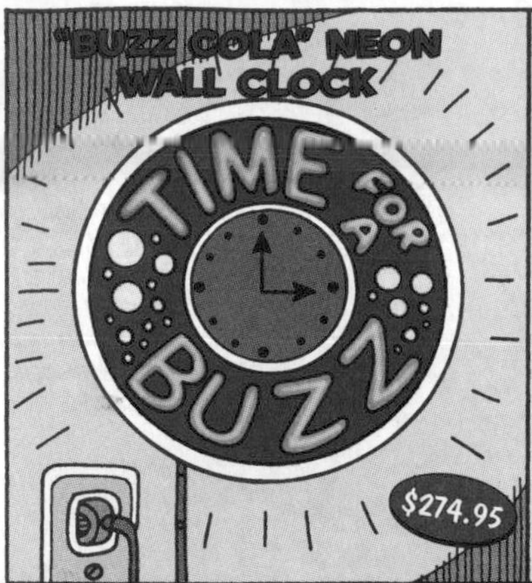
"BUZZ COLA" NEON WALL CLOCK
TIME FOR A BUZZ
$274.95

Straight out of a 1950's malt shop, this nifty wall clock is trés cool, daddy-O! It DOES run a little fast…like 10 times the normal rate! (And why not? It WAS created to advertise the soda with "all the caffeine and twice the sugar!") Hand movement is a bit shaky (no surprise there), but the clock's overall condition is very fine.

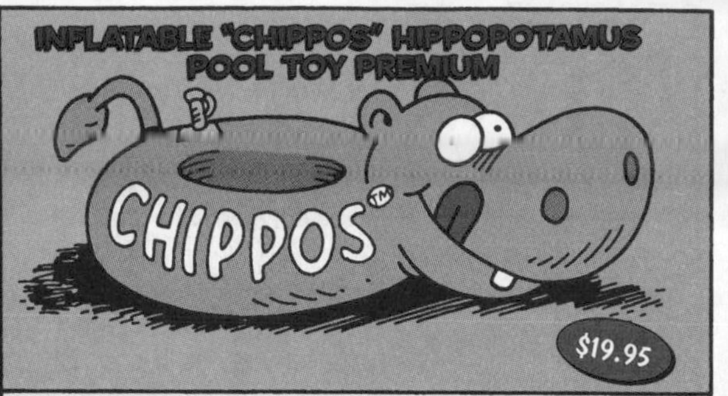
INFLATABLE "CHIPPOS" HIPPOPOTAMUS POOL TOY PREMIUM
CHIPPOS™
$19.95

Any serious snacker probably remembers these colorful mail-in giveaways, mainly because they tended to leave an orange ring around the pool. Available only in sizes XL through 6XL. Fine condition.

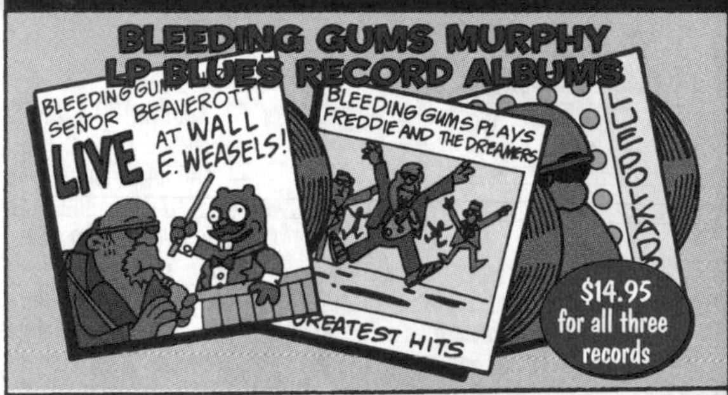
BLEEDING GUMS MURPHY LP BLUES RECORD ALBUMS
BLEEDING GUMS SEÑOR BEAVEROTTI LIVE AT WALL E. WEASELS!
BLEEDING GUMS PLAYS FREDDIE AND THE DREAMERS GREATEST HITS
BLUE POLKA
$14.95 for all three records

"Bleeding Gums Murphy And Señor Beaverotti LIVE At Wall E. Weasel's", "Bleeding Gums Plays Freddie And The Dreamers' Greatest Hits" and "Blue Polka-Dots With Bleeding Gums Murphy", are not exactly Bleeding Gums' finest hours, to say the least. However they ARE in excellent near-mint condition. Too bad we can't say the same for Bleeding Gums himself.

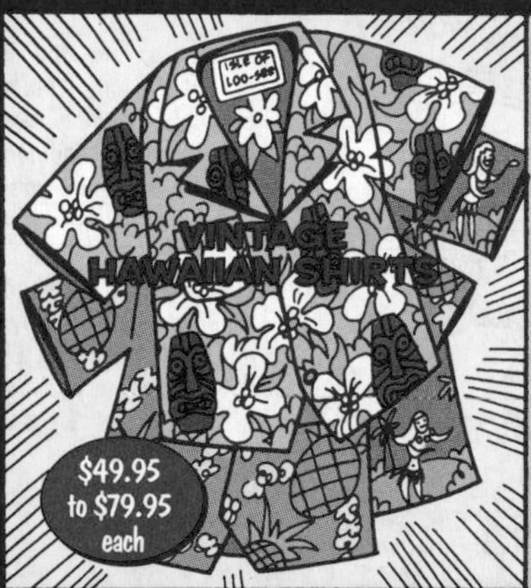
VINTAGE HAWAIIAN SHIRTS
ISLE OF LOO-SEB
$49.95 to $79.95 each

Aloha oy vey! As a certain someone (Homer Simpson, if you MUST know) once uttered, "There's only two kinds of guys who wear these shirts -- gay guys and big fat party animals!" Well, I don't know anything about big, fat, party animals, but I DO know that these vintage beauties will be the crown jewels of any SENSIBLE man's wardrobe.

Excellent condition.

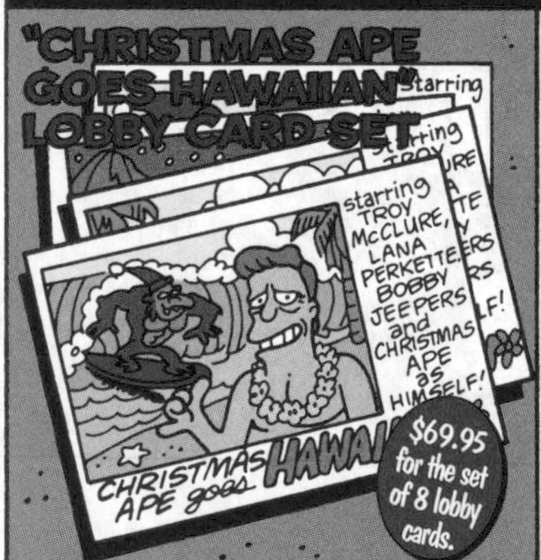
"CHRISTMAS APE GOES HAWAIIAN" LOBBY CARD SET
starring TROY McCLURE, LANA PERKETTE, BOBBY JEEPERS and CHRISTMAS APE as HIMSELF!
CHRISTMAS APE goes HAWAIIAN
$69.95 for the set of 8 lobby cards.

The "CHRISTMAS APE" films are beloved by Saturday-afternoon matinee-goers of all ages. This 1972 installment featured the hunky heartthrob TROY McCLURE in one of his finest roles as Camp Counselor Leakey.

Fine condition.

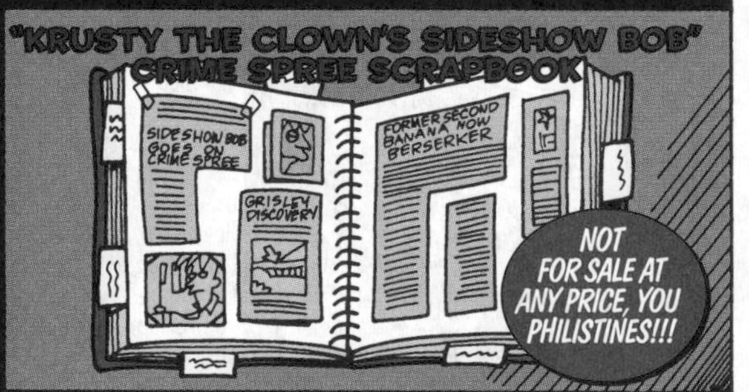
"KRUSTY THE CLOWN'S SIDESHOW BOB" CRIME SPREE SCRAPBOOK
SIDESHOW BOB GOES ON CRIME SPREE
FORMER SECOND BANANA NOW BERSERKER
GRISLEY DISCOVERY
NOT FOR SALE AT ANY PRICE, YOU PHILISTINES!!!

This collection of newspaper and magazine clippings document the multiple rampages of Springfield's favorite attempted SERIAL KILLER and slapstick sidekick, SIDESHOW BOB! Hundreds of hours have gone into the careful cutting, pasting, and annotations that have been--oh, this thing is just SO great, I can't make myself PART with it!

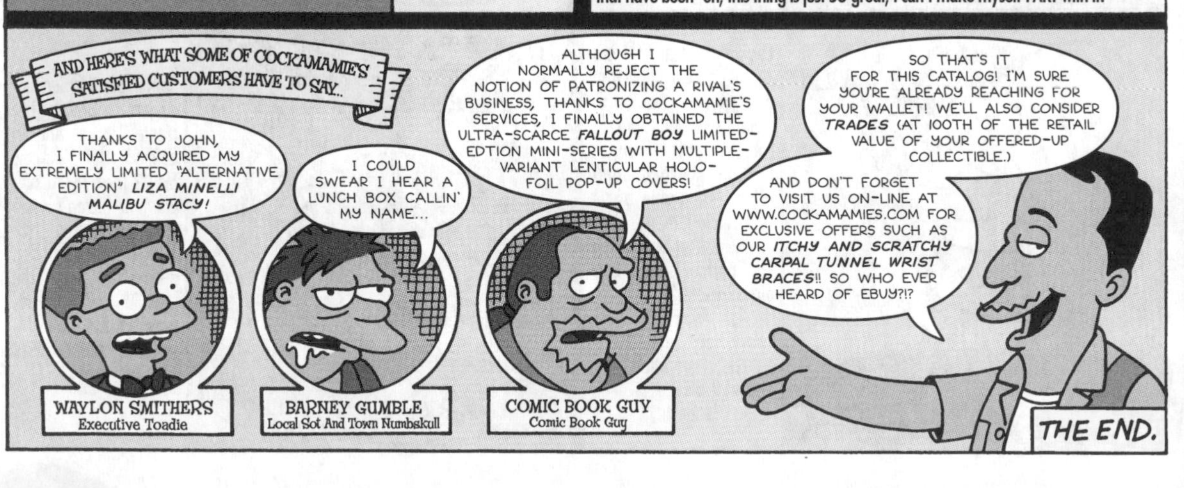
AND HERE'S WHAT SOME OF COCKAMAMIE'S SATISFIED CUSTOMERS HAVE TO SAY...
THANKS TO JOHN, I FINALLY ACQUIRED MY EXTREMELY LIMITED "ALTERNATIVE EDITION" LIZA MINELLI MALIBU STACY!
I COULD SWEAR I HEAR A LUNCH BOX CALLIN' MY NAME...
ALTHOUGH I NORMALLY REJECT THE NOTION OF PATRONIZING A RIVAL'S BUSINESS, THANKS TO COCKAMAMIE'S SERVICES, I FINALLY OBTAINED THE ULTRA-SCARCE FALLOUT BOY LIMITED-EDITION MINI-SERIES WITH MULTIPLE-VARIANT LENTICULAR HOLO-FOIL POP-UP COVERS!
SO THAT'S IT FOR THIS CATALOG! I'M SURE YOU'RE ALREADY REACHING FOR YOUR WALLET! WE'LL ALSO CONSIDER TRADES (AT 100TH OF THE RETAIL VALUE OF YOUR OFFERED-UP COLLECTIBLE.)
AND DON'T FORGET TO VISIT US ON-LINE AT WWW.COCKAMAMIES.COM FOR EXCLUSIVE OFFERS SUCH AS OUR ITCHY AND SCRATCHY CARPAL TUNNEL WRIST BRACES!! SO WHO EVER HEARD OF EBUY?!?
WAYLON SMITHERS
Executive Toadie
BARNEY GUMBLE
Local Sot And Town Numbskull
COMIC BOOK GUY
Comic Book Guy
THE END.